Canadian Manufacturing

Volume I

What are the causes of the decline in productivity in Canadian manufacturing? How can Canada formulate an industrial policy to make its products internationally competitive?

Answering these complex questions requires insight into the factors that contribute to growth or stagnation in industry. *Canadian Manufacturing: A Study in Productivity and Technological Change* examines the productivity of labour and capital in the nineteen industry groups that constitute the Canadian manufacturing sector.

Volume I, *Sector Performance and Industrial Strategy*, outlines the study's methodology and considers the explanations that have been proposed for Canada's productivity slowdown. The study's data suggest that the decline is attributable more to outdated capital equipment than to the commonly cited "slump" in labour productivity. Author Uri Zohar applies the study's findings to the problem of industrial strategy: since the performance of different industries is highly disparate and subject to rapid change, macroeconomic policy is unlikely to be beneficial to all of them at once. A more specialized policy is needed, one that backs "winner" industries identified on the basis of productivity measurements and national choices about social and economic development.

Volume II, *Industry Studies 1946-1977*, provides the most extensive time-series studies done to date on manufacturing industries. Performance in each of the nineteen industry groups — from food and beverage products to chemical industries — is studied, using four production functions that quantify various factors contributing to productivity, and each industry group is compared against a benchmark average for the entire sector. These detailed findings provide the basis for the discussion of industrial strategy in Volume I.

Uri Zohar is a professor of economics in the Faculty of Administrative Studies at York University in Toronto. He has written extensively on economic policy and has acted as a consultant or staff economist to government and industry in Canada, the U.S. and Israel.

The Canadian Institute for Economic Policy has been established to engage in public discussion of fiscal, industrial and other related public policies designed to strengthen Canada in a rapidly changing international environment.

The Institute fulfills this mandate by sponsoring and undertaking studies pertaining to the economy of Canada and disseminating such studies. Its intention is to contribute in an innovative way to the development of public policy in Canada.

Canadian Institute for Economic Policy
Suite 409, 350 Sparks St., Ottawa K1R 7S8

Canadian Manufacturing

A Study in Productivity and Technological Change

Volume I
Sector Performance and Industrial Strategy

Uri Zohar

Canadian Institute for Economic Policy

ISBN 0-88862-526-X paper
ISBN 0-88862-527-8 cloth

6 5 4 3 2 1   82 83 84 85 86 87

Canadian Cataloguing in Publication Data
Zohar, Uri, 1931-
    Canadian manufacturing: a study in productivity and technological change

Contents: v. 1. Sector performance and industrial strategy — v. 2. Industry studies 1946-1977.
ISBN 0-88862-527-8 (v. 1 bound). — ISBN 0-88862-526-X (v. 1 pbk.). — ISBN 0-88862-614-2 (v. 2 bound). — ISBN 0-88862-613-4 (v. 2 pbk.)

1. Canada — Industries. 2. Industrial productivity — Canada. 3. Canada — Economic policy — 1945-1971.* 4. Canada — Economic policy — 1971-   * I. Canadian Institute for Economic Policy. II. Title.

HC115.Z64 *1982*   338.0971   C82-095391-5

61, 492

Additional copies of this book
may be purchased from:
James Lorimer & Company, Publishers
Egerton Ryerson Memorial Building
35 Britain Street
Toronto, Ontario M5A 1R7
Printed and bound in Canada

Contents

v

vi

Tables

Figures

Foreword

For many years there has been an intense debate in Canada about the need for an industrial strategy, particularly in the manufacturing sector. Such a strategy, it is claimed, would increase productivity, encourage key sectors, and rationalize weak ones, and much of the debate has focused on general policies to stimulate the manufacturing sector.

While it has been generally accepted that different manufacturing industries would respond differently to a general stimulus, little work has been done to evaluate the different results. The author of this study, Uri Zohar, has analysed the productivity of labour and capital in, and the impact of technological change on, nineteen manufacturing industries to determine what factors drive them. Only through such an appreciation can a comprehensive industrial strategy be implemented.

The Institute is publishing this study to further the discussion about an industrial strategy for Canada. As in all our studies, the views expressed here are those of the author and do not necessarily reflect those of the Institute.

Roger Voyer
Executive Director
Canadian Institute for Economic Policy

Acknowledgements

This study summarizes the findings of my research on productivity questions and their relationship to economic policy.

I would like to express my appreciation to the Faculty of Administrative Studies at York University and, in particular, to its Dean, W.B. Crowston, for his continuing encouragement and support of this study. I am also grateful to Professor Abraham Rotstein for reading all the versions of this study and contributing to the clarity of this final product. I am also grateful to Professor S. Friedland for reading the manuscript, and Professor N. Biger for helping me in the verification of the data throughout the study. Professor Murray Brown's and Professor Zvi Griliches's comments and suggestions are also greatly appreciated. My research assistants, Bill Jamison and Amos Raz, have performed with dedication beyond their regular duties.

The Canadian Institute for Economic Policy has been most generous with its provision of an editorial assistant and other services. Specifically, Dr. Roger Voyer and Professor Abraham Rotstein have provided support and patience beyond description to make this project possible. The two referees selected by the Institute provided me with valuable comments.

Mrs. Michelle Srebrolow's willingness to bear with me through several revisions of the manuscript is greatly valued.

Needless to say, the responsibility for any errors lies exclusively with me.

Last, but not least, my daughter Lilach spent days and evenings helping me to record the many tables in this study; my daughter Ayelet and my son Asaf helped record the data base; and my wife Shlomit promoted the progress of the study through her patience and understanding of the task at hand. In many ways this was a family project.

On the Productivity Slowdown

1

The process of formulating public policy aimed at stimulating economic growth and enhancing social welfare is complex, involving economic, social, and environmental concerns. Such a process calls for increasingly profound analytical insight into factors contributing to growth or stagnation, not only in the economy as a whole but also at the sectoral or even industry level. Of particular interest in this field of inquiry is an understanding of the principal determinants of productivity growth, such as the quantity and quality of factor inputs, the specificity or substitutability of the factors, and the degree of returns to scale. Other factors that influence productivity growth are the nature of regulations to which an industry may be subjected and specific incentives such as preferential tax treatment or import tariffs from which an industry benefits.[1] All of these factors may affect productivity growth in different industries and to varying degrees.

Moreover, the determinants of productivity do not generally act independently of one another. Any of these factors, acting independently or together, may well induce a trend towards the introduction of technological changes to improve output per worker employed or "productivity." The pace and direction of technological change may in turn be influenced by several factors. Managers may anticipate and decide to adopt capital-using rather than labour-using production methods. The degree of market imperfection and the desire to increase competitiveness may also determine technological change. Clearly, policy-makers attempting to satisfy the competing demands of society are confronted with a complicated task when they begin to consider how to raise productivity growth. The issue is especially important today as growth rates have fallen off or stalled almost completely in many industrial economies.

In the past some of the determinants of productivity growth have been studied in a qualitative or impressionistic manner and others have been subjected to a degree of quantitative analysis. But few time series studies exist on Canadian manufacturing industries, and none covers more than two decades.

In the longest time series study of technical change and factor substitution during the postwar period in Canada, Kotowitz employed a constant elasticity of substitution-type production function.[2] He fitted the function to time series data for aggregate manufacturing and production in manufacturing industries. He assumed that technical change affects both capital and labour as a smooth trend and found that the elasticity of substitution between capital and labour was significantly different from both zero and unity in the postwar period and had declined considerably from the prewar to the postwar period. Kotowitz pointed out that the assumption of smooth technical progress required further research and testing in order to verify whether technical change is indeed induced by expectations of a rise in the real wage rate. He also recommended that the contribution of labour and capital quality to productivity growth be measured by some form of quality weighting of both the labour and capital.

Later H. Postner undertook to measure the effects of labour and capital on productivity in a study for the Economic Council of Canada.[3] By regressing the trend growth rates of labour productivity cross-sectionally for seventeen two-digit manufacturing industries in the Standard Industrial Classification, using the growth rates of measures of labour and capital quality, he found that productivity growth differentials could be explained to some extent by: growth of the ratio of non-production to production workers; growth of the ratio of male to female non-production workers; the trend of per worker capital intensity; and the trend of establishment size.

Further research is needed to gain greater understanding of longer term productivity and thus of the competitiveness of Canada's manufacturing industries both domestically and internationally.[4] Such research would, among other things, deepen our understanding of three major issues: the extent of induced technological change; the overall impact of factor quality changes on productivity changes; and the specific contribution of technological change to productivity in manufacturing industries.

The intent of this study is to analyse the productivity of labour and capital and the impact of technological change on Canadian manufacturing industries. To accomplish this objective, the variables and parameters involved in the manufacturing sector as a whole were examined. A benchmark average estimate for the sector was derived in

2

order that the performance of separate industries could be compared with the "average." This aggregate estimate may also facilitate future comparison of the performance of Canada's manufacturing sector with that of its major trading partners.

Some studies have been done on productivity growth in the United States, but the industrial product mix, the ease of factor substitution, and the length of production runs in Canada are considerably different from those of U.S. manufacturing industries. Thus, although trends in the United States have a pronounced effect on those in Canada, the results of such studies cannot be directly applied. Nevertheless, owing to the "openness" of the Canadian economy and to the country's proximity to the United States, the nature of technological change is somewhat correlated in the two countries. Perspective on productivity trends and technological change in Canada can, therefore, be gained from comparisons with studies done for U.S. industries.[5]

A quantitative assessment of the interactions of factor input requires a proper analytical framework to measure and explain the contribution of a specific set of inputs to productivity growth. In the classic case, Arrow sought a simple production function that would explain certain relationships between factor inputs.[6] This study uses four production functions to analyse various aspects of productivity. Use of the econometric production functions approach limits to a certain extent the understanding that can be gained of productivity and technological change. Needless to say, many more factors affect high or low productivity than can be "measured" or represented statistically. Nevertheless, econometric study of a set of important structural issues can and should be of great assistance in interpreting and understanding the sources of productivity growth.

This study comes in two parts. This volume, Volume I, contains the basic theoretical material and the general conclusions drawn from the production function analysis. Readers interested in the detailed data for the nineteen industry groups analysed should turn to Volume II, *Industry Studies, 1946-77*. Both volumes examine the concept of productivity and the variables that affect economic performance in the economy.

The Concept of Productivity and Change
In the course of my research I have discovered that the concept of "productivity" and the way in which it relates to the growth and well-being of society are not well understood. While certain notions surrounding this concept are widely accepted, on some issues there is

3

still no consensus. Generally, economists agree that productivity is the outcome of a process of production using a given technology by which a set of inputs are converted into final output. The set of inputs usually includes labour, capital, management, and intermediate inputs, such as energy, raw materials, research and development, education, and other items. All these inputs are measured in physical units or through their proxy — "real" prices.

Several interpretations may be ascribed to the meaning of productivity, simply because of the potentially long list of inputs that may be included to measure it. For the sake of clarity, productivity in this study involves three notions: labour productivity, which measures output per person-hour paid resulting from utilizing a specific factor of production; capital productivity, which is expressed as the output obtained per unit of capital; and total factor productivity, which is a global measure of output resulting from the interaction of the entire set of inputs, properly weighted according to their contribution to the production process. This study covers partial factor productivity — that is, labour and capital productivity together — and total factor productivity, as well as several other related measurements.

These measurements of factor productivity are particularly important for observations of output per man-hour and capital per man-hour (capital intensity). For example, an improvement in labour productivity has a direct bearing on growth of real per capita income.[7] Since labour is a major factor of production, an increase in real per capita earnings would reflect a trend of economic growth, while the type of technology used would imply a trend of changing employment.

With the available data, productivity can be measured by various methods, including interviews, direct computations of output-labour ratios, derivations of indices representing variables, and estimations of econometric production functions of different types. There are numerous problems of measurement biases and complications, depending upon the degree of aggregation and the type of information sought. For example, a productivity study of a single firm would vary in complexity and would utilize different information from a similar study of a sector or the economy as an aggregate. In this study I use estimation results from four different types of econometric production functions to point out the marginal contribution of individual factors of production in nineteen industry groups during the thirty-two-year timespan from 1946 to 1977. From these results, the sources of productivity growth may be identified.

The objective in the production process is to maximize output and

4

revenues. Output could grow simply because of an absolute increase in some or all factors of production. But such an increase could also derive from a rise in output per unit of input as a consequence of achieving the proper mix of available resources with the best available technology. Improvement might also result from better management in the production process or from the introduction of new and more efficient technology. Finally, the quality of labour and capital might rise. So far, most of these factors lend themselves to direct measurement, and thus recent performance can be evaluated. But studies of the sources of the productivity decline in the United States go far beyond directly measurable factors of production and deserve close attention, for some of these imponderables may have contributed as well to the similar slowdown in Canada.[8]

Some have argued, for example, that one possible explanation for the slowdown in productivity has been the reduction in expenditures for research and development. In addition, Orio Giarini observed that "we are more and more coming to the point where science-based technology has exploited all the major possibilities made available by the scientific advances of the last century, and that we may have to wait decades for the reservoir to be replenished." In partial agreement Schumpeter contended that innovation occurs in waves; that an idea spreads and is applied in many fields; and he supposes that we have come to the end of such a wave. But Denison, who undertook a comprehensive study of the productivity slowdown, claims that by every measurement, research and development expenditures have increased.[9] At the same time he admits that research and development contributed no more than 0.3 percentage points to the growth rate of private domestic GNP in the mid-1960s and probably considerably less, and thus retardation of such expenditures would have contributed little if anything to the decline in productivity. He rejects Giarini's hypothesis concerning the depletion of the scientific reservoir of advances, since the corresponding retardation in growth was not gradual but rather sudden. We shall see whether any of these arguments hold in Canada.

Government regulation is also often blamed for the slowdown in productivity growth. Denison listed an extensive number of government programs that imposed severe additional costs on private industry in order to comply with health and safety laws as well as to fulfil record-keeping obligations. Like Denison, I am sceptical about these cost burdens, since by themselves they could not have increased enough to explain depressed productivity from 1973 to 1976.

However, as he points out, the failure of business to find the cheapest way to conform with government regulations can be expensive, and efficiency and productivity are being lost because top management is devoting more time to regulatory constraints than to business considerations. Regulations often cause endless delays and sometimes even eventual abandonment of a project. Various provisions in the tax code and legislation affecting resource allocation, by distorting the market mechanism, may also contribute to inefficient capital allocation that eventually affects growth. The overall effect of regulation on productivity growth is not clear, though certainly some impact is visible.

In his attempt to explain the cause of the productivity slowdown, Denison also examined attitudes, inflation, energy prices, and decreased management productivity. Although all might be partly responsible, no one of these factors is totally responsible for slowing productivity growth. A decline in the work ethic might have contributed, though the effect may not be significant. The impact of inflation is difficult to assess. It is hard to know whether there has been any change in the level of competition in America, and discussion about competition levels and the quality of management are inconclusive. In the end, Denison turned to consideration of the sudden increase in OPEC oil prices, which occurred at about the same time as the productivity slowdown. But from his calculations it seems unlikely that higher energy prices caused more than a 0.2 per cent loss of labour productivity and potential output between 1973 and 1976. Thus we are still left with no clearcut explanation.

The literature signifies clearly that economists in the United States have reached no consensus as to the source of the slowdown, its significance, or its economic impact. Tatom considered four major factors that are frequently linked to the productivity slowdown: a decline in capital investment, a slowdown in the introduction of new technology, the changing composition of the labour force towards more inexperienced groups, and an increase in service employment relative to manufacturing employment.[10] But others have deemed them insignificant.[11] Lester Thurow attributes the slowdown in the rate of growth in capital intensity or capital per person-hour to the "speedup" in the rate of growth in the labour force in the United States.[12] He argues that during the 1948-64 period the price of labour relative to capital rose by 2.7 per cent per annum. Labour became more expensive, relative to capital, and thus in those years capital intensity increased. After 1965 that process reversed, because of growth in the

6

labour force, and thus capital intensity declined. Kendrick, using Denison's framework, found that advances in knowledge, education, and training of management and labour, resource allocations, and capital were the most significant positive contributors to growth.[13]

Most economists would agree about the importance of research and development and the accumulation of capital to productivity growth. They would also be fairly agreed that diffusion of technology and the rate at which it is diffused throughout the economy affect productivity. But since technology is embodied in capital, the quality of the diffused technology depends on the quality of capital. For example, the addition of new machinery with newer technology performing the "old" function of production would have a greater impact on productivity than simply new machines with the same capabilities as the old ones.

This overview of some of the current explanations of the productivity slowdown in the United States provides some useful guidelines for analysis of the similar phenomenon in Canada. Although some studies have looked at various aspects of productivity growth, no comprehensive analysis exists of the "qualitative" factors affecting productivity change utilizing the Denison-Kendrick framework, so that no evidence is available on the impact of such factors on changes in Canadian productivity. Nor does this study, which deals explicitly with the contributions of tangible capital and labour inputs to productivity changes, make any guesses about the impact of qualitative factors. Nevertheless, some conclusions are advanced that are consistent with the quantitative econometric analysis in this study.

One strong conclusion that derives from the econometric analysis is that the productivity decline in Canada is by no means similar to that in the United States. Neither all the causes nor all the symptoms are the same, with the obvious implication being that the policies followed in the United States to address the productivity slowdown may not be the proper prescription for Canada. For example, as we have seen, some U.S. economists see that a radical decrease in the level and the rate of change of capital intensity after the energy crisis in 1973 is the major cause of the slowdown. This study shows that the compounded annual rate of change in capital intensity in Canadian manufacturing during the 1973-77 subperiod increased in the manufacturing sector and in sixteen of the total nineteen industry groups. According to Kendrick's theory, this should have contributed to an increase in labour productivity in at least sixteen industries. Oddly enough that did not happen in the Canadian case; labour productivity declined in ten industries, did not change in two, and increased in seven industries.

7

Another notable difference appears in the changes in the labour forces in the two countries. In Canada, the structure of the labour force changed considerably during the last decade. But the trend of the increase seems not to resemble that of the United States. For instance, Ostry and Rao argue that "in part, the productivity slowdown in 1974-75 represented a cyclical phenomenon associated with the rate of labour hoarding. By 1976 the effects of the slowdown were beginning to wear off in manufacturing as output rose to 5.2 per cent over 1975 levels. Productivity increased by 5.8 per cent as the number of man hours worked declined slightly."[14] Thurow's argument for the United States is just the reverse.

In fact, the data in this study show that labour productivity is not the main problem in the Canadian economy. Chapters 2 and 3 contain the results of the aggregate econometric analysis of productivity in the manufacturing sector as a whole and the specific industry-level analysis. From them my main conclusion is that the productivity decline can be attributed more to a failure of an aspect of capital development; that is, much capital in the manufacturing sector is old and new capital has not always embraced newer and more efficient technology. One result is that growth in overall efficiency and labour productivity has stalled. Chapter 4 draws together all the conclusions of the study and suggests an approach to policy-making that would not only address the productivity issue but lead to a consistent, long-term program to promote competitiveness of Canadian manufactured products.

Aggregate Analysis of the Manufacturing Sector

2

This chapter addresses the difficult task of measuring aggregate productivity levels in the manufacturing sector using several production functions. The problem is complex for two overriding reasons. First, the sector is classified by Statistics Canada into nineteen industry groups, each of which in turn includes hundreds or even thousands of separate firms. Thus any aggregate measure can be justifiably criticized because of the diversity it masks. Second, productivity is affected by a myriad of factors that cannot all be measured through production functions. But since a production function represents the relationship between a set of inputs — usually capital, labour, and technological progress over time — and the resultant output, clearly no single production function can adequately reflect the diverse technologies in each plant or industry or the multitude of entirely different products generated by these varied technologies.

In the past many studies on productivity have concentrated on aggregates; that is, they "fitted" or analysed production in the whole economy or its various sectors. Such analyses are of little value for making decisions about specific production measures. Nevertheless, they do provide an "average" representation of an economy's or a sector's performance, which is useful because it allows a comparison among industries and among different countries. Therefore, before going on to analyse productivity in each of nineteen manufacturing industries, this chapter determines economies of scale, capacity utilization, and aspects of labour and capital productivity at the sectoral level in order to create benchmarks against which individual industries can be compared, to provide a basis for international comparisons, and to supply measures against which other studies can be analysed. But first, two important concepts that are often considered as requisites for growth and higher productivity — capacity utilization and economies of scale — are examined in some detail.

Productivity, Capacity Utilization, and Economies of Scale

A basic diversity of views prevails among economists over the concept of "capacity" operation and consequently over the best way of measuring it. A fair summary of all the different definitions would describe capacity as the level of output or gross national product that could be produced given the existing stock of plant and equipment, if the available labour force were appropriately distributed among industries.

The importance of the capacity concept lies in its relationship to actual output. The gap between the actual output of an industry or an economy in general and its potential output (or capacity) can be measured in terms of operating or utilization rates. High operating rates should, other things being equal, induce firms to add to their capacity, generally through investment. Since investment spending forecasts constitute an important part of forecasting, operating rates are useful to the extent that they enable forecasters to predict investment outlays. Furthermore, high operating rates should signal supply-related inflationary pressures to the extent that output is "pushing against" capacity limits. Thus measures of capacity utilization may provide significant assistance to the economic forecaster in predicting inflation and investment spending. But the usefulness of measures of capacity and of capacity utilization will vary from industry to industry. Moreover, aggregate measures of capacity utilization, such as measures of operating rates in all manufacturing, may conceal a great deal of irregularity in the positions of individual industries. For example, in the 1973 economy, "information from a variety of sources indicates that capacity limited the expansion of output in several industries such as paper, petroleum, steel and some lines of chemicals, while many others exhibited evidence of ample spare capacity."[1] Accordingly, the implication for both new investment and price pressures might be expected to be considerably different for these industries than for others.

But the quantification of potential output and of the accompanying "gap" between actual and potential "is at best an uncertain estimate." Significant differences exist among various capacity utilization measures.[2] Therefore it is important to understand how the different techniques measure capacity utilization and why they differ from each other.

A distinction can be drawn between measures of capacity utilization that are "production-based" and those that are "survey-based." Production-based measures involve the use of output statistics. In survey-based measures respondents from the industry report on the degree of capacity utilization in their operations based on the use of labour rather than output. Of the five major capacity utilization measures in use in the United States, the two production-based measures — the Federal Reserve and Wharton measures — show a greater amplitude of swing than the three survey measures — the McGraw-Hill, Bureau of Economic Analysis, and Census measures. Furthermore, of the two production-based measures, the Wharton shows slightly more amplitude than the Federal Reserve; of the survey-based measures, McGraw-Hill shows more amplitude than the BEA.[3] The differences between the two production-based methods result from the different ways in which capacity is measured. Wharton's method is a "trend-through-the-peaks" measure, which identifies historic peaks of production. The production peaks are joined graphically by lines taken as representative of the measure of potential output for the period between these peaks. A capacity measure for periods following the most recent peak can be obtained by extrapolating the latest segment of the trend. The Federal Reserve method is a "capital stock" measure in which capital stock is used as a proxy for capacity. While this eliminates the need for questionable forward extrapolation, the link between investment spending and capacity expansion is somewhat imprecise.[4]

In this study I have adopted the capital-stock method for two reasons. First, it is consistently used by Statistics Canada and thus my findings can be related to official publications. Second, and more important, labour unemployment cannot properly reflect decline in capacity; rather, it is the totality of unemployed resources that causes capacity utilization to fluctuate. This represents the maximum value of a ratio of output to gross capital stock; and only one such point occurred in our series of thirty-two years. With performance in this "maximum value year" established at 100 per cent capacity utilization, that in all other years is relative (see Appendix A for methodology). While the measure of capacity is complex and the precise relationship between investment spending and capacity expansion has not yet been established, the same method was used consistently throughout the study, so the results can be compared with other studies employing the same methodology.

The other variable that deserves special consideration is economies of scale. In general, the term "economies of scale" refers to the relationship between a change in a firm's total inputs and the resulting level of output, when technology and all other factors are held

11

constant. Such a measure indicates the existence of one of three probable situations. First, a firm may continuously be spending more for inputs than the value of the outputs. This result is defined as "diseconomies of scale" because an additional change of, say, 10 per cent in its total inputs would increase output by less than 10 per cent. Second, under "constant returns to scale," a firm may add 10 per cent more inputs and receive an identical 10 per cent increase in output. Third, "economies of scale" are achieved when a firm continuously gains more in output than it spends to change its total inputs. Economists consider the scale or scope of operation an important factor in minimizing the costs of operation and maximizing a firm's output. Economies of scale derive not only from the size of the firm or plant, but also from the size of available markets, the length of production runs, and the scope of sales, and credit. Consequently, economies of scale assume several forms that are rather complex and not always easily identified through empirical analysis.

In considerations of economies of scale there is a general awareness that the size and structure of Canadian manufacturing have contributed to the differences in the levels of real output per person employed between Canada and the United States. Daly, Keys, and Spence distinguished four different aspects of size — size of market; size of firm; size of plant; and size of production run — that may affect economies of scale. They concluded that the size of the market is an important factor, to the extent that it affects the possibility for specialization and long production runs and decided that greater product diversity in Canada contributes significantly to the higher costs and lower productivity than in the United States. They assumed that size of plant is probably not a dominant factor in explaining the productivity difference between the Canadian and U.S. economies. Finally, they concluded that the influence of the size of the firm on productivity differences is very uncertain and deserves further study.[5]

Paul Gorecki analysed economies of scale at the plant level and described two methods of estimating efficient plant sizes: the survivor and engineering techniques. The survivor method "estimates efficient plant size on an industry basis, by examining the share of industry output accounted for by each plant size group for two time periods: 1961-1966; 1966-1972. Those plant size groups which increased in relative importance are considered, according to this measure, to be efficient." The engineering technique "uses estimates made by engineers of the most efficient plant size, given factor prices and technology, excluding outbound transportation costs."[6] Using the survivor technique for fifty-six Canadian manufacturing industries, accounting for approximately 40 per cent of the value added in Canadian manufacturing industry, he concluded that, in general, efficient plant size is small in relation to market size. He also found that the most important determinant of plant size was the extent of the market rather than geography, market stability, or market growth. Using engineering estimates of minimum efficient plant size for seventeen industries, he discovered that the number of efficient plants compatible with domestic consumption varied considerably across the sample. He concluded that for a small number of Canadian manufacturing industries, the engineering estimate exceeds, sometimes substantially, the survivor estimate of minimum efficient plant size. As measured by the engineering technique, economies of scale at the plant level appear to be a much more important element of market structure in Canada than in the United States.

On the basis of this evidence, he suggested a pragmatic approach to the administration of competition policy in Canada, since the significance of economies of scale varies greatly from industry to industry. Second, he recommended trade liberalization, since his empirical evidence indicated that increases in market size would lead to a rise in Canadian plant sizes.

Le Craw, in a recent survey dealing with economies of scale that relates directly to industrial policy in Canada, identified five different levels of economies of scale: product, multi-product, plant, multi-plant, and firm. Le Craw concluded that plant-specific economies of scale have not imposed a significant cost disadvantage on Canadian firms. By contrast, product-specific economies of scale "may be the major source of production inefficiency in Canada."[7] Canadian firms produce a wider range of products than do firms of comparable size outside Canada, and thus each plant produces a more diverse line of products than similar-sized plants elsewhere, employing much less specialized equipment, requiring more set-up time, and experiencing fewer of the economies of scale that arise from learning by doing. Such diseconomies of scale have generally not been quantified, but he concludes that "on the basis of individual case studies they would seem to be quite large." In general, his conclusion is that firm-level economies in Canada may justify larger businesses than do plant-level economies. In drawing policy implications from the studies, Le Craw concludes that while large firms are neither necessary nor desirable in all industries, "public policy should not limit the size of firms to that necessary to achieve only plant-level economies of scale."[8]

In another study of scale economies, Scherer defined economies of scale as "reductions in cost per unit of product manufactured and sold associated with the operation of large as compared to small production, distribution and merchandising entities," with "entity" meaning anything from a production line to a firm. Focusing solely on manufacturing industries, Scherer concluded that although important scale economies exist, they are exhausted without requiring a high degree of seller concentration in a market the size of the United States. He stressed, however, that the variance from industry to industry is great and that, in designing an appropriate government policy towards the manufacturing sector, the unit-cost/scale relationship is not the only factor to consider; product quality, service, image, and innovation are other variables that also deserve attention in connection with entity size.

Scherer distinguished between "plant-specific" scale economies and "product-specific" scale economies and concluded that the "links between concentration and the realization of product-specific scale economies in production are quite intricate. Higher concentration may permit larger production lots and longer runs; but by paralyzing price incentive for specialization, it can also work in the opposite direction. We need to know much more about the conditions under which one propensity is stronger than the other."[9]

He also questioned whether decisions about size of capital investment are influenced systematically by such structural variables as the level of concentration within a relevant market and the extent of multiplant operation sustained by leading sellers. One of his own studies indicates that plant sizes tend to be larger when market concentration is high, other things such as the size of the market, the strength of scale economies, and the decentralizing pull of shipping costs being held equal. He noted too that, while certain cost savings can be obtained through the operation of a multiplant investment strategy or a multiplant specialization of production, such economies are "second-best economies" in the sense that they are realizable only to the extent that competitive market processes break down.

In relation to other economies of multiplant firm scale Scherer noted that the average cost of capital tends to vary inversely with firm size, but he questioned whether this benefit accrues to society as a whole or whether it represents a redistribution of income rather than real resource savings. In addition, plant procurement economies — the ability of large purchasers to pay lower prices for raw materials and for other inputs than those paid by small purchasers — tended to be negligible in most cases, and even when the economies were significant, the benefits were largely redistributional in character and nearly always resulted from some breakdown of competitive market processes. Sales promotional and market access advantages, class of scale advantages, while complex to measure, are slight or negligible. However, in most of the consumer goods industries, single-plant firms experience handicaps in competing toe-to-toe in the promotional arena with multiplant firms. Scherer found that there are advantages of scale in research and innovation but that they appear to be fully realized when firm size and concentration levels are well below the upper size and concentration ranges of existing U.S. industrial structures. He concluded that economies of scale in managerial factors cannot be adequately reviewed because the evidence is too scant to draw any firm conclusion.

The Report of the Royal Commission on Corporate Concentration directed special attention towards the issue of desirable economies of scale in large, diversified firms. Although recognizing that the nature of the Canadian market, combined with nationalistic government economic policies, has led to an economy whose firms and plants in many industries tend to be relatively small and unspecialized by international standards, the Commission concluded that plant-specific scale economies have not, in general, imposed a major cost disadvantage on Canadian firms serving the Canadian market. In contrast, the Report viewed product-related economies as an important source of scale inefficiency in Canada and concluded that, in many Canadian industries, firm-level economies justify larger-sized businesses than do plant-level economies.[10]

Daly, following Scherer's terminology, differentiated among three different concepts of economies of scale — product-specific economies, plant-specific scale economies, and company-wide scale economies — and drew some conclusions about the scope for higher productivity, given access to larger markets. Product-specific scale economies refer to changes in cost per unit of output with longer runs and although the phenomenon of greater product diversity in Canadian plants than in U.S. plants in the same industry is well established, there is less certainty regarding the effects of such diversity on productivity and cost differences between the two countries. Nonetheless, product diversity is the most important single source of the difference in cost and productivity between the two countries.[11] By contrast, plant-

15

specific scale economies — that is, the costs of alternative size plants producing a particular product or group of products in the same industry — are not a significant factor in causing productivity differences between Canadian and U.S. manufacturing industries.

Both plant-specific and product-specific scale economies are referred to by Daly as "production economies." Alternatively, the concept of company-wide scale economies refers to savings on non-production costs in a group of plants operated by one company in the same broad industry group. That is, there may be economies of scale in advertising, research and development, and capital fund-raising (for example) for a group of plants rather than for each plant by itself. He concludes that such financial and advertising cost differentials are generally not critical in the large cost differences in existing manufactured product prices. In conclusion, Daly suggests that the key implication presented by previous economies of scale studies is that "there are significant potential gains in increased productivity and reductions in costs per unit by a reduction in the current high degree of product diversity in Canadian manufacturing. However, there are no incentives for the individual firms to move in this direction if their selling prices to sell the additional volume would have to be cut more drastically than the expected reduction in average cost."[12]

Our brief discussion of these two concepts leads us naturally to examination of the basic methodology used in this study. Using the production functions we are able to see the effects of various factors on capacity utilization and economies of scale in manufacturing industries.

The Methodology

Comparisons of figures on productivity levels and changes within and among countries soon revealed that a certain degree of looseness prevails in the use of data. Different studies use different base years and employ diverse definitions of the variables. For example, studies defining labour in terms of "production activity" give higher figures for labour productivity per man-hour than those using "total activity" statistics. In Canada "production activity," as defined by Statistics Canada, includes direct production workers only. Conversely, Statistics Canada's "total activity" data include all wage and salaried workers, services workers, head-office employees, and sales force personnel. Further, "production activity" includes the value added only by direct production processes, whereas "total activity" includes the value added by all direct as well as indirect workers such as managers, engineers, personnel staff, and others.

The measurement of the various aspects of capital is perhaps the most complicated issue in a productivity study. The different methods employed range from the use of gross capital stock statistics, with and without deflation by capacity utilization indexes, to the use of net capital stock or a measure of capital services. The differences between the various methods are significant and have sparked considerable debate over the most appropriate measurement techniques. It is, however, beyond the scope of this study to expand on such a complex methodological issue.[13]

My intention here is to point out the significantly different productivity data obtained from statistical series of "production" and "total activity" and gross and net capital stock. To this end, estimates were made of four different measures. In this series of estimations, production activity represents primarily the labour and value added contributing to and resulting from the direct production process; on the labour side, it includes blue-collar wage workers only. Total activity, following the Statistics Canada definition, includes all salaried workers, services, head-office employees and sales staff. In assessing production performance for the purpose of formulating policy on international trade subsidies and other public interventions, my preference lies in measuring productivity using the total activity framework. An estimate based on direct production is needed, however, for comparison with other studies, since most productivity studies are based on production activity only. The other two categories are estimations with gross capital stock and with net capital stock. Two different base years — 1961 and 1971 — were introduced in order to show that each base year gives different results and that comparisons with other studies are possible only if data of the same base year are used.

Tables 2-1 through 2-5 and Appendix C present the statistical results of these four different estimates of productivity, using four production functions: Cobb-Douglas (CD), constant elasticity of substitution (CES), variable elasticity of substitution (VES), and the Translog approximation of the CES.[14] Each of these functions, which are fully explained in Appendix A, complements the others and provides additional information on productivity. Gathering information from all these functions gives us a wide spectrum of measures of productivity.

Economies of Scale

Economies of scale are often considered to be an important factor in the productivity equation. Tables 2-1 and 2-2 display the results of calculation of scale economies using the Cobb-Douglas production function. Scale economies are achieved when the figure representing scale $\alpha + \beta$ is larger than one; for example, a 1 per cent increase in factor inputs resulted in a 1.73 per cent increase in output in 1971 using total activity and gross capital stock inputs. The unrestricted estimates of labour and capital point clearly to economies of scale in Canadian manufacturing throughout the 1946-77 period. There are variations, however, in the size of the scale economies for several reasons. First,

TABLE 2-1
COBB-DOUGLAS PRODUCTION FUNCTION, TOTAL ACTIVITY
(1961 and 1971 dollars)
$$\ln Q = A + \alpha \ln L + \beta \ln k + \lambda \, T$$

	A	α	β	λ	$\bar{R}^2$
Gross capital stock	−5.0978	0.7793	0.8305		0.9975
(1961 constant $'s)	(38.1542)	(108.699)			
	−9.1737	1.01151	1.0779	−0.01512	0.9979
	(5.3056)	(10.2724)		(2.3634)	
Net capital stock	−4.1091	0.7476	0.7968		0.9932
(1961 constant $'s)	(20.0871)	(66.1650)			
	−0.3672	0.5272	0.5618	0.01491	0.9938
	(0.1711)	(4.1726)		(1.7509)	
Gross capital stock	−6.1111	0.9732	0.7657		0.9969
(1971 constant $'s)	(38.0340)	(97.5832)			
	−3.6203	0.8098	0.6371	0.00852	0.9971
	(2.4722)	(8.4345)		(1.71064)	
Net capital stock	−5.3538	0.9496	0.7471		0.9948
(1971 constant $'s)	(27.0755)	(75.4649)			
	−1.83158	0.71204	0.5602	0.00126	0.9953
	(0.9862)	(5.6876)		(1.9067)	

A—Efficiency parameter
α—Elasticity of response of output to labour
β—Elasticity of response of output to capital
λ—The contribution of technological change to output through time

A 1 per cent increase in labour, with the amount of capital held constant, will add α per cent to output. It follows that $\alpha + \beta$ represents returns to scale.

Source: Table B-1

18

TABLE 2-2
COBB-DOUGLAS PRODUCTION FUNCTION, PRODUCTION ACTIVITY
(1961 and 1971 dollars)

$$\ln Q = A + \alpha \ln L + \beta \ln K + \lambda T$$

	A	α	β	λ	$\bar{R}^2$
Gross capital stock (1961 constant $'s)	−4.0591 (18.0586)	0.5019 (59.7874)	0.9595		0.9917
	−0.1954 (0.5981)	0.3479 (2.6339)	0.6653	0.1548 (1.1675)	0.9921
Net capital stock (1961 constant $'s)	−2.9899 (12.1488)	0.4791 (50.2631)	0.9159		0.9883
	4.5636 (1.7299)	0.1652 (1.5077)	0.3158	0.0033 (2.8733)	0.9909
Gross capital stock (1971 constant $'s)	−4.8491 (17.5732)	0.6272 (52.0158)	0.9242		0.9890
	2.6204 (1.1962)	0.2805 (2.7599)	0.4133	0.00279 (3.4298)	0.9922
Net capital stock (1971 constant $'s)	−4.0138 (15.6716)	0.6105 (52.7807)	0.8997		0.9893
	3.0795 (1.1506)	0.2689 (2.0873)	0.3963	0.00282 (2.6604)	0.9914

A—Efficiency parameter
α—Elasticity of response of output to labour
β—Elasticity of response of output to capital
λ—The contribution of technological change to output through time

A 1 per cent increase in labour, with the amount of capital held constant, will add α per cent to output. It follows that $\alpha + \beta$ represents returns to scale.

Source: Table B-1

the base year differences (1961 and 1971) generate an upward bias of 0.09-0.12 for 1971 in the production activity and 0.13-0.15 in the total activity runs. Second, the coefficients of gross and net capital stock runs vary. Production activity gives a smaller figure than total activity by 0.07 for 1961 and 0.04 for 1971. The values of economies of scale in the different tests are summarized in Table 2-3. The degree of the scale economies is somewhat larger than expected, in part because the Cobb-Douglas function generally contains many potential upward biases in its coefficients caused by aggregation, specification, and

TABLE 2-3

COBB-DOUGLAS AVERAGE ECONOMIES OF SCALE

GROSS AND NET CAPITAL STOCK

(1961 and 1971 dollars)

	1961 Dollars	1971 Dollars
Production activity		
Net capital stock	1.3950	1.5102
Gross capital stock	1.4614	1.5514
Total activity		
Net capital stock	1.5444	1.6967
Gross capital stock	1.6098	1.7389

Source: Tables 2-1, 2-2

simultaneous equation biases, the equation biases, the instability of coefficients, and the methods of estimation.[15] Nevertheless, the economies of scale of 1.39 and 1.54 in the net capital stock series seem reasonable for the aggregate manufacturing sector.

The results of the economies of scale (V) calculations in the CES production function are consistent with those in the CD functions (see Tables 2-4 and 2-5). But the questions of the potential bias of the CES results cannot be ignored. For example Nerlove and others have argued that different estimation methods yield varying results and that problems of the instability, identification, and specification of the coefficients are present.[16] However, Diwan has suggested another method of estimating the CD and the CES functions and proved that his method has far less bias than other estimation techniques. This study follows Diwan's methodology and, as an additional safeguard, compares the results of economies of scale from the CD and the CES functions.[17] Consequently, the biases are minimized.

The inclusion of a time variable in the calculation indicates that an average of 1.5 per cent of overall productivity growth can be attributed to technological change in the 1961 dollar series and an average of 1.3 per cent in the 1971 series.[18] To verify that the results on economies of scale are indeed unbiased and stable, yet another form of a production function — the transcendental type that contains the properties of nonhomothetic function — was also employed. The advantage of this function is that it accounts for market imperfections because it is not constrained to homogenous production frontier measurements. The specific form selected was the Translog approximation of the CES suggested by Griliches, because it provides additional information on the changing level of economies of scale through time.[19] The results were entirely consistent with those obtained from the CD and the CES functions and are encouraging, since economies of scale were 1.4 and increased through time.

Two important conclusions can be drawn from the existence of economies of scale in the manufacturing sector and the greater economies in the "total activity" measure. First, it is clear that the increase in real manufacturing output is well beyond that in labour and capital inputs. Although it is difficult to identify from such an aggregative measure the kind of economies of scale involved, the results suggest the existence of product-specific economies of scale rather than necessarily firm-size scale. If so, it is safe to assume that, on aggregate, efficiency increased in part because of increased product specialization. Since such a process is never isolated from institutional and legislative events, tariff reductions from the Kennedy Round and the Canada-U.S. Automotive Agreement no doubt contributed to the efficiency gains. Second, the greater degree of economies of scale using "total activity" data points to a positive phenomenon in the manufacturing sector. Since the difference between the production activity and total activity measures consists of the non-direct labour force, such as engineers, head office and sales personnel, and management, and the addition of these persons not directly involved in production contributed to larger economies of scale, Canadian management was a positive contributor to economies of scale in manufacturing.

Capacity Utilization

Figure 2-1 shows that the manufacturing sector operated at full capacity in 1973, but that a gap between potential capacity utilization and actual output existed from then until 1976. Since the computation here is based on the ratio of capital stock to output, and Statistics Canada includes some of the depleted and unused capital stock in the capital stock figures, the capacity index may be somewhat biased upward. More important, however, is the fact that capacity utilization gaps do not tell us whether that "unused" capacity is due to weak supply or weak demand conditions. A gap between actual output and capacity utilization may result from weakening external demand for Canadian products, not the inability of the sector to produce at capacity. An answer to such a question calls for a complementary study of the demand side of the economic equation. Nonetheless, the findings are not in line with the often heard claim that current

21

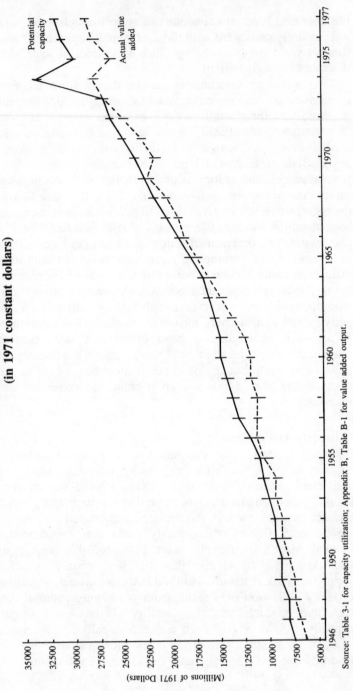

FIGURE 2-1
CANADIAN MANUFACTURING, POTENTIAL CAPACITY AND REAL VALUE ADDED, 1946-1977
(in 1971 constant dollars)

Source: Table 3-1 for capacity utilization; Appendix B, Table B-1 for value added output.

inflationary pressures in our economy are due to full capacity utilization of all inputs.

Elasticity of Substitution

The elasticity of substitution variable measures the ease with which factor inputs, such as capital and labour, can be substituted for one another in the production process. The larger the absolute value of the measure, the more easily factor inputs can be substituted for one another without a loss of output. Conversely, if the elasticity value registers close to zero, the production technology is such that labour cannot be substituted for capital to produce the same expected level of output or vice versa.

Tables 2-4 and 2-5 give the values of the elasticities of substitution computed from the CES production function. These aggregate elasticities vary between 1.46 and 1.59 for 1961 and 1971 base years, indicating that on average factor inputs appear similar and thus could be easily substituted for one another without loss of output. But if this were true, unemployment would not be so difficult to overcome, for if capital and labour were indeed easily substituted for one another without loss of output, the sector could easily switch to labour-

TABLE 2-4
CES PRODUCTION FUNCTION, MARGINAL CONDITION
(1961 dollars)

$$\ln Q = \ln A + V [\ln L - 1 \ln \{ \delta (K/L)^{-e} + (1 - \delta)\}]$$

	δ	σ	V	$\bar{R}^2$	D.W.
Total activity with Net capital stock	0.4017	1.4565	1.5540 (75.2345)	0.9288	0.6580
Total activity with Gross capital stock	0.3500	1.5293	1.6133 (109.7680)	0.9258	1.1732
Production activity with Net capital stock	0.4449	1.9514	1.4157 (53.9157)	0.9898	0.6564
Production activity with Gross capital stock	0.3664	2.1013	1.4737 (55.4705)	0.9269	0.7323

δ—A parameter measuring the distribution of factor inputs for a given production technology
σ—Elasticity of substitution between factor inputs
V—Returns to scale
$\bar{R}^2$—Adjusted R^2

Source: Table B-1.

23

TABLE 2-5
CES PRODUCTION FUNCTION, MARGINAL CONDITION
(1971 constant dollars)
$$\ln Q = \ln A + V [\ln L - 1 \ln\{\delta (K/L)^{-P} + (1 - \delta)\}]$$

	δ	σ	V	$\bar{R}^2$	$D.W.$
Total activity with Net capital stock	0.2883	1.5850	1.7098 (91.7206)	0.9964	0.8098
Total activity with Gross capital stock	0.2388	1.6656	1.7413 (88.7178)	0.9962	1.7539
Production activity with Net capital stock	0.3191	2.1901	1.5374 (55.4021)	0.9903	0.6671
Production activity with Gross capital stock	0.2500	2.3218	1.5631 (44.9320)	0.9854	0.7920

δ—A parameter measuring the distribution of factor inputs for a given production technology
σ—Elasticity of substitution between factor inputs
V—Returns to scale
$\bar{R}^2$—Adjusted R^2

Source: Table B-1.

intensive technology in times of high unemployment, thus absorbing the unemployed without losing output or reducing productivity. This is a good example of the bias of aggregate data and the lack of correspondence between the world of the CES function and reality; indeed, advanced production technologies are relatively capital intensive and the possibility of substituting men for machines without loss in output (while simultaneously maximizing profits) is very remote indeed. Clearly, in many cases factor inputs are dissimilar and are not easily interchangeable. An examination of in Table 2-4 shows the degree of similarity between factor inputs, or the distribution of factor inputs. The larger the number, the more capital-intensive the technology (the range is generally between zero and one) and the more dissimilar the factors of production. On average, the result was 0.29 in 1971 dollars and 0.40 in 1961 dollars, suggesting a relative similarity in factor inputs. But, once again, the aggregate data are unrepresentative of the majority of the two-digit manufacturing industry groups, for their inputs are not, in fact, easily substitutable.

The same questions were then examined by estimating the variable elasticity of substitution (VES) and the Translog functions, where all the parameters were allowed to vary. The resulting elasticity of substitution measure is far more realistic than that in the CES function.

24

Furthermore, a technological progress function is estimated to show the labour-saving or capital-saving bias of technology. The results of the VES calculations displayed in Table 2-6 and Figure 2-2 reveal that

TABLE 2-6
VES PRODUCTION FUNCTION,
ELASTICITY OF SUBSTITUTION AND TECHNICAL CHANGE,
TOTAL AND PRODUCTION ACTIVITY

Year	Total Activity with Net Capital Stock		Production Activity with Net Capital Stock	
	Elasticity of Substitution	Technological Progress Function	Elasticity of Substitution	Technological Progress Function
1946	0.989	0.924	2.549	1.000
1947	0.995	0.930	2.541	0.998
1948	1.009	0.945	2.458	0.979
1949	1.003	0.938	2.417	0.969
1950	1.013	0.949	2.322	0.946
1951	1.019	0.956	2.284	0.937
1952	1.002	0.937	2.381	0.961
1953	0.991	0.926	2.439	0.974
1954	0.991	0.926	2.365	0.957
1955	1.005	0.940	2.281	0.936
1956	1.007	0.943	2.263	0.932
1957	1.001	0.936	2.259	0.931
1958	1.007	0.942	2.187	0.913
1959	1.020	0.957	2.137	0.899
1960	1.019	0.955	2.126	0.897
1961	0.997	0.932	2.041	0.874
1962	1.011	0.947	2.076	0.868
1963	1.019	0.955	1.998	0.863
1964	1.027	0.963	1.983	0.859
1965	1.031	0.968	1.977	0.857
1966	1.032	0.969	1.974	0.856
1967	1.032	0.970	1.960	0.852
1968	1.043	0.981	1.927	0.843
1969	1.050	0.989	1.910	0.838
1970	1.042	0.980	1.933	0.845
1971	1.048	0.987	1.926	0.843
1972	1.053	0.991	1.924	0.842
1973	1.061	1.000	1.905	0.837
1974	1.060	1.013	1.913	0.839
1975	1.048	0.987	1.951	0.850
1976	1.058	0.998	1.874	0.828
1977	1.065	1.005	1.815	0.811

26

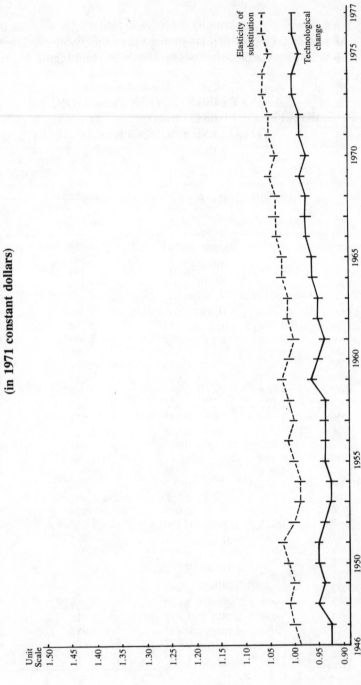

FIGURE 2-2
ELASTICITY OF SUBSTITUTION AND TECHNOLOGICAL PROGRESS,
TOTAL MANUFACTURING
(in 1971 constant dollars)

Note: $g+1$ implies technical change process in the direction of labour using
$g-$ implies technical change process in the direction of capital using

Source: Table 3-1 for capacity utilization; Appendix B, Table B-1 for value added output.

the value of the elasticity of substitution of the biased type, σ_b is around one and that the technological progress function (g) is slightly less than one. Thus, on aggregate, the sector was slightly capital intensive, and very little change in technological progress occurred in the whole sector. Capital and labour are shown in the VES function to be far less interchangeable than in the CES estimates. Since the VES is a more general and stable function and provides far more realistic information for policy decisions than the CD and the CES functions (see Appendix A), we therefore concentrate on the interpretation of its results.

Labour Productivity and Capital Intensity

Tables 2-7 and 2-8 containing the results of the VES production function estimations reveal that, on aggregate, capital intensity has been far less significant than labour in enhancing productivity in manufacturing. Technological progress, however, has contributed about 2.9 per cent to increased productivity during the last three decades (see Table 2-7, where $\alpha_3 = 0.0286$). Figure 2-3 (page 30) and Table 2-9 (page 31) illustrate the distinct differences between labour productivity and capital intensity levels, computed in both 1961 and 1971 dollars. While 1971 base year prices generate larger annual levels than those computed on 1961 base year, it is still desirable to show the actual biases in order to emphasize that care should be taken in comparing productivity figures derived from different base years.

Table 2-10 (page 32) summarizes the aggregate average performance of labour productivity and capital intensity in the various periods, reiterating the relatively large upward bias of productivity and capital intensity levels when these are computed on the basis of production activity rather than total activity. Using the more comprehensive total activity results we see that annual average productivity levels increased from one period to another throughout the entire thirty-two year period. The same pattern appears for the average annual level of capital intensity.

But average levels appear unjustifiably optimistic in assessing productivity performance during the last three decades when the post-energy crisis years are included. More useful is the assessment of the sector's continuous performance based on the computation of compounded annual rates of growth, which varied over the period. In the 1946-56 period, output per man-hour increased by a compounded annual rate of growth of 3.54 per cent, while capital intensity increased

27

TABLE 2-7
VES PRODUCTION FUNCTION, MARGINAL CONDITION, TOTAL ACTIVITY
$$Z = \alpha_0 + \alpha_1 k + \alpha_2 P_2 + \alpha_3 T$$

	α_0	α_1	α_2	α_3	$\bar{R}^2$
With net capital stock (1961 constant $'s)	0.6846 (9.2358)	−0.16974 (1.4234)	1.4164 (9.5826)		0.9919
	0.0766 (14.3368)	−0.03562 (0.41371)	0.3258 (1.4951)	0.02845 (5.6725)	0.9707
With gross capital stock (1961 constant $'s)	0.4449 (3.0927)	0.1169 (0.9526)	1.0741 (7.5620)		0.9916
With net capital stock (1971 constant $'s)	0.4716 (6.4627)	−0.1635 (1.3615)	1.4075 (9.5128)		0.9919
	0.8245 (10.3051)	−0.0294 (0.3402)	0.3146 (1.4451)	0.0286 (5.6916)	0.9962
With gross capital stock (1971 constant $'s)	0.2056 (1.7278)	0.1491 (1.4551)	1.0346 (8.5644)		0.9920
	0.6822 (6.0881)	0.1057 (1.5313)	0.1649 (0.9998)	0.02828 (6.0524)	0.9965

Z—Output/Man-hour; k — Capital/Labour; P — Hourly earnings; T — Time variable

α_0—A reduced form coefficient containing parameters of market imperfection and substitution (see relation (15) of Appendix A)

α_1—A reduced form coefficient containing parameters of labour efficiency and substitution (see relation (15) of Appendix A)

α_2—A coefficient which approximates elasticity of substitution of the neutral type

α_3—Technological change over time, a time variable T is used as a proxy to indicate such a change.

Source: Table B-1

an average of 3.75 per cent annually. In the 1957-66 period, there was a slight decline in the rate of growth of productivity from 3.54 per cent to 3.01 per cent, while the annual rate of growth in capital intensity dropped by more than 50 per cent from 3.75 per cent to 1.64 per cent per annum. During the 1967-73 period, there was a significant increase in the annual rate of growth of productivity to 4.23 per cent, while the annual rate of capital intensity accelerated from 1.64 per cent to 3.17 per cent.

TABLE 2-8
VES PRODUCTION FUNCTION, MARGINAL CONDITION, PRODUCTION ACTIVITY, 1946-1976
$$Z = \alpha_0 + \alpha_1 k + \alpha_2 P_2 + \alpha_3 T$$

	α_0	α_1	α_2	α_3	$\bar{R}^2$
With net capital stock (1961 constant dollars)	0.5281 (5.9882)	0.2946 (2.9494)	1.03198 (6.8864)		0.9902
	0.7603 (9.4115)	0.1093 (1.3127)	0.6516 (4.8045)	0.01916 (4.9327)	0.9948
With gross capital stock (1961 constant dollars)	0.1694 (1.3105)	0.4324 (4.7799)	0.8672 (6.8010)		0.9929
	0.5563 (3.6542)	0.2015 (2.0328)	0.6492 (5.2848)	0.01577 (3.6241)	0.9952
With net capital stock (1971 constant dollars)	0.2564 (3.1643)	0.2983 (2.9698)	1.0289 (6.8651)		0.9903
	0.6599 (6.4807)	0.11122 (1.3249)	0.6508 (4.8009)	0.01913 (4.9214)	0.9948
With gross capital stock (1971 constant dollars)	-0.01775 (0.1357)	0.3795 (3.9089)	0.9328 (6.7184)		0.9917
	0.5341 (3.1668)	0.1447 (1.5087)	0.6593 (5.1138)	0.01770 (4.1693)	0.9949

Z—Output/Man-hour; k — Capital/Labour; P — Hourly earnings; T — Time variable

α_0—A reduced form coefficient containing parameters of market imperfection and substitution (see relation (15) of Appendix A)

α_1—A reduced form coefficient containing parameters of labour efficiency and substitution (see relation (15) of Appendix A)

α_2—A coefficient which approximates elasticity of substitution of the neutral type

α_3—Technological change over time, a time variable T is used as a proxy to indicate such a change.

Source: Table B-1

The last decade was divided into two subperiods in order to observe whether or not the manufacturing sector as an aggregate suffered a serious setback in productivity and/or in capital intensity as a consequence of the 1973 energy crisis. Table 2-10 reveals a significant decline in the annual rate of productivity growth from 4.23 per cent in the 1967-73 period to 1.92 per cent in the 1973-77 subperiod. By

29

FIGURE 2-3
PRODUCTIVITY AND CAPITAL INTENSITY IN CANADIAN
MANUFACTURING, PRODUCTION ACTIVITY AND TOTAL ACTIVITY
(1961 constant dollars, net capital)

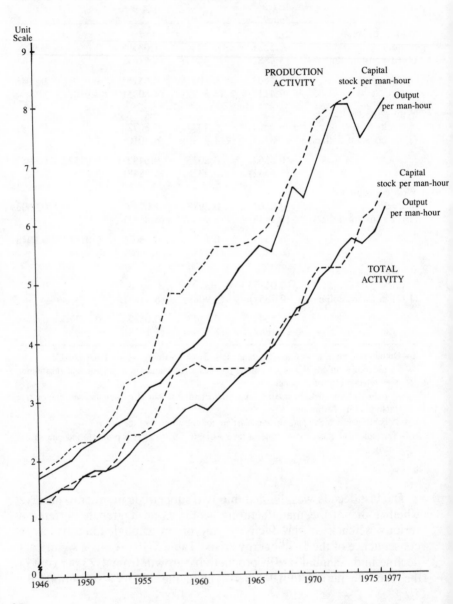

30

TABLE 2-9
VES PRODUCTION FUNCTION, PRODUCTIVITY
AND CAPITAL INTENSITY
(1971 dollars)

Year	Total Activity with Net Capital Stock		Production Activity with Net Capital Stock	
	Output/ Labour	Capital/ Labour	Output/ Labour	Capital/ Labour
1946	2.68	3.25	3.036	3.918
1947	2.80	3.21	3.157	3.866
1948	2.88	3.41	3.253	4.100
1949	2.92	3.55	3.378	4.379
1950	3.07	3.65	3.581	4.534
1951	3.19	3.67	3.718	4.565
1952	3.25	3.90	3.823	4.899
1953	3.39	4.12	4.078	5.283
1954	3.53	4.64	4.237	5.952
1955	3.75	4.73	4.508	6.071
1956	3.93	4.87	4.739	6.263
1957	4.02	5.42	4.878	7.019
1958	4.17	6.06	5.124	7.936
1959	4.41	6.12	5.390	7.967
1960	4.53	6.43	5.568	8.435
1961	4.42	6.20	5.780	8.656
1962	4.69	6.18	6.497	9.138
1963	4.86	6.19	6.669	9.054
1964	5.07	6.13	7.058	9.103
1965	5.24	6.16	7.294	9.152
1966	5.41	6.38	7.482	9.411
1967	5.62	6.89	7.419	9.707
1968	6.02	7.27	7.926	10.218
1969	6.38	7.46	8.631	10.773
1970	6.48	8.10	8.362	11.141
1971	6.90	8.56	9.023	11.928
1972	7.13	8.54	9.592	12.253
1973	7.51	8.57	10.165	12.365
1974	7.75	8.97	10.174	12.557
1975	7.57	9.74	9.498	13.040
1976	7.84	9.96	9.859	13.350
1977	8.26	10.42	10.362	13.945

contrast, the annual rate of growth in capital intensity continued to increase at a rate of 3.99 per cent after 1973. From these data and without referring to the structure of capital or its quality — extremely important issues into which production functions provide no insight —

31

TABLE 2-10
AVERAGE ANNUAL LEVELS AND COMPOUNDED RATES OF GROWTH IN PRODUCTIVITY AND CAPITAL INTENSITY

	Total Activity				Production Activity			
	Z	ΔZ	K	ΔK	Z	ΔZ	K	ΔK
	($)	(%)	($)	(%)	($)	(%)	($)	(%)
1961 Dollars								
1946-56	2.79	3.52	2.83	3.81	3.33	4.12	3.54	4.44
1957-66	4.06	3.03	4.45	1.67	5.45	4.35	6.24	2.99
1967-73	5.70	4.23	5.75	3.14	7.70	4.59	8.14	3.50
1973-77	6.75	1.92	6.93	4.06	8.83	0.38	9.49	2.50
1946-77		3.57		3.75		3.91		4.09
1971 Dollars								
1946-56	3.22	3.54	3.90	3.75	3.77	4.12	4.89	4.35
1957-66	4.68	3.01	6.13	1.64	6.17	4.36	8.59	2.97
1967-73	6.58	4.23	7.91	3.17	8.73	4.61	11.20	3.52
1973-77	7.79	1.92	9.53	3.99	10.01	0.37	13.05	2.43
1946-77		3.58		3.71		3.91		3.61

Δ—Stands for compounded annual rates of change.

Z—Output per man-hour (Q/L)

K—Net capital stock per man-hour (K/L)

Source: This table is computed from Tables 2-7 to 10 and Table 3-4.

we can conclude at this point only that labour productivity slowed after the 1973 energy crisis and the degree of capital intensity accelerated during this slowdown.

Nevertheless, several tentative explanations of this phenomenon should be considered. For example, a time lag of several years between the increase in capital intensity and its impact on labour productivity may account for the difference in the growth rates in these two inputs, though this proposition will not be tested. Moreover, qualitative factors that affect productivity growth, such as managerial skills and performance levels and efficiency in allocating and reallocating resources in a changing socioeconomic environment, may also contribute. These factors are implicit in production function analyses and appear correlated. Managerial ability and efficiency probably increased significantly during the last three decades, since a comparison of the results of the Cobb-Douglas function for production activity and total activity shows that management and service contributed significantly to rising economies of scale (see Table 2-3).

32

Daly and Globerman argue further that a potentially more important factor could be the dynamic aspects of greater output in relation to total factor input — the more rapid adoption of new technology, more aggressive, younger, and better-trained management, and a greater degree of competition within the Canadian market.[20] Other interpretations of the causes of productivity growth are extremely important for the understanding of productivity changes but are "outside" a production function analysis. One suggests that the impact of tariff reductions from the Kennedy Round and the Canada-U.S. Automotive Agreement led to an increase in efficiency, longer runs of production, and an implied increase in productivity.[21]

Although the explanations for the changes since 1973 are only tentative, since the 1973-77 subperiod covers only four years and thus may contain relatively large random errors in statistical tests, certain conclusions can be drawn about the behaviour of average labour productivity and capital intensity in manufacturing over the 1946-77 period. First, the evidence shows a definite trend towards increasing productivity and capital intensity. Second, with the exception of the 1966-69 and 1973-76 subperiods, capital intensity was higher than labour productivity, and on average the rate of growth in the former was higher than that in the latter. Third, on average over the whole period, production activity registered much higher rates of growth than total activity. However, higher growth rates are misleading and do not reflect "true" productivity ratios, because they contain only a subset of total employees engaged in manufacturing activity. These data cannot therefore be considered to represent accurately the competitiveness in the sector.

This evidence suggests that if the upward trend of capital intensity, which became more pronounced during recent years, were to continue, Canadian manufacturing might become more competitive abroad. It also indicates that if the trends were accompanied by continuous improvement in managerial skill, available economies of scale may be exhausted by the expansion of Canadian enterprises. In addition, Canadian manufacturing could not be considered a future contributor to a reduction in the economy's general unemployment problem if the recent capital-intensification trend were to continue.

Labour Share of Value Added and Real Wages

The phenomenon of unemployment and its relation to productivity and capital intensity poses a "chicken-and-egg" type of problem. Our data show that the absolute number of employees in manufacturing declined from 1.786 million in 1974 to 1.742 million in 1977. Real value added increased from $14,275.5 million in 1974 to $25,079.3 million in 1977. Real wages (in 1961 constant dollars) rose from $2.91 per hour in 1974 to $3.04 per hour in 1977. The puzzle is whether unemployment was a contributing factor, however small, to increases in labour productivity, or whether an increase in productivity, through the increase in capital intensity, was a contributing factor, again however small, to unemployment.

The share of wages in total output exhibited a general downward trend. We see from Table 2-11 that labour's share of value added decreased from 61 per cent in 1946 to 49 per cent in 1977. This means that payments to capital increased from 39 per cent in 1946 to 51 per cent in 1977. What this signifies is a definite structural change on aggregate with labour receiving a decreasing share of total value added (Figure 2-4, page 36). Coinciding with this changing trend, we observe in Figure 2-5 (page 37) an ever-increasing real wage per person throughout the period, from $1.65 in 1946 to $4.06 in 1977, which may be consistent with the increasing rate of capital intensity. The corresponding rates of increase in real wages and labour productivity are shown in Table 2-12 (page 37).

Although labour's share in value added declined from 0.61 in 1946 to 0.49 in 1977, technological change was slightly labour saving until 1962, and very mildly capital saving (close to neutral) from 1962 to 1977. The elasticity of substitution, in the "production activity" data declined from 2.11 in 1946 to 1.72 in 1977, indicating that changes in production technology rendered the factors of capital and labour increasingly dissimilar; that is, less substitutable. For total activity, however, the picture is entirely different. The elasticity of substitution variable did not diverge much from one, signifying almost neutral technological change.

Conclusion
Several conclusions emerge from the myriad of numbers presented in this chapter. First, capital intensity has been increasing faster than labour productivity. In the short run, there are likely to be lags between the introduction of new capital stock and its influence on productivity. In the longer run, however, the fruits of added capital per man-hour are expected to contribute to higher labour productivity. But even if new and higher quality capital is added at a rapid pace, older and less productive capital may not be discarded from the production processes. If depleted capital stock is largely unused but still included in net

34

TABLE 2-11
EARNINGS RATE AND SHARE OF EARNINGS
IN VALUE ADDED
(1971 constant dollars)

	Total Activity with Net Capital Stock		Production Activity with Net Capital Stock	
Year	Earnings	Earnings Share in Value Added	Earnings	Earnings Share in Value Added
	($/hr)	(%)	($/hr)	(%)
1946	1.65	0.613	1.52	0.500
1947	1.69	0.605	1.57	0.499
1948	1.69	0.586	1.58	0.488
1949	1.74	0.595	1.62	0.481
1950	1.78	0.580	1.66	0.464
1951	1.82	0.571	1.70	0.457
1952	1.94	0.596	1.82	0.475
1953	2.07	0.611	1.97	0.484
1954	2.15	0.611	2.00	0.472
1955	2.22	0.592	2.06	0.457
1956	2.31	0.589	2.15	0.453
1957	2.40	0.597	2.21	0.452
1958	2.46	0.589	2.24	0.437
1959	2.51	0.569	2.29	0.425
1960	2.59	0.572	2.35	0.422
1961	2.66	0.603	2.30	0.398
1962	2.73	0.583	2.54	0.391
1963	2.78	0.572	2.57	0.385
1964	2.83	0.559	2.68	0.380
1965	2.90	0.553	2.76	0.378
1966	2.98	0.551	2.82	0.377
1967	3.09	0.549	2.76	0.372
1968	3.21	0.533	2.85	0.360
1969	3.31	0.519	3.05	0.353
1970	3.46	0.533	3.03	0.362
1971	3.61	0.523	3.25	0.360
1972	3.67	0.515	3.44	0.359
1973	3.75	0.499	3.57	0.352
1974	3.89	0.501	3.61	0.355
1975	3.96	0.523	3.50	0.369
1976	3.95	0.504	3.34	0.338
1977	4.06	0.491	3.22	0.311

capital stock figures, the rate of growth in the measured productivity of capital would decline over time.

To determine whether or not depleted capital is included in the net

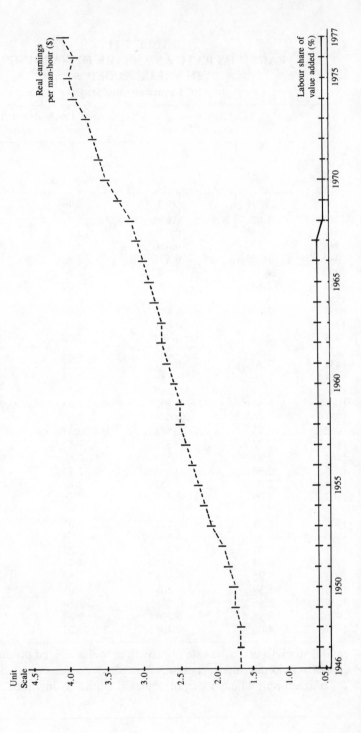

FIGURE 2-4

LABOUR SHARE OF VALUE ADDED AND REAL WAGES,

TOTAL MANUFACTURING, 1946-1977

(in 1971 constant dollars)

Real earnings per man-hour ($)

Labour share of value added (%)

Unit Scale

4.5

4.0

3.5

3.0

2.5

2.0

1.5

1.0

.05

1946   1950   1955   1960   1965   1970   1975   1977

36

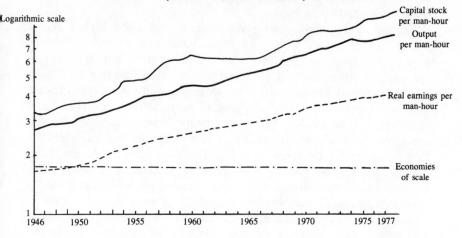

FIGURE 2-5
LABOUR PRODUCTIVITY, CAPITAL INTENSITY, REAL WAGES,
AND ECONOMIES OF SCALE, TOTAL MANUFACTURING
(in 1971 constant dollars)

TABLE 2-12
COMPOUNDED ANNUAL RATE OF CHANGE IN HOURLY REAL
WAGES AND LABOUR PRODUCTIVITY

	Labour Productivity	Real Wage Per Hour
	(%)	
1946-77	3.58	2.85
1946-60	3.56	3.05
1960-70	3.31	2.67
1970-77	3.08	2.02
1973-77	1.92	1.60

capital stock figures, it is necessary to examine the fluctuations in capital-output rates over the last three decades. If these ratios increased over time, added output per added capital stock decreased; that is, the average productivity of capital fell.

In fact, the average capital productivity rate in the manufacturing sector declined slightly. This is undesirable, since it means that the rise in capital intensity has not "paid off" in corresponding productivity increases. Information from two trade associations revealed that their

37

industries commonly retain obsolete capital in their plants, despite the fact that it is mostly unused. If this is true for most industries in the sector, then current statistical practices in recording capital stock will result in a downward bias in the output-capital ratios derived from Statistics Canada data banks.

Second, the manufacturing sector demonstrated a high level of economies of scale, with only small variations over the 1946-77 period. This indicates that there was no significant structural change in the sector. It is difficult to interpret the exact meaning of such aggregate economies of scale, since we do not know what type of scale economies exist and such an aggregate measure does not reveal any plant-specific behaviour. But some combination of product-specific economies of scale and interindustry complementarities likely contribute to overall economies of scale. The data point to a significant contribution to the rise in economies of scale from management. Further, calculations based on Diwan's method show increased labour productivity can be attributed to economies of scale.

Third, the analysis examined the impact of technology on labour efficiency — a measure of the elasticity of response of labour efficiency to technological change. Since increased labour efficiency implies increased productivity, we were interested in knowing the degree to which technology or its proxy, capital per man-hour, contributed to productivity. The data showed that aggregate labour efficiency did not depend upon capital in a major way. Indeed, the coefficient of elasticity of 0.40 demonstrates that an additional one per cent of new capital generated an increase of only 0.4 per cent in labour efficiency. Clearly, capital was not highly complementary to labour efficiency, and various other factors must account for increased labour efficiency. Although such factors as managerial ability and economies of scale contributed to rising productivity, little is known about other factors that may account for productivity increases.

Finally, in light of the above tests, I examined the distribution of payments to labour and capital during the last three decades, to see whether there was a gain in labour share in the manufacturing sector. From the evidence it was obvious that the rate of returns to labour fell below that to capital, indicating that labour is receiving a lower share of productivity gains than capital.

Further, the technological progress function was almost constant throughout the thirty-two year period, exhibiting a very slight capital-using or labour-saving bias. This is somewhat a puzzling phenomenon, for the impact of capital intensification does not show, raising a question about the effectiveness of such a process on productivity. If such a trend were to continue, expansion in the manufacturing sector would likely generate much less than a proportionate increase in labour employment. Thus expansion in the sector is unlikely to solve unemployment problems.

Although these aggregate data are useful for some purposes, the following chapters establish that an industrial policy should not be guided by results from such an aggregate, because the values of these important parameters vary tremendously from one industry to another. Thus policy decisions should be based mainly on the industry-specific considerations analysed in Chapter 3 and Volume II.

Industry Analysis

3

This chapter contains a disaggregated analysis of the nineteen industry groups at the two-digit level of the Statistics Canada Standard Industrial Classification (SIC). During the 1946-77 period, the classification of Canadian manufacturing industries was refined and redefined in 1948, 1960, and 1970, so that an industry group might not contain the same mix of subgroups throughout the period. However, the periods in this study — 1946-60, 1960-70, and 1970-77 — were selected to coincide with the dates of the reclassification, and thus the industry groups remain statistically consistent throughout the thirty-two years of the analysis.[1]

The sections following assess the performance of manufacturing industries in terms of the variables estimated and computed from the production functions discussed in Chapter 2. The analysis covers absolute, average, and marginal values of productivity performance and shows that industries belonging to a "high performance" group using average productivity measures might rank with a lower performance group when rate-of-change or marginal data are used. All industries were evaluated in terms of total activity and net capital stock. All calculations were made in 1971 constant dollars. For the sake of clarity, value added was used as a measure of output throughout the study, drawing on Griliches's conclusions:

> [Value added] facilitates the comparison of results for different industries with different material use intensities, and it improves the comparability of data for individual establishments even within the same industry as long as they differ in their "thickness" (amount of vertical integration).
>
> It facilitates the aggregation of output measures across industries through the reduction of "double-counting".
>
> It reduces the probability of estimation and interpretation by eliminating the intermediate input (M) from both sides of the equation. "Materials" are asymmetric input.

Any short-run fluctuation in demand may be met without such change in the work force or machinery in place, but will usually induce a similar fluctuation in the use of raw material or energy input. In this sense intermediate input (*M*) is more endogenous than labour (*L*) or capital (*K*), and its use as an independent variable is more likely to lead to simultaneous equation biases.[2]

This issue is controversial and not all economists would agree with Griliches. Consequently, some studies use value added data and others use total output figures that include intermediate inputs. Using value added consistently gives somewhat different productivity results from a study that is based on total output figures. Therefore, it is difficult to compare two studies using different variables to measure output. Here the results of the nineteen industry groups are assessed in terms of absolute levels and rates of change.

Capacity Utilization

The question of capacity utilization and its implications for productivity performance has been raised often in discussions among economists over the last few years. In 1979 Edward Carmichael, writing for the Conference Board in Canada, claimed that

> by the end of 1978 the Canadian economy [had] been operating substantially below its potential (capacity) for over four years. The cost of allowing resources to be idle for such a long period has been substantial. On the assumption that there has been no change in long-run productivity growth, the cumulative loss in real GNP has been $32.2 billion since 1974.[3]

The next year the Economic Council confirmed that the economy was operating below its potential and pointed out that production activity is inefficient when the economy operates below full capacity. The Council reasoned that weaknesses on the demand side were a cause of below capacity performance, arguing that during periods of temporarily falling demand for products, firms do not lay off workers, and this excess manpower causes inefficient production.[4] Both views were helpful but tended to concentrate on short-run observations.

The findings in this study show that the situation is much more severe when viewed in a long-run perspective. Clearly, Carmichael's key assumption that productivity did not change in the long run was inaccurate for, in fact, productivity varied substantially between 1946 and 1977. Second, all the manufacturing industries operated below

41

capacity for most of the thirty-two year period and, if workers are not laid off, the sector faces a long period of redundant employment because the economy remains in a "permanent" state of inefficient production. My own view is that it is capital that stays idle in periods of low capacity utilization and perpetuates that condition. From my analysis it is more likely that labour is a variable and, unless the industry experiences extremely short periods of low capacity utilization, workers are laid off. The evidence of higher unemployment rates during low capacity utilization years does not seem to be a coincidence.

Table 3-1 (pages 44-45) shows fluctuations in capacity utilization in every single industry. These fluctuations often but not always reflect the economy's business cycle trends. The Canadian economy as an aggregate reached full capacity output in 1973. The manufacturing sector also reached full capacity output in the same year (see Figure 2-1). A close examination of Table 3-1 reveals, however, that only four of the nineteen industry groups conform with the aggregate pattern, demonstrating clearly the inapplicability of aggregative results to the behaviour of single industries. Much too often statements refer to the performance of the whole economy or the entire manufacturing sector, even though there is no necessary relationship between the behaviour of the aggregates and that of the specific industries. Thus no policy implications derived from the aggregate would be reliable for the various separate industries. Indeed, individual manufacturing industries achieved full capacity during four different periods. Food and beverage, rubber plastic, leather, electrical and electronic, petroleum and coal, and paper and paper products industries produced at full capacity in the 1946-1951 period. Tobacco products, printing and publishing, and wood industries reached full capacity output in 1955-56. The primary metals, non-metallic minerals, furniture and fixtures, and metal fabrication industries attained full capacity output in 1965-66. Finally, in 1973, knitting mills, textile, transportation equipment, and chemical and chemical products industries reached peak capacity output.

This result is a source of some concern, since six manufacturing industries operated below capacity for over three decades, and three others functioned below capacity for at least twenty-five years. These nine industries represent 49 per cent of the manufacturing sector's value added. An additional group of four industries reached capacity in the mid-1960s and diverged from full capacity afterwards. This means that thirteen of the nineteen manufacturing industries, representing 71 per cent of the sector's value added, operated below capacity after 1965.

The message that emerges is that much of the sector has retained, for almost a generation, varying levels of idle productive resources that represent an enormous loss of potential income for the country. In addition, since optimal efficiency in resource allocation is closely related to full capacity operation, had productive resources been better utilized in the past, productivity levels would have been higher and Canada's competitiveness in world markets would have been substantially greater. These findings also challenge the belief that price increases are inevitable, since the "economy" has reached full capacity output and any increase demand by consumers "by definition" would result in increased inflationary pressures. Such arguments stem from a firm commitment to demand management policy and a neglect of the supply side of our economy that should be overcome.

Table 3-2 (page 46) provides further insights into the dynamic behaviour of capacity utilization. For the total manufacturing sector from 1946 to 1960 capacity utilization increased by 0.02 per cent annually and in the 1960-70 period, by 1.15 per cent annually. Between 1970 and 1977 capacity utilization declined at an annual rate of 0.34 per cent. After the energy crisis in 1973 the gap between actual and potential output increased considerably to 2.57 per cent annum. This pattern is alarming, since it points out an increasing rate in capacity build-up in 1973-74 that was unaccompanied by a corresponding increase in output. After 1975 the rate of increase in output and capacity utilization was about the same, but the gap between the two remained constant. The causes of the trend in total manufacturing are difficult to glean from the aggregates. Thus we turn our attention to trends in different industry groups.

Table 3-2 shows that the highest annual rate of decline in capacity utilization occurred from 1973 until 1977. During that period seven industries — furniture and fixtures, primary metals, metal fabricating, machinery, electrical and electronic products, petroleum and coal products, chemical and chemical products — exhibited a rate of decline in capacity utilization that was greater than the sectoral average. In all other industries, with the exception of tobacco products, rubber and plastic, and clothing, the rate declined, but by less than in the overall sector. But the most alarming phenomenon, exhibited in twelve of the nineteen industries — food and beverage, rubber and plastic, leather, wood, furniture and fixtures, paper and paper

TABLE 3-1
CAPACITY UTILIZATION, BY INDUSTRY
(%)

Year	Total manu.	Food and bev.	Tobacco	Rub. and Plas.	Leather	Text.	Knit-ting	Cloth.	Wood	Furn. and fix.
1946	82.1	100.0	83.9	78.9	100.0			72.0		
1947	88.7	92.8	81.9	100.0	85.1			65.3		
1948	88.7	87.8	77.6	83.2	71.9			64.4		
1949	87.8	83.3	80.4	94.0	74.1			63.7		
1950	91.1	82.6	80.5	76.6	70.9			62.8		
1951	95.6	83.0	74.6	78.8	68.6			60.5		
1952	93.6	85.1	85.9	69.6	76.7			66.1		
1953	94.6	84.6	91.0	74.7	80.8			64.3		
1954	87.9	84.1	93.1	59.9	74.9			59.6		
1955	96.2	83.1	99.2	65.6	80.0			61.2		
1956	94.1	84.2	100.0	69.7	86.3			63.6		
1957	87.6	83.9	99.1	61.5	83.8			63.7	89.4	
1958	81.7	84.2	96.8	58.7	83.6			64.5	90.1	
1959	85.1	84.8	93.9	64.9	87.2			67.6	92.2	
1960	82.3	82.5	94.8	52.3	82.6			68.3	91.5	
1961	82.4	81.3	93.9	48.3	91.2	61.7	59.5	70.2	89.8	75.0
1962	87.1	81.1	94.1	61.1	94.4	68.7	63.0	72.5	93.1	79.9
1963	90.1	80.7	95.9	62.8	94.7	73.8	68.7	74.6	96.3	85.2
1964	95.0	82.1	96.4	66.3	97.8	77.8	70.4	76.1	100.0	90.2
1965	98.0	81.1	96.1	66.9	98.8	76.1	70.8	75.9	97.5	97.3
1966	98.3	82.0	93.9	70.2	98.1	72.9	69.3	75.9	94.4	100.0
1967	94.8	82.6	93.5	71.7	93.0	72.1	67.7	73.9	92.9	93.6
1968	95.8	80.8	86.6	73.3	96.0	78.3	79.3	76.5	92.7	89.2
1969	98.5	80.0	86.0	74.9	93.2	86.1	85.0	77.6	90.6	89.6
1970	92.3	78.9	88.5	69.9	85.8	79.9	87.3	77.9	80.0	80.8
1971	92.0	78.8	87.0	67.4	87.5	85.3	94.2	86.6	82.5	80.0
1972	95.7	78.7	88.3	69.6	85.2	95.2	97.6	94.3	83.1	89.5
1973	100.0	77.4	90.8	73.4	83.8	100.0	100.0	97.2	85.4	91.2
1974	83.1	74.1	94.6	68.3	82.5	95.8	93.3	94.6	74.9	86.9
1975	89.1	72.4	91.1	59.5	79.0	90.2	92.0	95.5	65.5	74.1
1976	90.0	73.1	92.1	67.9	73.7	90.5	92.2	100.0	75.7	77.0
1977	90.1	72.6	95.1	75.2	76.0	93.1	97.1	98.1	80.3	76.0

products, primary metals, metal fabricating, machinery, electrical and electronic products, petroleum and coal products, and chemical and chemical products — is that, since their full-capacity year, although their rates of potential output increased, their rates of capacity utilization decreased at a faster rate. This pattern implies the presence of structural bottlenecks that prevent industries from approaching their potential output levels.

TABLE 3-1 (Continued)

Year	Paper	Print. and Pub.	Prim. Metals	Metal Fab.	Mach-inery	Trans. Equip.	Electric. and Electron.	Non-Met. Min.	Petrol. and Coal	Chem-ical
1946	83.0	65.6				40.9	79.1	56.6	100.0	71.5
1947	88.0	70.3				52.1	100.0	66.5	96.6	71.3
1948	89.9	75.2				55.0	91.6	67.4	96.5	68.8
1949	91.4	77.5				56.7	87.7	70.5	92.2	68.2
1950	96.9	82.5				60.8	89.9	77.4	96.3	71.7
1951	100.0	81.5				72.0	86.8	82.6	99.2	77.6
1952	90.7	80.3				79.6	78.5	82.5	94.5	75.7
1953	90.8	87.8				84.6	84.3	86.8	91.3	73.2
1954	89.7	92.2				65.1	76.9	86.0	87.3	74.0
1955	88.5	93.0				67.1	81.4	92.6	88.5	77.6
1956	87.4	100.0				70.0	65.8	93.8	93.3	78.8
1957	77.6	97.6				66.6	71.7	84.7	87.9	77.4
1958	72.5	92.2				57.4	65.6	83.3	81.4	76.1
1959	75.2	96.9				55.4	66.2	85.8	82.1	74.6
1960	75.8	96.5				52.0	65.5	78.5	80.5	74.9
1961	73.7	96.6	81.7	64.9	67.5	50.1	67.0	79.1	82.7	76.1
1962	73.9	96.0	84.7	72.1	73.3	58.2	75.9	87.8	86.5	78.7
1963	75.2	94.1	87.6	79.6	75.7	64.8	78.5	86.5	90.2	81.7
1964	78.7	90.6	95.2	88.3	82.7	67.0	83.3	94.6	89.5	90.3
1965	77.1	92.7	100.0	77.0	85.6	75.8	87.8	100.0	91.3	92.5
1966	76.1	95.7	97.9	100.0	90.6	73.9	91.2	96.1	93.0	92.7
1967	60.5	95.3	88.2	93.6	85.0	78.6	84.4	83.3	90.1	88.5
1968	68.8	94.2	92.8	99.9	81.2	85.8	82.6	85.2	95.2	88.8
1969	73.7	95.6	91.3	92.4	88.3	91.5	84.8	84.4	94.2	92.3
1970	70.4	93.6	92.4	87.3	83.3	75.5	77.4	76.5	90.4	89.4
1971	67.1	93.7	86.7	85.5	81.8	83.9	77.6	84.7	88.6	90.4
1972	70.0	96.5	85.4	85.4	87.6	89.4	80.5	88.3	89.4	93.0
1973	72.4	98.9	88.5	90.6	93.5	100.0	85.7	94.6	95.0	100.0
1974	75.1	98.4	91.0	93.6	100.0	94.7	86.6	93.0	90.5	99.6
1975	58.6	95.6	78.7	81.8	93.2	86.9	76.9	86.8	82.9	85.8
1976	64.8	95.9	74.0	82.8	85.0	91.5	78.5	85.5	80.0	80.1
1977	66.9	94.5	77.4	80.2	78.6	94.6	74.1	87.9	80.6	78.2

Three factors that may shed light on the problem are the relationship of decreasing capacity utilization with capital intensity, and the rates of change of average capital productivity and labour productivity. For example, we found that seven of these twelve industries had lower than average capital intensity; all of them, except rubber and plastic products, demonstrated a declining rate of average capital productivity; and five industries exhibited "low" labour productivity. These findings reveal some serious difficulties, whose solutions lie in the domain of industrial policy.

TABLE 3-2
COMPOUNDED ANNUAL RATE OF GROWTH
IN CAPACITY UTILIZATION
(%)

	1946-60	1960-70	1970-77	1973-77
Total manufacturing	0.02	1.15	−0.34	−2.57
Food and beverage	−1.36	−0.45	−1.18	−1.59
Tobacco	0.88	−0.69	1.03	1.16
Rubber and plastic	−2.89	2.94	1.05	0.61
Leather	−1.36	0.38	−1.72	−2.41
Textile	n.a.	2.91	2.21	−1.77
Knitting	n.a.	4.35	1.53	−0.73
Clothing	−0.38	1.32	3.35	0.23
Wood	n.a.	1.33	0.05	−1.53
Furniture and fixtures	n.a.	0.83	−0.87	−4.46
Paper	−0.65	−0.74	−0.73	−1.96
Printing and publishing	2.80	−0.30	0.14	−1.13
Primary metals	n.a.	1.38	−2.50	−3.29
Metal fabricating	n.a.	3.35	−1.20	−3.00
Machinery	n.a.	2.36	−0.83	−4.25
Transportation equipment	1.73	3.80	3.27	−1.38
Electrical and electronic	−1.34	1.68	−0.62	−3.57
Non-metallic mineral	2.36	−0.26	2.00	−1.82
Petroleum and coal	−1.54	1.17	−1.63	−4.03
Chemical	0.33	1.79	−1.89	−5.96

Source: Table 3-1.

Among the problems, the declining rate of capital productivity could very well be the major factor causing Canadian industries to lose ground in world markets. But even if Canadian labour productivity increased favourably relative to that of our major competitors abroad, the rise would not compensate for the loss in capital productivity enough to raise total productivity above the level in manufacturing in, say, the United States. To aggravate their problems further, Canadian industries pay about 25 per cent more than their American counterparts for capital goods, because most of them are imported and subject to tariffs. Thus just to stay at par with producers in our major export market the marginal productivity of capital must be at least 25 per cent higher in Canada than the United States. In order to make our final exportable products competitive, both labour and capital must be more productive than their U.S. counterparts. Since this is unlikely in the near future, Canadian governments should consider a reduction in tariff rates for capital goods.

Several possible explanations of low capital productivity are current. One is that manufacturing industries are "overloaded" with excess quantities of capital they cannot readily utilize. Another is that industries are not replenishing old, low productive capital quickly enough to overcome declining capital productivity stemming from increasing accumulations of unused and low productive capital in the plants. Yet another is that technology is having a questionable impact on labour efficiency, an issue examined later in this chapter. My discussions with representatives of trade associations and several industries indicate that the second possibility — a slow capital replacement rate — is likely to prevail in the majority of the industries in the sector. The undesirable combination of the absolute cost of new capital, coupled with unjustifiably high domestic interest rates, seems to be a major cause for obsolescence of plant and equipment in Canadian manufacturing industries.[5]

Economies of Scale

Economies of scale are often thought to be directly related to productivity performance, and many argue that the Canadian economy is too small to enable industries to attain sufficient economies of scale to achieve optimum levels of productivity. We used three types of production functions — the Cobb-Douglas (CD), the constant elasticity of substitution (CES), and the translog form — to assess these arguments.

Table 3-3 presents results of the calculations of scale economies in the three functions (see also Appendix D). With the exception of those for the textile industry most of the results are consistent in the three functions and could reliably be used for policy formation. The textile industry is a special case because of the 1976 decision to impose import quotas to protect the industry, a step that may throw off the stability of statistical results. Specifically, and without the introduction of a time variable, all three functions gave a strong degree of economies of scale (1.7-1.9) for Total Manufacturing. When time variable was introduced into the functions, CD and CES continued to show the same degree of scale economies, but the Translog function showed only a result of 1.17 (see Tables D-1, D-2, D-4 in Appendix D). Table 3-3 also shows the tremendous variations in the degree of scale economies among the manufacturing industries, from those that registered very strong economies of scale (1.54-1.86) through to some that exhibited diseconomies of scale throughout the period analysed.

The industries are divided into four groups. The first contains nine

47

TABLE 3-3
ECONOMIES OF SCALE,
THREE PRODUCTION FUNCTIONS

	Cobb-Douglas	Constant Elasticity of Substitute	Translog
Total manufacturing	1.75	1.73	1.86
Food and beverage	1.53	1.54	1.41
Tobacco	1.98	1.86	1.07
Rubber and plastic	1.13	1.13	1.06
Leather	1.00	1.04	0.80
Textile	1.16	0.90	0.36
Knitting	0.88	0.98	0.82
Clothing	0.96	1.09	1.24
Wood	1.30	1.32	1.35
Furniture and fixtures	1.40	1.39	1.45
Paper	1.21	1.21	1.18
Printing and publishing	1.63	1.61	1.34
Primary metals	1.38	1.38	1.59
Metal fabricating	1.62	1.62	1.73
Machinery	1.06	1.01	1.46
Transportation equipment	1.56	1.64	1.92
Electrical and electronic	1.70	1.72	1.61
Non-metallic mineral	1.39	1.38	1.67
Petroleum and coal	1.57	1.85	1.94
Chemical	1.45	1.49	1.45

industries that show very strong economies of scale (1.54-1.86). These are: tobacco products, transportation equipment, food and beverage products, machinery, metal fabrication, printing and publishing, electrical and electronic products, petroleum and coal products, and chemical and chemical products. The second group consists of industries with economies of scale ranging from 1.13 to 1.39: furniture and fixtures, wood, rubber and plastic products, non-metallic minerals, primary metals, paper and paper products. The third group consists of two industries, clothing and leather products, which show constant returns to scale. The fourth group contains the textile industries and knitting mills which exhibit diseconomies of scale throughout the period analysed. We should note that the Translog function shows the leather products industries in this category as well (with a scale value of 0.8).

In Chapter 1 where I described the issue of economies of scale and its many complexities I assumed that the scale economies were of the "product" type. However, another possible type of economies of scale exists in the total industry group. This phenomenon, the "externalities internal to the industry," is rather straightforward, though it may seem contradictory. Certain firms in the same industry produce complementary products, thereby generating higher capacity utilization and growth in various sections in the industry; that is, one firm's production becomes another firm's input for its final products. Demand for inputs extends beyond a single industry's boundaries to another complementary industry. Indeed, some of the industries' economies of scale are probably due to this process of internalization of a firm's externalities within the industry group.

Tables 3-4 to 3-6 provide further insight into the behaviour pattern of economies of scale through time. Table 3-4 reveals two interesting points. First, economies of scale did not change radically after 1946 or, indeed, after the early 1960s in the industries with no data from the 1940s and 1950s. Second, two-thirds of Canadian manufacturing industries enjoyed various degrees of increases in their scale, and only seven industries showed a very small decline in scale during the thirty-year period. This is encouraging in a young economy, for the positive growth trend shows that many industries have not yet reached "maturity" of scale and their potential for expansion is not yet fully utilized.

Table 3-5 (page 52) outlines the compounded rate of annual growth in scale economies during various periods. While the average for the whole sector over the whole period is a decline of 0.01 per cent per annum, only four industries exhibited a similar decrease. All industries experienced an increase in the rate of growth in scale economies during the 1970s. The growth rate after 1973 was, however, somewhat different. Total manufacturing declined by 0.07 per cent per annum; more important, eight industry groups showed a decline in their yearly rate. The exact causes for this decline cannot be pinpointed without a careful and comprehensive study of these industries. The energy crisis seems not to be the only explanation, although these eight particular industries are indeed energy intensive. Pure speculation suggests that demand factors in the United States could well be an important factor.

Tables 3-4 and 3-5 exhibited two trends, based on absolute numbers and annual rates of change. The significance of these trends was assessed using the Translog production function. The detailed econometric results of this function are found in Appendix D, while Table 3-6 (page 53) summarizes the results. The absolute levels of

49

TABLE 3-4
CES PRODUCTION FUNCTION, ECONOMIES OF SCALE
(1971 constant dollars)

Year	Total manu.	Food and bev.	Tobacco	Rub. and Plast.	Leather	Text.	Knit-ting	Cloth.	Wood	Furn. and fix.
1946	1.7379	1.5670		1.1189	0.9671					
1947	1.7382	1.5575		1.1403	0.9592					
1948	1.7358	1.5519		1.1304	0.9490					
1949	1.7328	1.5465		1.1470	0.9532					
1950	1.7355	1.5460		1.1269	0.9521					
1951	1.7352	1.5447		1.1285	0.9540					
1952	1.7306	1.5457		1.1224	0.9573					
1953	1.7290	1.5454		1.1292	0.9648					
1954	1.7286	1.5455		1.1156	0.9643					
1955	1.7315	1.5440		1.1229	0.9675					
1956	1.7310	1.5447		1.1294	0.9739					
1957	1.7263	1.5443	1.9096	1.1251	0.9751			0.9969	1.3057	
1958	1.7257	1.5442	1.8993	1.1273	0.9755			0.9971	1.3083	
1959	1.7294	1.5447	1.8933	1.1362	0.9795			0.9993	1.3094	
1960	1.7293	1.5435	1.8983	1.1223	0.9779			1.0002	1.3131	
1961	1.7243	1.5386	1.8952	1.1140	0.9801	0.3569	0.5805	1.0021	1.3165	1.3854
1962	1.7290	1.5395	1.8919	1.1323	0.9842	0.3648	0.5876	1.0076	1.3202	1.3890
1963	1.7308	1.5401	1.8954	1.1330	0.9852	0.3710	0.5984	1.0111	1.3223	1.3896
1964	1.7322	1.5488	1.8980	1.1369	0.9884	0.3768	0.6031	1.0134	1.3248	1.3889
1965	1.7310	1.5306	1.9013	1.1374	0.9899	0.3783	0.6054	1.0150	1.3234	1.3914
1966	1.7283	1.5310	1.8985	1.1406	0.9906	0.3780	0.6075	1.0175	1.3240	1.3924
1967	1.7265	1.5413	1.8952	1.1451	0.9897	0.3793	0.6082	1.0167	1.3254	1.3896
1968	1.7302	1.5413	1.8898	1.1514	0.9930	0.3881	0.6203	1.0206	1.3262	1.3900
1969	1.7332	1.5423	1.8918	1.1532	0.9943	0.3972	0.6261	1.0218	1.3267	1.3907
1970	1.7302	1.5425	1.8959	1.1278	0.9946	0.3948	0.6309	1.0224	1.3240	1.3887
1971	1.7326	1.5444	1.8982	1.1261	0.9980	0.4014	0.6373	1.0267	1.3252	1.3883
1972	1.7335	1.5452	1.9010	1.1271	0.9988	0.4097	0.6415	1.0288	1.3197	1.3916
1973	1.7362	1.5455	1.9042	1.1296	1.0004	0.4136	0.6453	1.0307	1.3189	1.3936
1974	1.7353	1.5437	1.9054	1.1277	1.0037	0.4115	0.6418	1.0307	1.3169	1.3895
1975	1.7279	1.5428	1.9007	1.1202	1.0019	0.4086	0.6421	1.0312	1.3152	1.3823
1976	1.7284	1.5449	1.9071	1.1307	0.9980	0.4099	0.6443	1.0336	1.3226	1.3898
1977	1.7311	1.5450	1.9140	1.1410	1.0092	0.4127	0.6531	1.0363	1.3275	1.3970

economies of scale estimated by this function are generally consistent with the results of the two other functions (CD and CES). Indeed, it is quite striking to learn that fourteen out of nineteen industries enjoy significantly high degrees of economies of scale. Turning to the dynamics of economies of scale through time, the results show highly significant changes in nine industries. Rubber and plastic products, clothing, transportation equipment, electrical and electronic products,

TABLE 3-4 (Continued)

Year	Paper	Print. and pub.	Prim. Metals	Metal Fab.	Mach- inery	Trans. Equip.	Electric. and Electron.	Non- Met. Min.	Petrol. and Coal	Chem- icals
1946	1.2193	1.6059				1.6303	1.7533	1.3715	1.8153	1.4970
1947	1.2182	1.6081				1.6462	1.7520	1.3798	1.8680	1.4959
1948	1.2168	1.6097				1.6500	1.7459	1.3783	1.8019	1.4926
1949	1.2167	1.6022				1.6516	1.7399	1.3800	1.7932	1.4820
1950	1.2190	1.6060				1.6655	1.7354	1.3839	1.7952	1.4952
1951	1.2192	1.6037				1.6602	1.7253	1.3876	1.7969	1.4967
1952	1.2137	1.6027				1.6558	1.7162	1.3875	1.7863	1.4922
1953	1.2154	1.6070				1.6523	1.7154	1.3878	1.7840	1.4862
1954	1.2157	1.6074				1.6362	1.7145	1.3857	1.7796	1.4775
1955	1.2151	1.6071				1.6370	1.7177	1.3863	1.7834	1.4933
1956	1.2149	1.6097				1.6356	1.6967	1.3863	1.7905	1.4947
1957	1.2903	1.6105				1.6303	1.7029	1.3813	1.7976	1.4937
1958	1.2068	1.6066				1.6241	1.7051	1.3790	1.7888	1.4926
1959	1.2103	1.6074				1.6256	1.7080	1.3794	1.7972	1.4926
1960	1.2124	1.6058				1.6234	1.7139	1.3765	1.7968	1.4949
1961	1.2112	1.6051	1.3744	1.6120	0.9680	1.6262	1.7074	1.3770	1.7913	1.4875
1962	1.120	1.6060	1.3772	1.6131	0.9720	1.6350	1.7131	1.3837	1.7977	1.4980
1963	1.2137	1.6048	1.3789	1.6157	0.9731	1.6400	1.7144	1.3823	1.8059	1.4919
1964	1.2160	1.6021	1.3814	1.6168	0.9793	1.6356	1.7174	1.3854	1.8090	1.4982
1965	1.2148	1.6013	1.3818	1.6168	0.9805	1.6411	1.7178	1.3861	1.8162	1.4977
1966	1.2134	1.6019	1.3704	1.6159	0.9805	1.6349	1.7155	1.3814	1.8132	1.4962
1967	1.2091	1.6019	1.3747	1.6149	0.9863	1.6384	1.7116	1.3740	1.8110	1.4923
1968	1.2111	1.6026	1.3708	1.6138	0.9849	1.6453	1.7139	1.3772	1.8152	1.4920
1969	1.2159	1.6046	1.3814	1.6153	0.9854	1.6480	1.7160	1.3782	1.8140	1.4946
1970	1.2145	1.6053	1.3812	1.6139	0.9915	1.6483	1.7162	1.3747	1.8102	1.4925
1971	1.2136	1.6065	1.3798	1.6153	0.9909	1.6459	1.7155	1.3829	1.8079	1.4958
1972	1.2173	1.6077	1.3806	1.6153	0.9980	1.6477	1.7197	1.3858	1.8073	1.5001
1973	1.2204	1.6083	1.3839	1.6183	1.0011	1.6521	1.7216	1.3904	1.8079	1.5050
1974	1.2213	1.6096	1.3850	1.6195	1.0056	1.6504	1.7217	1.3896	1.7993	1.5035
1975	1.2065	1.6099	1.3777	1.6128	1.0104	1.6497	1.7184	1.3872	1.7908	1.4909
1976	1.2139	1.6107	1.3757	1.6136	1.0062	1.6525	1.7239	1.3881	1.7900	1.4854
1977	1.2203	1.6127	1.3790	1.6152	1.0025	1.6547	1.7273	1.3940	1.7869	1.4821

non-metallic minerals, and the chemical and chemical products industries all demonstrate growth in scale economies at an increasing rate as time progresses. Textile, metal fabrication, and the petroleum and coal products industries show growth in scale economies but at a diminishing rate through time. The remaining ten industries show no significant change in economies of scale throughout the period. Overall, economies of scale rose in the manufacturing sector at an accelerating rate and in a statistically significant way.

TABLE 3-5
COMPOUNDED ANNUAL RATE OF GROWTH
IN ECONOMIES OF SCALE

	1946-77	1946-60	1960-70	1970-77	1973-77
Total manufacturing	−0.01	−0.04	0.01	0.01	−0.07
Food and beverage	−0.05	−0.11	−0.01	0.02	−0.02
Tobacco	0.01	−0.20	−0.01	0.14	0.13
Rubber and plastic	0.06	0.64	0.05	0.17	0.25
Leather	0.14	0.08	0.17	0.21	0.22
Textile	0.86	n.a.	1.13	0.63	−0.24
Knitting	0.70	n.a.	0.93	0.49	0.31
Clothing	0.19	0.11	0.22	0.19	0.14
Wood	0.08	0.19	0.08	0.04	0.17
Furniture and fixtures	0.05	n.a.	0.03	0.09	0.06
Paper	0.003	−0.04	0.02	0.07	0.002
Printing and publishing	0.22	0.27	0.14	0.24	0.18
Primary metals	0.02	n.a.	0.06	−0.02	−0.09
Metal fabricating	0.01	n.a.	0.01	0.01	−0.05
Machinery	0.21	n.a.	0.26	0.16	−0.08
Transportation equipment	0.05	−0.03	0.15	0.06	0.05
Electrical and electronic	−0.05	−0.16	0.01	0.09	−0.38
Non-metallic mineral	0.05	0.03	−0.01	0.17	0.07
Petroleum and coal	−0.05	−0.07	0.07	−0.19	−0.29
Chemical	−0.03	−0.01	−0.02	−0.10	−0.38

Labour Productivity and Capital Intensity

Detailed sets of data on labour productivity and capital intensity from the more general variable elasticity of substitution production function are contained in Table D-5, where labour productivity is defined as value added output per-hour, both in terms of "total activity" rather than production workers only. This table reveals an absolute increase in both productivity and capital intensity in all manufacturing industries. It is, however, difficult to trace variations among industries with respect to average and marginal fluctuations and to find whether they contain any causal relationship.

Average labour productivity and its compounded rate of change are analysed in Tables 3-7 and 3-8. Over the thirty-two-year span, on average seven industry groups had "below sectoral average" productivity: leather products, textiles, knitting mills, clothing, wood, furniture and fixtures, and electrical and electronic products. The same phenomenon persisted during the 1946-60 period. In the 1960-70 decade the same industry groups still remained below average;

TABLE 3-6
TRANSLOG PRODUCTION FUNCTION
ECONOMIES OF SCALE AND THEIR SIGNIFICANCE, 1946-77

	Economies of Scale	Growing at an Increasing Rate	Growing at a Declining Rate
Total manufacturing	1.86	V*	
Food and beverage	1.41	V	
Tobacco	1.07	V	
Rubber and plastic	1.06	V*	
Leather	0.80	V	
Textile	−0.36		V*
Knitting	0.82		V
Clothing	1.24	V*	
Wood	1.35		V
Furniture and fixtures	1.45	V	
Paper	1.18	V	
Printing and publishing	1.34	V	
Primary metals	1.59		V
Metal fabricating	1.73		V*
Machinery	1.46		V
Transportation equipment	1.92	V*	
Electrical and electronic	1.61	V*	
Non-metallic mineral	1.67	V*	
Petroleum and coal	1.94		V*
Chemical	1.45	V*	

V*—growing or declining at the 95%-99% level of confidence interval; i.e., highly significant statistically.

V—growing or declining rates, but not statistically significant.

however, productivity in machinery industries fell from "higher than average" to "below average" status. In the 1970s this lower productivity subset expanded to nine industries with the addition of metal fabrication industries. The picture was somewhat different in the 1973-77 subperiod, when the order reversed and nine industries had above sectoral average performance, and ten industry groups fell below that level.

Table 3-8 shows the compounded annual rate of change in labour productivity over the same periods. Based on rates of change throughout the 1946-77 period industries were grouped into three subsets. Two industries — food and beverage, and rubber and plastic — performed at about the same level as the sector. "High" performance was registered in tobacco products, textile, knitting mills,

53

TABLE 3-7
AVERAGE LABOUR PRODUCTIVITY
(1971 dollars)

	1946-60	1960-70	1970-77	1973-77	1946-77
Total manufacturing	3.50	5.34	7.43	7.79	4.93
Food and beverage	4.08	6.67	8.33	8.82	5.55
Tobacco	5.05	9.65	14.19	15.09	8.49
Rubber and plastic	4.80	7.55	7.57	8.01	6.27
Leather	2.46	3.23	4.26	4.46	3.09
Textile	1.83	3.43	5.67	6.01	3.15
Knitting	n.a.	2.80	4.42	4.70	3.88
Clothing	2.12	3.32	4.21	4.44	2.95
Wood	2.17	4.39	5.68	5.92	3.63
Furniture and fixtures	n.a.	3.89	4.91	5.13	4.31
Paper	4.57	6.08	7.56	7.73	5.70
Printing and publishing	4.10	5.72	7.53	7.91	5.36
Primary metals	n.a.	6.70	8.18	8.44	7.31
Metal fabricating	n.a.	5.42	6.91	7.15	5.92
Machinery	n.a.	4.96	7.07	7.41	5.83
Transportation equipment	3.28	5.80	9.54	10.17	5.44
Electrical & electronic	3.26	5.03	7.17	7.62	4.67
Non-metallic mineral	4.30	6.25	8.86	9.52	5.91
Petroleum and coal	4.72	9.87	14.23	15.03	8.41
Chemical	4.36	7.34	11.06	11.81	6.76

TABLE 3-8
COMPOUNDED ANNUAL GROWTH RATE
IN LABOUR PRODUCTIVITY
(%)

	1946 -77	1946 -60	1960 -70	1970 -77	1970 -73	1973 -77
Total manufacturing	3.70	3.82	3.64	3.53	5.04	2.41
Food and beverage	3.83	4.99	2.91	6.22	4.71	7.37
Tobacco	5.68	7.32	3.94	4.92	5.10	4.78
Rubber and plastic	3.77	5.04	0.98	5.30	3.83	6.42
Leather	2.52	1.59	2.70	4.16	3.84	4.39
Textile	5.01	4.38	5.83	5.11	6.15	4.34
Knitting	6.36	n.a.	6.67	5.96	5.51	6.30
Clothing	3.26	3.47	2.38	4.12	4.10	4.14
Wood	4.88	5.99	4.00	3.94	1.02	6.19
Furniture and fixtures	3.61	n.a.	3.56	3.68	3.38	3.91
Paper	2.65	2.81	2.48	2.57	4.81	0.92
Printing and publishing	3.23	3.47	2.58	3.67	3.55	3.76
Primary metals	2.54	n.a.	3.01	1.95	3.78	0.59
Metal fabricating	2.73	n.a.	3.20	2.13	3.98	0.77
Machinery	3.51	n.a.	3.39	3.65	7.35	0.96
Transportation equipment	5.05	3.57	7.01	5.24	7.44	3.61
Electrical and electronic	3.91	3.76	3.71	4.50	5.41	3.82
Non-metallic mineral	4.28	4.52	2.64	6.17	7.89	4.89
Petroleum and coal	5.73	8.30	3.72	3.56	7.48	0.72
Chemical	4.77	5.59	3.51	4.96	8.38	2.46

wood, transportation equipment, electrical and electronic products, non-metallic minerals, petroleum and coal products, and chemical and chemical products. The remaining industry groups fell into the "low" performance category. In the 1960s there was a radical change in the rate of productivity growth, and only four industry groups remained in the high performance category: textiles, knitting mills, wood, and transportation equipment. Tobacco, electrical and electronic products, and petroleum and coal products slipped from high to average performance, and non-metallic minerals, and chemical and chemical products retreated from "high" to "low" performance. Twelve industry groups out of the nineteen in the sector had lower than average labour productivity. In the 1970-77 period the picture changed radically towards an increased rate of productivity growth in most industries, although the petroleum and coal products industry remained in the average performance category, and the paper and paper products, primary metals, and metal fabrication industries stayed in the low productivity growth category. The remaining fifteen industries accelerated their rate of productivity growth into the "high" category. The 1973-77 subperiod looks much the same, with three exceptions: petroleum and coal products industries moved from average to low productivity, chemical and chemical products moved from high to average productivity, and machinery industries moved from high to low productivity.

The increase in the labour productivity growth rate in some industries is striking because it seems to contradict the general belief in a productivity slowdown in Canadian manufacturing after 1970, and in particular after 1973. For example, in its *Seventeenth Annual Review*, the Economic Council of Canada argued that the rate of growth in "output per person-hour dropped sharply in the 1974-76 period as did the growth rates of material and energy per person-hour. But capital per person-hour in manufacturing actually increased slightly faster from 1974 to 1976 than it did from 1967 to 1973." [6] The Council went on: "National aggregate data suggest that the decline in productivity growth began in about 1973-74. This is confirmed by the detailed industry data we have examined." [7] The Council's explanation of the sources of productivity slowdown was interesting but neither new nor particularly helpful.

The findings in this study diverge considerably from those of the Economic Council. Although the aggregate rate of productivity growth did slow down in manufacturing in the 1973-77 subperiod, it would be wrong to generalize about what happened in specific industries. Table

3-8 shows clearly that since 1973 a significant slowdown in productivity growth appeared only in ten of nineteen industry groups. Further, the Economic Council grossly underestimated the rate of growth in capital intensity per man-hour. In Table 3-9 the divergence between my findings and those of the Economic Council grow further, because clearly the marginal productivity of labour decreased without exception overall and in all industry groups in the 1970-73 period. The 1973-77 subperiod showed an *increase* in the marginal productivity of labour in all the industries of the sector. Thus the slowdown in labour productivity ''on the margin'' did not occur at all in the subperiod after the energy crisis.

These data indicate that the rate and the pattern of productivity slowdown are much lower and structurally different in Canada than in the United States, suggesting that most recent studies relied too heavily

TABLE 3-9
MARGINAL PRODUCTIVITY OF LABOUR
(%)

	1946 -47	1946 -60	1960 -70	1970 -77	1970 -73	1973 -77
Total manufacturing	4.60	3.27	4.98	6.93	6.54	7.27
Food and beverage	3.76	2.76	4.52	5.64	5.20	5.98
Tobacco	1.98	1.57	2.07	2.72	2.55	1.85
Rubber and plastic	3.03	2.32	3.65	3.66	3.36	3.87
Leather	1.98	1.57	2.07	2.72	2.55	2.85
Textile	2.68	1.55	2.91	4.82	4.43	5.10
Knitting	3.30	n.a.	2.38	3.75	3.45	3.99
Clothing	1.94	1.40	2.19	2.77	2.57	2.93
Wood	2.83	1.69	3.42	4.42	4.12	4.61
Furniture and fixtures	3.06	n.a.	2.76	3.48	3.30	3.64
Paper	3.73	2.99	3.98	4.95	4.89	5.06
Printing and publishing	4.90	3.75	5.23	6.89	6.41	7.24
Primary metals	5.48	n.a.	5.03	6.14	5.93	6.33
Metal fabricating	5.45	n.a.	4.99	6.36	6.11	6.58
Machinery	3.85	n.a.	3.27	4.67	4.40	4.89
Transportation equipment	5.34	3.22	5.69	9.36	8.59	9.98
Electrical and electronic	4.93	3.44	5.31	7.56	6.97	8.04
Non-metallic mineral	3.78	2.75	3.99	5.66	5.15	6.08
Petroleum and coal	5.74	2.99	5.04	7.59	7.01	8.10
Chemical	4.64	2.99	5.04	7.59	7.01	8.10

Note: The figures in this table are derived from the estimated results of the Cobb-Douglas production function. The function is of the form $Q = AL^\alpha K^\beta$, where $\frac{\partial Q}{\partial L} = \alpha \left(\frac{Q}{L}\right)$ is the marginal product of labour (MPL). The values of α appear in Table D-1.

on figures from the United States. Probably, too, the Economic Council's conclusions were derived from average performance data rather than from compounded rates of change (see Table 3-7 for similarity with the Council's findings). Among the sources contributing to changes in the rate of productivity growth, it is feasible that energy prices have been a factor. At present the importance of this factor is unknown, but the Economic Council's claim that it contributed significantly to the slowdown should not be overlooked.

To measure the sources of productivity growth, we used Diwan's method in which he extended Solow's proposition to cases with increasing returns to scale.[8] This method disaggregates the contribution to growth in labour productivity into two sources: economies of scale and "all other factors." Later we measure part of "all other factors." Table 3-10 gives a detailed account of the contribution of economies of scale to the growth in labour productivity in each

TABLE 3-10
CONTRIBUTION TO GROWTH IN LABOUR PRODUCTIVITY, ECONOMIES OF SCALE AND OTHER FACTORS
(%)

	Economies of Scale	All Other Factors
Total manufacturing	31	69
Food and beverage	7	93
Tobacco	30	70
Rubber and plastic	−21	121
Leather	−23	123
Textile	−44	144
Knitting	−43	143
Clothing	−17	117
Wood	6	94
Furniture and fixtures	11	89
Paper	4	96
Printing and publishing	23	77
Primary metals	26	74
Metal fabricating	34	66
Machinery	−9	109
Transportation equipment	25	75
Electrical & electronic	23	77
Non-metallic mineral	−9	109
Petroleum and coal	31	69
Chemical	10	90

Note: These figures were derived using Diwan's method.

industry group. This table shows that economies of scale have not contributed at all to increased productivity in rubber and plastic products, leather industries, textile industries, knitting mills, clothing industries, machinery, and non-metallic mineral products industries. It has contributed between zero and 10 per cent to productivity growth in five industry groups: food and beverage products, wood, furniture and fixtures, paper and paper products, and chemical and chemical products industries. The contribution of economies of scale to productivity growth in the remaining seven industries was between 23 and 31 per cent.

Among "all other factors," one parameter — the impact of technology on labour efficiency — is of great interest: in the VES function m represents the value of the elasticity of the response of labour efficiency to technological changes (see Appendix A). When $m = 0$ labour efficiency does not depend on capital; that is, capital is not complementary to labour efficiency. These technological changes may occur in various forms as a result of an effective R & D program, the introduction of new plant and equipment purchased from abroad, or a significant improvement in managerial ability in an industry. It is indeed impossible to pinpoint the exact source of technological change without undertaking detailed micro level studies, and even then ambiguities would prevail about the exact impact of, say, R & D on productivity growth.[9] It is, therefore, vital to emphasize that in this study m is a global proxy for the impact of technological change; that is, the result and not the causes of technological change.

No consistent pattern of the technological impact on labour efficiency exists among the nineteen industry groups (Table 3-11). Industries most responsive to technological change are: leather products, non-metallic mineral products, wood, primary metals, tobacco products, petroleum and coal products, furniture and fixtures, and chemical and chemical products industries. From a policy point of view, the payoffs to increased productivity would be greater in the industries where the impact of technological change is higher then the sectoral average.

Turning now to the average level of capital intensity in manufacturing, defined as the amount of net capital stock per person-hour paid in each industry, all in constant prices using the appropriate deflators, Table 3-12 indicates consistent increases throughout the four periods including the post-energy crisis years. However, it would be somewhat hasty to conclude from these average level figures that the energy crisis had no effect on new investments, for most investment programs

58

TABLE 3-11
VES PRODUCTION FUNCTION, IMPACT OF TECHNOLOGY ON LABOUR EFFICIENCY

	Technological Change
Total manufacturing	0.4013
Food and beverage	0.9317
Tobacco	1.8397
Rubber and plastic	0.8484
Leather	2.7464
Textile	0.1944
Knitting	0.3887
Clothing	1.8619
Wood	1.5861
Furniture and fixtures	1.0803
Paper	0.2095
Printing and publishing	0.8473
Primary metals	1.3167
Metal fabricating	0.8379
Machinery	0.3484
Transportation equipment	0.3214
Electrical & electronic	0.4457
Non-metallic mineral	2.1294
Petroleum and coal	1.1965
Chemical	2.1715

TABLE 3-12
AVERAGE CAPITAL INTENSITY

	1946-77	1946-60	1960-70	1970-77	1973-77
Total manufacturing	5.58	4.47	6.67	9.11	9.53
Food and beverage	5.95	4.16	6.33	9.29	9.95
Tobacco	5.07	3.23	5.80	7.98	8.28
Rubber and plastic	5.05	3.74	6.14	6.31	6.66
Leather	1.46	1.30	1.35	1.98	2.12
Textile	5.41	4.34	5.55	7.49	7.88
Knitting	3.19	n.a.	2.02	2.73	2.93
Clothing	0.66	0.62	0.68	0.76	0.82
Wood	3.87	2.10	4.27	7.07	7.76
Furniture and fixtures	1.85	n.a.	1.45	2.22	2.35
Paper	13.37	9.40	14.75	19.94	20.40
Printing and publishing	3.90	2.93	4.29	5.41	5.58
Primary metals	15.80	n.a.	14.24	17.94	18.83
Metal fabricating	4.24	n.a.	3.80	4.86	4.99
Machinery	3.70	n.a.	3.30	4.28	4.38
Transportation equipment	4.83	3.26	5.59	7.13	7.17
Electrical and electronic	2.93	2.21	3.09	4.23	4.44
Non-metallic mineral	9.31	6.82	10.09	13.53	14.08
Petroleum and coal	39.81	23.28	45.52	57.33	72.48
Chemical	13.33	9.08	14.05	21.41	23.37

cannot instantly be changed because of the long-term commitments and duration of major projects. For example, average growth in 1974 may reflect purchase orders initiated in 1972 or earlier. In other cases, a company might find itself already committed to complete a project started several years back. Average levels are therefore only useful to identify trends over longer periods of time, such as a decade or more.

The compounded annual rates of change of capital intensity within each period and over the long run are in Table 3-13. Several fluctuations occurred in the process of capital intensification. The 1946-60 period shows a consistently higher annual rate of growth than the whole period. In the 1960-70 period, the annual rate of growth declined in all industries except leather and printing. In the 1960s the rate of growth of capital intensity decreased significantly. The general trend reversed in the 1970s but wood industries and non-metallic mineral products industries maintained the same growth rates as in the 1960s. Tobacco products industries, furniture and fixtures, paper and

TABLE 3-13
COMPOUNDED ANNUAL RATE OF GROWTH
IN CAPITAL INTENSITY
(%)

	1946 -77	1946 -60	1960 -70	1970 -77	1970 -73	1973 -77
Total manufacturing	3.83	4.99	2.34	3.66	1.90	5.01
Food and beverage	4.99	5.35	3.29	6.73	4.59	8.37
Tobacco	4.66	6.34	3.58	2.92	3.48	2.50
Rubber and plastic	4.14	8.15	−0.97	3.73	3.29	4.07
Leather	2.72	1.88	2.33	4.99	4.32	5.49
Textile	3.39	4.21	2.11	3.59	−1.13	7.28
Knitting	3.27	n.a.	1.99	4.94	3.57	5.98
Clothing	1.89	2.45	−0.71	4.57	1.45	6.98
Wood	5.66	6.20	5.18	5.28	0.95	8.65
Furniture and fixtures	4.19	n.a.	4.30	4.05	−1.15	8.13
Paper	4.10	5.32	3.26	2.89	3.80	2.22
Printing and publishing	2.81	2.74	2.95	2.76	0.99	4.11
Primary metals	2.36	n.a.	1.22	3.85	4.05	3.69
Metal fabricating	1.68	n.a.	1.13	2.40	1.68	2.95
Machinery	2.21	n.a.	0.99	3.79	2.68	4.64
Transportation equipment	3.00	4.05	3.14	0.75	−3.13	3.77
Electrical and electronic	4.67	7.48	0.87	4.68	1.75	6.92
Non-metallic mineral	3.38	3.80	3.00	3.09	−0.78	6.10
Petroleum and coal	7.39	12.95	1.18	5.70	6.39	5.19
Chemical	5.63	6.96	2.29	7.88	3.45	11.33

paper products industries, transportation equipment industries, and printing and publishing industries experienced a declining growth rate. All the eleven other industries had substantially increased rates of growth. In the 1973-77 subperiod, only the tobacco and paper industries showed a slower rate of growth than in the 1970-77 period. All the other seventeen industry groups, and total manufacturing, showed an accelerated rate of growth in capital intensity. In the light of this evidence, the Economic Council's statement that capital intensity rose in only nine of twenty-two industries is puzzling.[10]

Tables 3-14 and 3-15 clarify the distinctively different behaviour in the average and rates of growth and illustrate the capital intensification

TABLE 3-14
AVERAGE ANNUAL LEVELS OF
CAPITAL INTENSITY AND PRODUCTIVITY

	Years in Which Average Capital Intensity was Higher than Productivity	Years in Which Average Capital Intensity was Lower than Productivity
Total manufacturing	All periods	
Food and beverage	All periods	
Textile	All periods	
Wood	1946-77, 1970-77, 1973-77	
Paper	All periods	
Primary Metals	All periods	
Transportation equipment	1960-70	
Non-metallic mineral	1960-70	
Petroleum and coal	1960-70	
Chemical	1960-70	
Tobacco		All periods
Rubber and plastic		All periods
Leather		All periods
Knitting		All periods
Clothing		All periods
Wood		1946-60, 1960-70
Furniture and fixtures		All periods
Printing and publishing		All periods
Metal fabricating		All periods
Machinery		All periods
Electrical and electronic		All periods
Transportation equipment		1946-77, 1946-60, 1960-70, 1973-77

TABLE 3-15
COMPOUNDED ANNUAL RATES OF GROWTH
IN CAPITAL INTENSITY AND PRODUCTIVITY

	Years in Which Rates of Growth of Capital Intensity were Higher than those of Productivity	*Years in Which Rates of Growth of Capital Intensity were Lower than those of Productivity*
Total manufacturing	1946-77, 1946-60, 1970-77, 1973-77 (twice productivity growth)	1960-70
Food and beverage	All periods	
Tobacco		All periods
Rubber and plastic	1946-77, 1946-60	1960-70, 1970-77, 1973-77
Leather	1946-77, 1946-60, 1970-77, 1973-77	1960-70
Textile	1973-77	1946-77, 1946-60, 1960-70, 1970-77
Clothing	1970-77, 1973-77	1946-77, 1946-60, 1960-70
Wood	All periods	
Furniture and fixtures	All periods	
Paper	All periods	
Printing and publishing	1960-70, 1973-77	1946-77, 1946-60, 1970-77
Primary metals	1970-77, 1973-77 (six times productivity growth)	1946-77, 1960-70
Metal fabricating	1970-77, 1973-77 (four times productivity growth)	1946-77, 1960-70
Machinery	1970-77, 1973-77 (five times productivity growth)	1946-77, 1960-70
Transportation equipment	1946-60, 1973-77	1946-77, 1960-70, 1970-77
Electrical & electronic	1946-77, 1946-60, 1970-77, 1973-77	1960-70
Non-metallic mineral	1960-70	1946-77, 1946-60, 1970-77, 1973-77
Petroleum and coal	1946-77, 1946-60, 1970-77, 1973-77 (seven times productivity growth)	
Chemical	1946-77, 1946-60, 1970-77, 1973-77 (six times productivity growth)	1960-70

process and its effect on productivity growth. The annual average level of capital intensity in nine industries was higher than the annual average of labour productivity during most of the period, although in transportation equipment industries this was true only in the 1960-70 period. The ten remaining industries had lower annual average levels of capital intensity than productivity during the whole period. Wood products industries showed lower capital intensity from 1946 until 1970, and transportation equipment industries had lower capital intensity than productivity except during the 1960s.

The picture changed entirely with the rates of change and marginal analyses in Tables 3-15 and 3-16. Only in the 1960-70 decade was the annual rate of change in total manufacturing productivity lower than that in capital intensity; in all other periods the rate of increase in capital intensification far exceeded that in productivity. In fact, after the energy crisis, the annual rate of growth in capital intensity was

TABLE 3-16
MARGINAL PRODUCTIVITY OF CAPITAL (%)

	1946 -77	1946 -60	1960 -70	1970 -77	1970 -73	1973 -77
Total manufacturing	0.59	0.59	0.59	0.60	0.61	0.60
Food and beverage	0.78	0.84	0.78	0.77	0.78	0.76
Tobacco	2.18	n.a.	2.14	2.19	2.19	2.33
Rubber and plastic	0.82	0.86	0.80	0.77	0.58	0.78
Leather	0.76	0.68	0.87	0.78	0.80	0.60
Textile	0.22	n.a.	0.20	0.24	0.24	0.24
Knitting	0.48	n.a.	0.49	0.52	0.53	0.51
Clothing	1.80	n.a.	1.71	2.14	2.21	2.11
Wood	0.45	n.a.	0.49	0.39	0.42	0.36
Furniture and fixtures	1.08	n.a.	1.12	1.02	1.06	1.01
Paper	0.25	0.28	0.23	0.21	0.22	0.21
Printing and publishing	0.99	1.00	0.95	1.00	0.98	1.02
Primary metals	0.29	n.a.	0.55	0.29	0.29	0.28
Metal fabricating	1.00	n.a.	1.00	1.00	1.00	1.00
Machinery	0.63	n.a.	0.60	0.66	0.65	0.68
Transportation equipment	0.71	0.66	0.65	0.85	0.81	0.90
Electrical and electronic	1.06	1.02	1.08	1.10	1.10	1.11
Non-metallic mineral	0.49	0.47	0.43	0.49	0.48	0.51
Petroleum and coal	0.20	n.a.	0.21	0.20	0.21	0.20
Chemical	0.38	0.38	0.36	0.41	0.43	0.40

* The marginal product of capital (MPK) is derived from our Cobb-Douglas production function $Q = AL^\alpha K^\beta$, $\frac{\partial Q}{\partial K} = \beta \left(\frac{Q}{K}\right)$ is the marginal productivity of capital (MPK). The values of β are the estimated values of Table D-1.

double that in labour productivity with the average again masking fluctuations among industries. During the 1960s there was a distinct slowdown in the rate of capital intensity, with an annual rate of growth in capital intensity exceeding the annual rate of growth in productivity in only five industry groups: food and beverage products, wood, furniture and fixtures, paper and paper products, and non-metallic minerals.

During the 1970s the pattern of capital intensification changed with over half the industry groups showing an accelerated rate of annual growth far exceeding that of productivity. The 1973-77 subperiod exhibited a surprising change, with fifteen of nineteen industry groups having exceedingly high rates of capital intensification that were far higher than those in labour productivity. There were five extreme cases: in the primary metals industries, the annual growth rate in capital intensity exceeded that in labour productivity by six times; in metal fabrication industries, by four times; in machinery industries, by four times; in petroleum and coal products industries, by seven times; and in chemical and chemical products, by six times. This evidence varies distinctly from that of the Economic Council.[11]

Technological Progress and Substitutability of Factor Inputs

Generally it is reasonable to assume that capital is complementary to labour efficiency and that the process of capital intensification represents technological progress. But the degree of complementarity between capital and labour is crucial, for it dictates the effectiveness of capital on labour efficiency. If the impact of capital on labour efficiency were low, then a substantial addition of capital would have little effect on labour efficiency and labour productivity would not improve much. The estimation results of the VES production function show (see Table D-3) that the capital coefficients were highly significant only in six of nineteen industries; that is, increased capital stock per labour hour did not contribute much to raising total factor productivity.

The same estimation results gives us a quantitative measure that represents the average annual technological improvement during the tested period (Table 3-17). Technological improvement, or the introduction of new technology, is generally conceived to be a catalyst in boosting total factor productivity and, effectively managed, it should indeed be so. But the impact of technological improvement on total productivity varies drastically among industries. For the sector, technological improvement accounted for 2.86 per cent of the rise in

64

TABLE 3-17
TOTAL FACTOR PRODUCTIVITY GROWTH ATTRIBUTABLE TO
TECHNOLOGICAL IMPROVEMENT, 1946-77
(%)

Total manufacturing	2.86*
Food and beverage	2.05
Tobacco	2.36*
Rubber and plastic	0.65
Leather	1.39*
Textile	3.40*
Knitting (1961-77)	9.85*
Clothing (1957-77)	1.23*
Wood (1957-77)	1.51
Furniture and fixtures (1961-77)	5.16*
Paper	1.36*
Printing and publishing	1.97*
Primary metals (1961-77)	2.57*
Metal fabricating (1961-77)	−2.22
Machinery (1961-77)	2.27
Transportation equipment	4.05*
Electrical and electronic	6.21*
Non-metallic mineral	1.10
Petroleum and coal (1957-77)	8.26*
Chemical	3.53*

Note: * Significant 1 and 5 per cent probability levels.

Source: Table 3-3.

total output between 1946 and 1977. New technology was statistically significant and above the sector's average only in seven industries: textiles, knitting mills, furniture and fixtures, transportation equipment, electrical and electronic products, petroleum and coal products, and chemical and chemical products. The impact of new technology on total output per man-hour was statistically significant and below the sector's average in tobacco products, primary metals industries, and leather products, clothing industries, paper and paper products, and printing and publishing industries. In six industries, technological improvement had no significant impact on total factor productivity.

Before rushing to any conclusions about the implied effectiveness of research and development (R & D) on productivity, we must analyse the structure of the industries with regard to capital and labour intensities and the ease with which capital could be substituted for

65

labour in their production processes. This will help to explain why the effects of new technology vary so much among industries. The technological progress function g (see Appendix A) defines the nature of each industry's technology and generates numerical values that signify the degee of "labour-saving," "neutral," and "capital-saving" technologies. For example, if the value of g is less than one, the industry is using labour-saving or capital-intensive technology. If the value of g is equal to one, technology is neutral, so that the industry may choose to use either labour or capital to produce a given level of output. When the value of g is greater than one, the industry has labour-intensive (or capital-saving) technology. Table D-6 demonstrates that eleven industry groups employed capital-using technology over the thirty-two-year period; five industry groups had labour-using technology for the entire period.

Once again, however, fluctuations in the degree of technology used are important, for a dynamic trend might be established, and knowledge of the industry in question may help forecast a future direction of technological change. The annual rate-of-change data for three periods revealed the behaviour of the industries (Table 3-18). In the 1946-77 period, six industries adopted increasingly labour-saving technology. Eight industry groups moved in the opposite direction, continuously employing more capital-saving technology. During the 1960s, six industry groups utilized increasingly labour-saving technology, while eleven moved towards labour-using technology. There was no noticeable change in the extent of technology used in rubber and plastic products, and in printing and publishing industries.

The picture changed again in the 1970-77 period. Ten industry groups experienced an annual rate of change towards labour-saving technology; printing and publishing, and petroleum and coal products industries experienced no change; and the remaining seven industry groups experienced a continuous change towards labour-using technology. Comparing these findings with the high-growth capital intensity industries in Table 3-15, six of the twelve in that category belong to the labour-saving technology group, whereas tobacco products, rubber and plastic products, knitting mills, and non-metallic mineral products, which had lower capital intensity growth, are included in the labour-saving technology group in Table 3-18. This implies that, although six industries have shown a higher-rate of growth in capital intensity than in productivity during this period, this additional growth has not dictated a change in production technology. Conversely, four industry groups that had slower rates of growth in

66

TABLE 3-18
COMPOUNDED ANNUAL RATE OF CHANGE IN
TECHNOLOGICAL PROGRESS FUNCTION

	1946-77	1960-70	1970-77
Total manufacturing	0.271	0.259	0.361
Food and beverage	0.062	−0.132	0.159
Tobacco (1957-77)	−0.359	0.146	−0.419
Rubber and plastic	0.032	0.098	−1.39
Leather	−0.003	−0.010	0.014
Textile (1957-77)	2.799	1.861	0.591
Knitting (1961-77)	−2.192	−2.562	−1.715
Clothing (1957-77)	0.137	0.636	−0.380
Wood (1957-77)	−0.306	−0.459	−1.206
Furniture and fixtures (1961-77)	0.264	0.237	0.298
Paper	0.127	0.099	0.278
Printing and publishing	0	0	0
Primary metals (1961-77)	0.212	0.982	−0.769
Metal fabricating (1961-77)	0.136	0.361	−0.153
Machinery (1961-77)	−1.034	−0.664	−1.534
Transportation equipment	1.269	2.282	0.427
Electrical and electronic	0.976	1.572	1.517
Non-metallic mineral	−0.065	0.101	−0.288
Petroleum and coal (1957-77)	−0.887	−1.866	0
Chemicals	−1.444	−0.106	−1.594

capital intensity switched towards labour-saving technology in the 1970s. This is puzzling and may indicate an innovative managerial decision to use existing capital more effectively. But since I did not measure the managerial impact on productivity at the industry level here, I cannot be certain.

We turn next to examine the results of the VES elasticity of substitution variable, which measures the ease with which factors of production (in this case, capital and labour) can be substituted for one another in a given technology without affecting total output or the volume of output (see Table D-6). If the value of this variable is less than one, the factors of production are relatively dissimilar, so that it would be difficult to substitute the expanding factor, say labour, for the constant factor, say capital, without affecting total productivity. Even though labour may increase indefinitely, the future growth of the total product is restrained by the technologically scarce (constant) factor, capital. When the elasticity of substitution variable is greater than one, factors of production resemble each other from a technological point of view, so that if one increases indefinitely while the other is held constant, the technology permits the expanding factor to be substituted relatively easily for the constant factor of production. All this means for policy is that industries whose elasticity of substitution variable is greater than one could be induced by the government to employ more labour in times of high unemployment without jeopardizing their output, their total output, and thus their total earnings. In order to see how successful the manufacturing sector could be in easing the problem of high unemployment, an assessment of the degree of elasticity of substitution and the size of the industry as an employer in needed.

Table D-6 shows that in total manufacturing the elasticity of substituion variable is not significantly different from one and thus has "neutral" technology with substitutable factors of production. Observing the various sizes of the variable in all other industries, one can immediately see how disastrous it would be, from an employment point of view, to recommend policy based upon the value of elasticity of substitution in total manufacturing. Note, too, that fluctuations in the elasticity of substitution are consistent with those of the technological progress function. Thus it should be clear that as technological advances occur in an industry, factors of production become more dissimilar and harder to substitute for each other; therefore, the value of elasticity of substitution variable would decrease.

The nature of technology in the industries was as follows: the value of the elasticity of substitution variable was around one only in the food and beverage products and leather products industries. The elasticity of substitution was greater than one in six industry groups: tobacco products, rubber and plastic products, clothing, machinery, non-metallic minerals, and chemical and chemical products industries. In the remaining eleven industry groups in the sector, the elasticity of substitution was smaller than one, and thus substitution between factors of production would be unlikely to occur. In terms of value added and number of employees, this last group represents most of the manufacturing sector. Prospects for the future seem to be that the manufacturing sector cannot be expected to contribute significantly to the reduction of unemployment nationwide.

Real Earnings, Labour Share, and Productivity

The examination of average levels and trends in real wages and salaries and the share of labour earnings in value added through time reveals structural factors that are worth exploring. Two basic questions arise: Have real earnings in manufacturing industries gone up, and at what rate of increase each year? Has the labour force of this sector received its marginal product in terms of real wages? If we can adequately answer these questions, we may see more clearly whether the labour wage level and and its rate of growth have outstripped the labour contribution to productivity levels and rates of growth. Furthermore, if the rate of increase in real wages exceeds that in productivity, labour earnings may not only cut into industrial profitability, but also endanger Canadian competitiveness in world markets.

Table D-7 demonstrates that real earnings in all manufacturing industries increased constantly after 1946 and that total payments to labour as a share of value added increased only in three industry groups: food and beverage products, leather products, and paper and allied industries. In the remaining sixteen industry groups, labour earnings as a proportion of value added decreased consistently after 1946. Thus the share of payments to capital increased during the period as the labour and capital share always total 100 per cent. This is consistent with the capital intensity data.

Table 3-19 displays the averages of real earnings and productivity per man-hour in each industry in all periods, bringing into focus the differentials in both earnings and productivity among the industries, as well as the changes through time in both categories. These data clearly show that average productivity per man-hour was much higher than average wages per man-hour paid to labour in each and every industry, and for each year during the thirty-two years and all the periods.

Table 3-20 illustrates the relationship between average productivity and real earnings per man-hour in the form of the ratio of average productivity per man-hour to average real earnings per man-hour. If the ratio is greater than one, average productivity was greater than average earnings per man-hour and average hourly labour earnings lagged behind average hourly productivity per man-hour. In fact, in most cases average hourly productivity was one and one half times greater than average hourly earnings in the manufacturing industries.

Again, however, no serious conclusions can and should be drawn on the basis of averages. Rather, compounded rates of annual growth, which describe marginal changes over time, are more appropriate for policy purposes. Indeed, economists have been trying for years to convince governments to use rates of change or marginal analyses for policy purposes. Marginal findings on productivity and earnings are demonstrated in Tables 3-21 (page 72) and 3-22 (page 73).

TABLE 3-19
AVERAGE REAL EARNINGS AND PRODUCTIVITY PER MAN-HOUR
(1971 dollars)

	Average Earnings						Average Productivity				
	1946-77	1946-60	1960-70	1970-77	1970-73	1973-77	1946-77	1946-60	1960-70	1970-77	1973-77
Total manufacturing	2.75	2.07	2.96	3.79	3.62	3.92	4.93	3.50	5.34	7.43	7.79
Food and beverage	2.51	1.77	2.65	3.77	3.36	4.05	5.55	4.08	6.67	8.33	8.82
Tobacco	2.92	1.96	3.15	4.47	4.21	4.66	8.49	5.05	9.65	14.19	15.09
Rubber and plastic	2.70	2.13	2.97	3.46	3.32	3.56	6.27	4.80	7.55	7.57	8.01
Leather	2.00	1.56	2.09	2.72	2.52	2.87	3.09	2.46	3.23	4.26	4.46
Textile	2.22	1.69	2.37	3.05	2.88	3.16	3.15	1.83	3.43	5.67	6.01
Knitting	2.20	n.a.	1.95	2.52	2.31	2.66	3.88	n.a.	2.80	4.42	4.70
Clothing	2.01	1.57	2.10	2.71	2.51	2.85	2.95	2.12	3.32	4.21	4.44
Wood	2.45	1.63	2.61	3.82	3.44	4.09	3.63	2.17	4.39	5.68	5.92
Furniture and fixtures	2.63	n.a.	2.37	2.98	2.80	3.11	4.31	n.a.	3.89	4.91	5.13
Paper	3.17	2.37	3.40	4.41	4.14	4.59	5.70	4.57	6.08	7.56	7.73
Printing and publishing	3.04	2.24	3.33	4.24	3.99	4.41	5.36	4.10	5.72	7.53	7.91
Primary metals	4.01	n.a.	3.60	4.52	4.29	4.70	7.31	n.a.	6.70	8.18	8.44
Metal fabricating	3.44	n.a.	3.08	3.90	3.70	4.05	5.92	n.a.	5.42	6.91	7.15
Machinery	3.65	n.a.	3.34	4.06	3.94	4.13	5.83	n.a.	4.96	7.07	7.41
Transportation equipment	3.22	2.42	3.49	4.42	4.25	4.55	5.44	3.28	5.80	9.54	10.17
Electrical and electronic	2.86	2.25	3.07	3.80	3.63	3.90	4.67	3.26	5.03	7.17	7.62
Non-metallic mineral	2.74	1.99	2.94	3.95	3.67	4.15	5.91	4.30	6.25	8.86	9.52
Petroleum and coal	3.81	2.74	4.16	5.46	5.08	5.71	8.41	4.72	9.87	14.23	15.03
Chemical	3.11	2.26	3.45	4.35	4.17	4.46	6.76	4.36	7.34	11.06	11.81

Source: Table 3-4

TABLE 3-20
RATIO OF AVERAGE PRODUCTIVITY TO AVERAGE REAL
EARNINGS PER MAN-HOUR

	1946 -77	1946 -60	1960 -70	1970 -77	1973 -77
Total manufacturing	1.79	1.69	1.80	1.96	1.99
Food and beverage	2.21	2.31	1.77	2.21	2.18
Tobacco	2.91	2.58	3.06	3.17	3.24
Rubber and plastic	2.32	2.25	2.56	2.19	2.25
Leather	1.55	1.58	1.55	1.57	1.55
Textile	1.42	1.08	1.45	1.86	1.90
Knitting	1.76	n.a.	1.44	1.75	1.77
Clothing	1.47	1.35	1.58	1.55	1.56
Wood	1.48	1.33	1.68	1.49	1.45
Furniture and fixtures	1.64	n.a.	1.64	1.65	1.65
Paper	1.80	1.93	1.79	1.71	1.68
Printing and publishing	1.76	1.83	1.72	1.78	1.79
Primary metals	1.82	n.a.	1.86	1.81	1.80
Metal fabricating	1.72	n.a.	1.76	1.77	1.77
Machinery	1.60	n.a.	1.49	1.74	1.79
Transportation equipment	1.69	1.36	1.66	2.16	2.24
Electrical and electronic	1.63	1.45	1.64	1.89	1.95
Non-metallic mineral	2.16	2.16	2.13	2.24	2.29
Petroleum and coal	2.21	1.72	2.37	2.61	2.63
Chemical	2.17	1.93	2.13	2.54	2.65

Source: Table 3-13

Considerable differences emerge in the rates of growth of real wages and salaries among different industries over the whole period. In addition, there is no clear or consistent trend in the rate of change in real earnings for the nineteen industry groups in the five periods. For example, the decreasing trend in the rate of change for total manufacturing is not representative because only four of nineteen industries share such a trend: tobacco products industries, electrical and electronic products industries, chemical and chemical products industries, and transportation equipment industries. Some other industries showed an increase in the rate of change in earnings in all five periods, and in the rest, the rate of change from one period to another fluctuated in both directions.

Table 3-22 takes up the question of the relationship between changes in productivity and earnings. In this calculation, if the value of the ratio of the change in productivity to the change in earnings exceeds one, on the margin, real wages and salaries in manufacturing lagged behind

71

TABLE 3-21
COMPOUNDED ANNUAL RATE OF GROWTH
IN REAL EARNINGS
(%)

	1946 -77	1946 -60	1960 -70	1970 -77	1970 -73	1973 -77
Total manufacturing	3.83	4.99	2.34	3.66	5.01	1.90
Food and beverage	4.99	5.35	3.29	6.73	4.59	8.37
Tobacco	4.66	6.34	3.58	2.92	3.48	2.50
Rubber and plastic	4.14	8.15	−0.97	3.73	3.29	4.07
Leather	2.72	1.88	2.33	4.99	4.32	5.49
Textile	3.39	4.21	2.11	3.59	−1.13	7.28
Knitting	3.27	n.a.	1.99	4.94	3.57	5.98
Clothing	1.89	2.45	−0.71	4.57	1.45	6.98
Wood	5.66	6.20	5.18	5.28	0.95	8.65
Furniture and fixtures	4.19	n.a.	4.30	4.05	−1.15	8.13
Paper	4.10	5.32	3.26	2.89	3.80	2.22
Printing and publishing	2.81	2.74	2.95	2.76	0.99	4.11
Primary metals	2.36	n.a.	1.22	3.85	4.05	3.69
Metal fabricating	1.68	n.a.	1.13	2.40	1.68	2.95
Machinery	2.21	n.a.	0.99	3.79	2.68	4.64
Transportation equipment	3.00	4.05	3.14	0.75	−3.13	3.77
Electrical and electronic	4.67	7.48	0.87	4.68	1.75	6.92
Non-metallic mineral	3.38	3.80	3.00	3.09	−0.78	6.10
Petroleum and coal	7.39	12.95	1.18	5.70	6.39	5.19
Chemical	5.63	6.96	2.29	7.88	3.45	11.33

productivity. If the value of this ratio were significantly less than one, on the margin, the rise in real earnings was higher than that in productivity. Such a phenomenon may have some bearing on the financial viability of the respective industries. The food and beverage products industries, and paper and paper products industries were the only two groups in which the rate of growth in earnings consistently exceeded that in labour productivity. The situation in the leather products industry was the same until 1970, when productivity growth caught up with the change in real wages and even rose somewhat above it.

Estimation of the trends during the different periods reveals some important factors. The ratio for the whole period shows that labour received an increase in real income that was approximately equal to the increase in its productivity in three industry groups. In two industry groups, labour received an increase in its real income that was well above the increase in its productivity. In the remaining fourteen

72

TABLE 3-22
RATIO OF ANNUAL RATE OF GROWTH
IN LABOUR PRODUCTIVITY TO ANNUAL RATE OF GROWTH
IN REAL EARNINGS
(1971 dollars)

	1946 -77	1946 -60	1960 -70	1970 -77	1970 -73	1973 -77
Total manufacturing	1.30	1.17	1.24	1.53	1.85	1.20
Food and beverage	0.95	1.57	0.88	0.84	1.12	0.75
Tobacco	1.32	1.52	0.90	1.26	1.25	1.28
Rubber and plastic	1.46	1.49	0.48	2.39	1.96	2.64
Leather	0.93	0.73	0.93	1.18	1.36	1.09
Textile	1.70	1.58	1.90	1.66	2.46	1.18
Knitting	2.01	n.a.	2.32	1.69	2.21	1.46
Clothing	1.32	2.63	1.27	1.10	1.31	0.98
Wood	1.18	1.73	0.88	0.79	0.23	1.14
Furniture and fixtures	1.29	n.a.	1.25	1.36	1.41	1.33
Paper	0.78	0.77	0.90	0.67	1.57	0.21
Printing and publishing	1.04	1.01	0.90	1.35	1.55	1.25
Primary metals	1.08	n.a.	1.54	0.68	0.96	0.29
Metal fabricating	1.08	n.a.	1.25	0.85	1.62	0.31
Machinery	1.45	n.a.	1.22	2.59	3.87	0.51
Transportation equipment	1.78	1.17	2.43	2.21	2.90	1.63
Electrical and electronic	1.38	1.06	1.53	1.98	4.43	1.24
Non-metallic mineral	1.19	1.20	0.82	1.61	2.29	1.19
Petroleum and coal	1.59	1.90	1.41	1.01	3.07	0.17
Chemical	1.42	1.40	1.04	2.43	26.19	0.73

Source: Tables 3-6 and 3-15

industry groups, the increase in labour's real income was well below the increase in its productivity. The situation was much the same during the 1946-60 period. Several changes occurred, however, during the 1960s. In nine industry groups, or almost one half of the sector, the rate of change in income rose much faster than that in productivity. In ten industry groups, however, the rate of change in real income was much slower than the rate of change in productivity. These two variables coincided only in one industry.

The possible effects of these differences are complex. When workers in the nine industry groups received additional real income not earned through additional real productivity, two possibilities existed. Employers could pay that additional income beyond labour's increased productivity out of the company's potential profits. But when these were too low to cover that additional financial burden, they might

73

either encounter severe liquidity problems or turn to governments for aid. Alternatively, if the products of these industries were vital to consumers — that is, they possessed low price elasticity of demand — then the employers' burden of paying excess wage increases would be largely passed on to consumers. But if either situation persisted for a few years, no one would benefit. The industries in the first case would become a constant public burden paid for by consumers' increased taxes and their motivation for increasing productivity would be weakened. Inefficiency would increase over time, and further policy measures such as subsidies, would become necessary to prevent the industries from closing down. Generally the result would be higher prices for the domestic consumers.

The second case is less complicated for producers, since no public authorities or policies would be involved. Under labour pressure for higher income or for other reasons, employers who raise labour's real income "artificially" increase the purchasing power of their employees who can pay higher prices in the marketplace for goods and services. The process is termed artificial, because if real income rose faster than productivity, a vacuum would be created on the supply side and would develop without true structural cause. In sum, society would lose no matter which situation occurred, because both would create an unjustified public burden and inflationary pressures.

In the 1970s Canada faced a very different situation. Labour's rate of change in real earnings exceeded that in productivity in only five industry groups. In one industry — petroleum and coal products — labour earnings and productivity increased at the same rates. In the remaining thirteen industries the rate of change in productivity exceeded that in real earnings, and in four of them by more than twice as much. In the short period following the energy crisis seven industry groups, all of which are energy intensive, increased their employees' real earnings by a rate that was several times faster than the rate of increase in their productivity: by 5.28 times in the petroleum industry; 3.23 times in metal fabricating industries; 4.76 times in paper industries; 3.45 times in primary metals; 1.96 in machinery and equipment; 1.37 in chemicals; and 1.33 in the food and beverage products industries. The products of this group of industries are probably price inelastic and, if so, consumers and not the industries themselves paid for these unjustly high increases in real income. Furthermore, this phenomenon placed an extra obstacle in the way of government attempts to fight inflationary pressures. In the remaining twelve industry groups, the rate of increase in workers' real earnings grew at a slower rate than that in productivity (see Table 3-22). The most extreme case during this period was in the rubber and plastic products industries in which workers received only 42 per cent of the increased productivity.

Table 3-23 adds some further information on the relationship between the marginal productivity of labour and average hourly real earnings. While labour is expected to be paid its marginal product, it would be reasonable if employers paid labour its marginal product minus their fixed costs for hiring and so forth. Assuming arbitrarily that such fixed costs amount to 35 per cent of labour earnings, an employer would break even if the ratio of the marginal product of labour to average real earnings were 1.35. The table shows that in the 1970s, that ratio was around 1.0 in seven industry groups, 1.35 to 1.60 in seven industry groups, and between 1.80 to 2.00 in five groups. The conclusion to be drawn is that even under generous assumptions,

TABLE 3-23
RATIO OF MARGINAL PRODUCT OF LABOUR TO AVERAGE
EARNINGS PER MAN-HOUR

	1946 -77	1946 -60	1960 -70	1970 -77	1970 -73	1973 -77
Total manufacturing	1.67	1.58	1.68	1.83	1.81	1.85
Food and beverage	1.37	1.56	1.71	1.50	1.55	1.48
Tobacco	2.04	1.81	2.15	2.22	2.16	2.27
Rubber and plastic	1.12	1.09	1.23	1.06	1.01	1.09
Leather	0.99	1.01	0.99	1.00	1.01	0.99
Textile	1.21	0.92	1.23	1.58	1.54	1.61
Knitting	1.50	n.a.	1.22	1.49	1.49	1.50
Clothing	0.97	0.89	1.04	1.02	1.02	1.03
Wood	1.16	1.04	1.31	1.16	1.20	1.13
Furniture and fixtures	1.16	n.a.	1.16	1.17	1.18	1.17
Paper	1.18	1.26	1.17	1.12	1.18	1.10
Printing and publishing	1.61	1.67	1.57	1.63	1.61	1.64
Primary metals	1.37	n.a.	1.40	1.36	1.38	1.35
Metal fabricating	1.58	n.a.	1.62	1.63	1.65	1.62
Machinery	1.05	n.a.	0.98	1.15	1.12	1.18
Transportation equipment	1.66	1.33	1.63	2.12	2.02	2.19
Electrical and electronic	1.72	1.53	1.73	1.99	1.92	2.06
Non-metallic mineral	1.38	1.38	1.36	1.43	1.40	1.47
Petroleum and coal	1.51	1.18	1.62	1.78	1.80	1.80
Chemical	1.49	1.32	1.46	1.74	1.68	1.82

Source: Tables 3-14 and 3-16

workers in the majority of industry groups did not receive in earnings the equivalent to their contributions to productivity increases.

Capital Intensity and Capital Productivity

Attempts to isolate the source of changes in productivity call for further disaggregation of total factor productivity and examination of the implied complementarity between labour productivity and capital intensity. This led to an examination of the levels and the rates of change in capital-output ratios and the levels and rates of changes in output-capital ratios. A compounded annual rate of change in the latter gives a dynamic indication of the average productivity of capital.

The question is whether the capital-intensive path taken by most industries in the sector resulted in correspondingly high capital productivity. While the Canadian manufacturing sector is among the most capital-intensive in the world, it is far from the most productive. Table 3-12 showed ever-increasing average levels of capital intensity in most industries in the sector and also revealed an accelerated rate of

TABLE 3-24
AVERAGE CAPITAL-OUTPUT RATIO

	1946 -77	1946 -60	1960 -70	1970 -77	1970 -73	1973 -77
Total manufacturing	1.25	1.26	1.26	1.23	1.20	1.22
Food and beverage	1.08	1.01	1.08	1.11	1.09	1.12
Tobacco (1957-77)	0.58	n.a.	0.60	0.56	0.58	0.54
Rubber and plastic	0.79	0.77	0.74	0.83	0.82	0.84
Leather	0.48	0.53	0.42	0.46	0.45	0.47
Textile (1961-77)	1.47	n.a.	1.59	1.32	1.31	1.31
Knitting (1961-77)	0.66	n.a.	0.67	0.62	0.61	0.62
Clothing (1957-77)	0.19	n.a.	0.19	0.18	0.17	0.18
Wood (1957-77)	1.06	n.a.	0.88	1.24	1.13	1.31
Furniture and fixtures (1960-77)	0.42	n.a.	0.37	0.45	0.43	0.45
Paper	2.28	2.02	2.42	2.64	2.60	2.65
Printing and publishing	0.72	0.67	0.75	0.72	0.73	0.70
Primary metals (1961-77)	2.16	n.a.	2.00	2.20	2.11	2.23
Metal fabricating (1961-77)	0.70	n.a.	0.64	0.70	0.70	0.70
Machinery (1966-77)	0.64	n.a.	0.66	0.60	0.61	0.59
Transportation equipment	0.92	0.98	0.88	0.75	0.79	0.70
Electrical and electronic	0.62	0.66	0.62	0.59	0.59	0.58
Non-metallic mineral	1.57	1.59	1.60	1.54	1.58	1.47
Petroleum and coal	4.80	n.a.	4.66	4.70	4.45	4.81
Chemical	1.96	2.01	1.93	1.93	1.80	1.97

TABLE 3-25
COMPOUNDED ANNUAL RATE OF GROWTH IN
CAPITAL-OUTPUT RATIO

	1946 -77	1946 -60	1960 -70	1970 -77	1970 -73	1973 -77
Total manufacturing	0.13	1.15	−1.27	0.15	−2.998	2.57
Food and beverage	1.28	2.61	0.00	0.48	−0.685	0.93
Tobacco	n.a.	n.a.	0.08	−1.89	−0.122	−2.14
Rubber and plastic	0.36	2.97	−1.92	−1.49	−0.579	−2.17
Leather	0.20	0.30	−0.37	0.80	0.588	0.97
Textile	n.a.	n.a.	−2.80	−1.46	−6.88	2.81
Knitting	n.a.	n.a.	−4.39	−0.96	−1.783	−0.34
Clothing	n.a.	n.a.	−3.08	0.38	−2.399	2.52
Wood	n.a.	n.a.	0.85	1.30	0.000	2.28
Furniture and fixtures	n.a.	n.a.	0.70	0.40	−4.314	4.09
Paper	1.42	2.45	0.76	0.30	−0.985	1.28
Printing and publishing	−0.41	−0.71	0.34	−0.87	−3.290	0.32
Primary metals	n.a.	n.a.	−1.73	1.85	0.261	3.06
Metal fabricating	n.a.	n.a.	−2.01	0.28	−2.199	2.18
Machinery	n.a.	n.a.	−2.33	0.11	−4.417	4.04
Transportation equipment	−1.94	0.46	−3.62	−4.26	−9.876	0.19
Electrical and electronic	0.73	3.54	−2.73	0.13	−3.504	2.96
Non-metallic mineral	−0.85	−0.68	0.35	−2.90	−8.070	1.17
Petroleum and coal	n.a.	n.a.	−2.44	2.05	−1.037	4.44
Chemical	0.81	1.28	−1.18	2.77	−4.577	8.66

TABLE 3-26
AVERAGE OUTPUT-CAPITAL RATIO

	1946 -77	1946 -60	1960 -70	1970 -77	1970 -73	1973 -77
Total manufacturing	0.81	0.80	0.81	0.82	0.83	0.82
Food and beverage	0.92	0.998	0.92	0.90	0.92	0.89
Tobacco	1.70	n.a.	1.67	1.71	1.71	1.82
Rubber and plastic	1.28	1.34	1.24	1.20	0.90	1.21
Leather	2.12	1.90	2.42	2.16	2.23	1.67
Textile	0.69	n.a.	0.63	0.76	0.77	0.77
Knitting	1.50	n.a.	1.53	1.62	1.65	1.60
Clothing	4.67	n.a.	4.43	5.55	5.72	5.47
Wood	0.95	n.a.	1.04	0.82	0.89	0.77
Furniture and fixtures	2.37	n.a.	2.46	2.23	2.33	2.20
Paper	0.45	0.50	0.41	0.38	0.39	0.38
Printing and publishing	1.376	1.39	1.33	1.39	1.37	1.42
Primary metals	0.463	n.a.	0.88	0.46	0.47	0.45
Metal fabricating	1.429	n.a.	1.43	1.42	1.42	1.43
Machinery	1.57	n.a.	1.51	1.65	1.63	1.70
Transportation equipment	1.12	1.05	1.03	1.34	1.28	1.42
Electrical and electronic	1.64	1.59	1.67	1.70	1.70	1.72
Non-metallic mineral	0.66	0.63	0.57	0.65	0.64	0.68
Petroleum and coal	0.209	n.a.	0.22	0.21	0.22	0.21
Chemical	0.497	0.49	0.47	0.53	0.56	0.52

annual increase during the 1973-77 subperiod. The question is whether that process can be considered a cause of the slowdown in productivity in Canadian manufacturing. It seems from Tables 3-24 to 3-27 that the productivity of capital is inversely related to the rate of capital intensity (see also Tables D-8, D-9). The larger the capital-output ratio, the further the industry is from its full capacity utilization level. The gap between potential and actual output became more apparent after 1973 when the rate of change on capital-output ratios became larger and output-capital ratios became negative.

There was little change from 1973 until 1977. But an entirely different picture is created in Table 3-27, where it is clear that the rate of change in capital productivity fell drastically in all industries after 1973. Table 3-14 showed that during the 1973-77 subperiod the marginal productivity of capital declined in ten industries, remained constant in three industry groups, and increased in six of the sector's nineteen industries. Although the rate of change in output-capital ratio may be partly explained by a cyclical downturn in the post-1973

TABLE 3-27

**COMPOUNDED ANNUAL RATE OF GROWTH IN
OUTPUT-CAPITAL RATIO**

	1946 -77	1946 -60	1960 -70	1970 -77	1970 -73	1973 -77
Total manufacturing	−0.14	−1.14	1.30	−0.16	2.95	−2.43
Food and beverage	−1.27	−2.55	0.00	−0.46	0.00	−0.91
Tobacco	n.a.	n.a.	0.36	1.93	1.58	2.19
Rubber and plastic	−0.35	−2.88	1.96	1.52	0.59	2.22
Leather	−0.20	−0.29	0.37	−0.80	−0.58	−0.97
Textile	n.a.	n.a.	2.87	1.49	7.38	−2.72
Knitting	n.a.	n.a.	4.59	0.96	1.83	0.34
Clothing	n.a.	n.a.	3.18	−0.38	2.46	−2.46
Wood	n.a.	n.a.	−1.12	−1.28	0.00	−2.23
Furniture and fixtures	n.a.	n.a.	−0.70	−0.40	4.50	−3.92
Paper	−1.40	−2.39	−0.76	−0.30	1.02	−1.27
Printing and publishing	0.41	0.72	−0.33	0.87	2.50	−0.33
Primary metals	n.a.	n.a.	1.78	−1.82	−0.27	−2.96
Metal fabricating	n.a.	n.a.	2.06	−0.28	2.23	−2.12
Machinery	n.a.	n.a.	2.39	−1.11	4.61	−3.51
Transportation equipment	1.98	−0.46	3.74	4.45	10.97	−0.19
Electrical and electronic	−0.72	−3.46	2.81	−0.14	3.61	−2.87
Non-metallic mineral	0.86	0.68	−0.36	2.98	8.80	−1.18
Petroleum and coal	n.a.	n.a.	2.47	−2.01	1.02	−4.23
Chemical	−0.81	−1.26	1.19	−2.70	7.79	−7.95

period, the variations in the marginal productivity of capital imply structural problems in some industries. Indeed, the fall in capital productivity is a far more crucial factor than changes in labour productivity in the temporary slowdown experienced in Canadian manufacturing.

Conclusion

Having looked at all these data, the task is now to determine what conclusions can be drawn. Several policy prescriptions emerged from the evidence. First, the technological process function indicates that the government's support for research and development would be more effective if grants were awarded to industries where the impact of new technology on labour efficiency is the greatest. Second, if the trend of technological development that characterized the 1970s continues to have the same direction and magnitudes in the 1980s, an expansion of at least twelve manufacturing industries will not generate a significant demand for labour. This means that only seven industry groups — food and beverage products, leather products, textiles, furniture and fixtures, paper and paper products, transportation equipment, and electrical and electronic products industries — would be potential contributors to a fall in the unemployment rate in Canada and in varying degrees. Third, the capital-intensification process happened too quickly in some industries and productivity has not yet increased in them.

A complicating factor for policy-makers is that national averages conceal special problems in the Canadian economy. For example, a few industry groups are regionally located and thus determine the welfare of the population in their respective regions. The leather products industry, for instance, indicated a high responsiveness of technology to labour efficiency, yet the industry fell within the labour-using technology category. However, because of its location in areas where jobs are needed, a regional policy to expand such an industry while introducing new technology would increase labour's employment in the region and its efficiency simultaneously. The same process would hold in the transportation equipment and electrical products industries. Needless to say, this problem is symmetrical so the inverse would hold. The transportation equipment industries are now experiencing such a phenomenon.

A further finding from the analysis is that a priority item on the government's agenda should be to investigate the reasons for the decline or constancy in the marginal productivity of capital in most

79

industries after 1973. An understanding of the dichotomy between capital and labour productivity is vital in order to find ways to make improvements in specific areas. The findings here point out that the weak link in the process of raising productivity in manufacturing is indeed capital and not labour. Empirical evidence shows that the capital-output ratio in manufacturing industries (except in three industries) increased after 1973. More explicitly, the output-capital ratio decreased in sixteen out of the nineteen manufacturing industry groups, and the marginal productivity of capital fell in ten industries. More important, the decline in the productivity of capital did not start with the energy crisis. Data indicate that this decline started in four industries in the 1960s and in twelve in the 1970s. Perhaps the conditions for new R&D grants should include an indication by the industry of a reversal in this process, because the productivity of capital is declining on the margin, and additional capital will promote further decline.

With regard to changes in productivity and real earnings in the manufacturing sector, we have not found global evidence that the major source of inflationary pressure is caused by labour's excess earnings. Perhaps there is more validity to this argument in the services sector of the economy. Seven industry groups, headed by petroleum and coal products, and the paper and paper products industries, stepped far out of line in paying income increases that were not generated by corresponding increases in productivity during the 1973-77 subperiod. The Canadian government must find a way to prevent such increases in the future if fighting inflation is as important as claimed. The remaining twelve industry groups in the sector in fact contributed to higher profits in their respective industries, as well as (perhaps unknowingly) dampening inflationary pressures.

Productivity, Technology, and Industrial Policy

4

This study undertook to analyse various aspects of the performance of nineteen industry groups that comprise the manufacturing sector in Statistics Canada's Standard Industrial Classification in an attempt to explain the persistent lagging productivity growth and to find a prescription for an industrial strategy that would address this problem. The main finding of this study is that the problem of declining productivity growth relates more to inefficiencies in the use of capital than labour. For example, although the annual rate of change in labour productivity declined in a majority of industries after 1973, the marginal productivity of labour increased in all of them. At the same time, the increase in hourly real earnings fell below that of labour's marginal productivity in almost all industries. In the case of capital, a comparison between the 1960-70 and 1970-77 periods shows that, in spite of continued overall growth in capital per man-hour, the marginal productivity of capital remained constant in more than half of the industry groups. In a small group of industries the marginal productivity of capital actually declined.

What emerges from these figures is that one reasonable explanation for the stall or decline in productivity growth in the manufacturing sector is that the stock of capital in some industries is depleted. Depleted capital stock signifies outdated technology, which in turn lowers the level of labour productivity or at least precludes an increase from prevailing levels. In addition, if capital is not properly replaced and such plant and equipment are still contained in capital stock figures, the potential figures for the industry will be inflated.

A related factor is that not only does the quantity of capital replacement affect advances in productivity, but also the quality of such capital determines to a large extent the resultant increase in productivity. For example, if a company replaced an old machine with an identical new machine, the probability is high that there would be no growth in productivity, for the same technology prevails in both the old and new machines. The constancy in marginal productivity of capital in many industry groups may be attributable to this phenomenon.

Technological innovations, which are embodied in new machinery that performs the same functions as older equipment but far more efficiently, usually enhance productivity. This brings us to the next related issue of complementary research and development to raise productivity for marketable products. In Canada R&D appropriations are insignificant in comparison with the value of the manufacturing sector's output. They are also declining, a trend that does not bode well for future potential productivity increases. Although this study did not consider directly the impact of R&D on productivity, the measured impact of new technology on labour efficiency was significant in several industries. By inference, the failure to introduce much new technology into the manufacturing sector is likely a factor in the decline of labour productivity.

What these findings indicate is that there is an opportunity in Canada to stimulate productivity through technological innovation. How this can best be achieved is a important issue in the perennial Canadian debate over appropriate government policy towards the manufacturing sector and the question of industrial strategy. The results of this study point to a new direction for an industrial policy, based on a method of "picking winners" from the spectrum of the manufacturing sector using a micro-level approach that would satisfy a complex set of social and political as well as economic objectives.

A Direction for Industrial Policy

Since the term "industrial strategy" first became a part of Canadian economic dialogue, the phrase has appeared with increasing frequency in government pronouncements, think-tank studies, and business publications.[1] Particularly in recent years, Canadian business leaders, economists, and politicians all seem to have become preoccupied with the need to develop an industrial strategy for Canada. Indeed, the amount of print devoted to the subject can only be described as prodigious.

Yet, despite the many attempts to define "industrial strategy," the term remains vague and elusive. In fact, the *Financial Times* once compared the search for an industrial strategy for Canada with the hunting of the snark — which nobody could describe — in Lewis Carroll's nonsense verse.[2] The few attempts to define the term have produced economic jargon but little enlightenment.[3] For example, a consortium of business groups, presenting their views in 1974 to then industry Minister Alastair Gillespie, defined industrial strategy as "a consistent program to achieve the development and optimum coordination of policies and decisions on the use of productive resources in order to achieve defined and accepted goals."[4]

As might be expected, the lack of clarity in defining "industrial strategy" has been accompanied by considerable confusion over the appropriate goals of government industrial policy. To the limited extent that policy goals have been explicitly addressed, they have been couched in catch phrases such as "economic efficiency." The Canadian Manufacturers' Association, for instance, once described the proper objective of an industrial strategy as the achievement of an "efficient economic system in the broad sense that the maximum usefulness is obtained from available resources to meet the material needs of our society both in terms of quality and quantity."[5] Such prescriptions cannot be disputed, but they are much too vague to provide concrete policy guidance.

It should not be surprising, then, that a multitude of spokesmen and "experts" have advocated many different and often conflicting policies. But among all the rhetoric two common themes seem to emerge. First, Canada does not have an "industrial strategy" but needs one.[6] Second, the prescriptions for an appropriate strategy, though differing tremendously, all promote the self-interest of those advancing the program. For example, scientists call for increased government funding for research and development; spokesmen for weak industries call for protective tariffs and government grants; and competitive industries argue that free trade is the answer to Canada's economic ills. The profusion of objectives indicates that what is needed first is a clear statement of the goals of industrial policy. Then a strategy can be developed in line with those aims.

My own belief is that adoption of an industrial strategy to promote higher productivity in capital and labour should be the most important single item on the agenda of the Canadian government. But an industrial policy cannot be formulated and function in a vacuum; rather, it must be consistent with overall national objectives and goals and supported by an institutional framework that will allow the realization of pre-set targets. By the same token, if a national-regional set of objectives and goals is not clearly formulated and explicitly articulated, it will be impossible to derive an explicit and clear industrial policy. When a long-term socioeconomic policy does not exist and is replaced by a constellation of policies contained in budgets and minibudgets for the short term and directed primarily towards currently pressing issues, industrial policy cannot exist. In fact, this type of approach, which the government has been following, does not guarantee consistency between industrial policies and the fulfilment of basic socioeconomic goals of the country, except coincidently from time to time. Instead, it would be better to have finite sets of changing ''tactics'' to solve momentarily pressing problems within an overall strategy, since the continuity and consistency of any given policy are basic conditions for any government to acquire and maintain the credibility of its people and enterprises.

Granted, the Canadian situation is unique and complex because of the lack of a federal-provincial consensus on economic goals and objectives. Nonetheless, the existing institutional framework that governs the Canadian economy, effected through federal government control over fiscal measures and the central banking system, for example, would more readily support a national industrial policy than a set of independent regional policies.

The problem of developing an industrial policy is made even more complex in the manufacturing sector than in non-producing sectors because any policy adopted must encompass both domestic and international economic activity. A strategy for the domestic front must promote employment, efficient utilization of resources, relative price stability, equitable distribution of economic activity across regions, expansion of secondary manufacturing, and technological innovation.[7] In the foreign trade sector an industrial strategy must, among other objectives, increase the competitiveness of Canadian manufactured goods, prescribe the degree of foreign investment, and foster the expansion of existing markets and the penetration of new ones. The policies adopted on the two fronts need not necessarily be compatible, complicating further the government task of devising and executing an industrial policy.

Many economists propose simply that government refrain from acting in the economy to let the market perform its ''true'' mission in promoting efficiency through reallocation of resources. Sooner or later, they claim, the law of comparative advantage would come into play and balance-of-payments difficulties would disappear. They argue that governments always mess up the economy rather than effectively augment the market function. Since we live in an age of oligopolistic market structures, this view of a completely ''free market'' mechanism is highly unrealistic and inapplicable to Canada or to any industrial nation.

In broad terms, my recommendation is, therefore, that governments should act as the guardians of competitive market conditions when considering an industrial strategy. Furthermore, a solution to Canadian socioeconomic problems has a much higher probability of success if policies and controls are dominated by the federal rather than provincial governments — though this does not moderate my criticism of the steps the federal government has pursued in the past. In addition, the enhancement of the efficient use of economic resources calls for action and co-operation by governments and the private sector. Without doubt the manufacturing sector is highly heterogeneous and no one blanket policy could satisfy all the industries contained within it. For example, some serve important regional objectives, such as employment and income distribution; others earn foreign exchange; yet others exploit available natural resources. Governments support certain less productive industries in all three groups for social and political as well as economic reasons. Clearly, any policy should be based on a long-term social cost-benefit analysis. Finally, the strategy adopted must always remain flexible enough to meet changing social and economic objectives.

One approach to industrial policy that is often suggested is to chose potentially successful industries and to promote their growth and development. In the past high-technology industries have usually been picked as the promising ones for Canada's future economic success. But their selection has not been systematic, and policy-makers have only assumed that high-technology industries are by definition highly productive and also score well in other major important variables. Such assumptions need to be scrutinized carefully. Perhaps more important is the problem that picking the winners in terms of one or two dimensions at most carries a high risk that very costly mistakes will be made. Often the mere act of picking a winner is an explicit substitution for the dynamic and changing market function of picking its own winners, and in any case, today's winner may be tomorrow's loser. On the other hand, arbitrary government decisions picking winners made in terms of only one dimension may determine the future industrial structure of the country. The possible effect is that there may be no chance for change over time, since subsidies and other supports tend to perpetuate themselves. Further, by providing all the needed support for their future development, designated industries may benefit from special government support and favourable regulations so that they may win eventual control over the domestic market to the detriment of other competing industries. In view of the possibility of such problems, any policy should be based on a broad assessment of the social and economic costs and benefits.

This study examined the various aspects of industry performance using four production functions as a guide to the industries that could be expected to be potential winners. Their behaviour was analysed at both the average and the marginal performance levels in terms of capacity utilization, economies of scale, elasticity of substitution, labour productivity, capital intensity, and labour share in value added output. On this basis a proposal is made for a method of devising a means of establishing which manufacturing industries might be picked as winners and developed through a clear and consistent government development strategy. The key element in this approach is to select those industries that fulfil the largest set of goals or whose performance is high in the most important objectives.

Table 4-1 records average performance levels in five variables for the nineteen industry groups in the manufacturing sector. From the table it is obvious that none of the industries scored high in all the variables. Twelve had high labour productivity. But among them only five — paper and paper products, primary metals, non-metallic minerals, petroleum and coal products, and chemical and chemical products — had high capital intensity as well. Supposedly, these capital-intensive industries are the high-technology industries that might be picked as winners. The question to consider is whether the other industries with high labour productivity should be abandoned. Clearly, on almost all grounds, the answer would be no.

Turning to the other variables, we see that in these same five industries — paper and paper products, primary metals, non-metallic minerals, petroleum and coal products, and chemical and chemical products — economies of scale rose after 1973, but only one had high labour productivity, capital intensity and economies of scale during that period. Surprisingly, there is generally no consistency between average high productivity and average scale attainment, and thus no reason to select industries only on the basis of significant scale economies.

In terms of their contribution to increased employment, industries with relatively large and average elasticities of substitution offer the most potential, since the relationship between low capital intensity and high elasticity of substitution is consistent. High elasticity of substitution means that labour can be substituted for capital without

86

TABLE 4-1
AVERAGE PERFORMANCE IN SELECTED VARIABLES

	Labour Productivity		Capital Intensity		Labour Share		Economies of Scale		Elasticity of Substitution	
	1946-77	1973-77	1946-77	1973-77	1946-77	1973-77	1946-77	1973-77	1946-77	1973-77
Food & bev.	H	H	A	L	L	H	L	A	A	A
Tobacco	H	H	L	L	L	L	H	L	L	L
Rub. & plast.	H	H	H	L	L	L	L	H	H	H
Paper	H	A	H	H	L	L	L	H	L	L
Print. & pub.	H	H	L	L	L	H	A	A	L	L
Prim. met.	H	H	H	H	H	L	L	L	L	L
Metal fab.	H	L	L	L	L	H	A	L	L	L
Machinery	H	H	L	L	L	H	L	H	H	H
Transport equip.	H	H	H	L	L	H	L	A	L	L
Non-met. min.	H	H	H	H	L	H	L	A	L	L
Petrol. and coal	H	H	H	H	L	L	A	L	L	L
Chemical	H	H	H	H	L	H	L	L	H	H
Leather	L	L	L	L	H	H	L	A	A	A
Textile	L	L	A	L	H	H	L	A	L	L
Knitting	L	L	L	L	H	H	L	H	H	H
Clothing	L	L	L	L	H	H	L	H	H	H
Wood	L	L	L	L	L	H	L	L	L	L
Furniture	L	L	L	L	H	H	L	A	L	A
Electrical & electron.	L	A	L	L	L	H	A	A	A	A

Notes: H - Higher than manufacturing sector average
       L - Lower than manufacturing sector average
       A - Same as manufacturing sector average

decreasing total output. Only nine industries could substitute labour for capital while maintaining their average product. But five of them had low capital intensity and low productivity. Three — leather products, textiles, and clothing industries — were crucial for regional employment. If employment and income distribution were the most important socioeconomic objectives, the government would have to abandon the high-technology objective in order to fulfil them.

These conclusions are drawn on the basis of average performance. But the importance of analysing marginal changes in industries when developing policy should not be forgotten. Dynamic growth rates signify industrial development or lack of it and also the success of government programs to certain industries over time. Tables 4-2 and 4-3 (page 90) contain the same variables but in terms of compounded rates of growth and give us an entirely different picture than that based on average performance in Table 4-1. Now, for example, a new group of industries has low labour productivity performance. But all the industries that would have been rejected on their average performance would be winners based on their labour productivity growth rates.

Summing up the results of the analysis, Table 4-3 shows that the consistency between capacity utilization and labour productivity is somewhat questionable only in three industry groups — furniture and fixtures, electrical and electronic products, and chemical and chemical products — where their rate of decrease in capacity utilization is greater than that of the manufacturing sector as a whole, though they remain in the high-productivity category. The connection between the rate of change in economies of scale and that of labour productivity is clearly positive in the high-productivity group, but there is no correlation between these two in the low-productivity group. A worrisome problem emerges from analysis of the relation between the rate of change in real earnings and productivity. In three out of the five industries with a declining rate of productivity growth — paper and paper products, primary metals, and petroleum and coal products — the rate of change in earnings continued to increase. Clearly, either these industries faced difficulties in covering the rising share of the wage bill in earnings, or consumers were paying the difference through higher prices. The rates of change in the average productivity of capital are more encouraging. Compared with the manufacturing sector as a whole, almost half of the industries had higher productivity of capital in the 1970s, while slightly more than half did better than the sector after 1973. The technological progress function shows that half the

TABLE 4-2
COMPOUNDED RATE OF CHANGE IN SELECTED VARIABLES

	Capacity Utilization Rate				Productivity				Real Wage				Economies of Scale				Capital Intensity			
	1946-60	1960-70	1970-77	1973-77	1946-77	1960-70	1970-77	1973-77	1946-77	1960-70	1970-77	1973-77	1946-77	1960-70	1970-77	1973-77	1946-77	1960-70	1970-77	1973-77
Total manufacturing	(+)	(+)	(-)	(-)	(+)	(+)	(+)	(+)	(+)	(+)	(+)	(+)	(-)	(O)	(+)	(-)	(+)	(+)	(+)	(+)
Food and beverage	(-)L	(-)L	(-)H	(-)L	A	L	H	H	H	H	H	H	(-)H	(-)H	H	H	H	H	H	H
Tobacco	H	(-)L	(+)H	(+)H	H	A	H	H	H	H	H	H	(+)A	(-)H	H	(+)H	H	H	L	L
Rubber and plastic	(-)H	H	(+)H	(+)H	A	L	H	H	L	L	L	H	(+)H	H	H	(+)H	H	L	A	L
Leather	(-)H	L	(-)H	(-)L	L	L	H	H	H	A	H	H	(+)H	H	H	(+)H	L	(-)L	H	H
Textile	H	H	(+)H	(-)L	H	H	H	H	A	H	H	H	(+)H	H	H	(-)L	L	A	L	H
Knitting	n.a.	H	(+)H	(-)L	H*	L	H	H	A*	L	H	H	(+)H	H	H	(+)H	L*	L	L	H
Clothing	(-)H	(+)H	(+)H	(+)H	L	H	H	H	L	H	H	H	(+)H	H	H	(+)H	L	L	H	H
Wood	H	(-)H	(+)H	(-)L	H	L	H	H	L*	H	H	H	(+)H	H	H	(+)H	L	(-)L	H	H
Furniture and fixtures	n.a.	L	(-)H	(-)H	L*	L	L	L	H	L	H	H	(+)H	H	H	(+)L	H*	H	H	H
Paper	(-)H	(-)L	(+)H	(-)L	L	L	L	L	H	A	H	H	(+)H	(O)	H	(O)	H	H	H	H
Printing and publishing	H	(-)H	(+)H	(-)H	L*	L	L	L	L*	L	H	A	(+)H	H	H	(+)H	L	L	L	L
Primary metals	n.a.	H	(-)H	(-)H	L*	L	L	L	L	L	H	H	(+)H	H	(-)H	(-)L	L*	L	L	L
Metal fabricating	n.a.	H	(-)H	(-)H	L*	L	L	L	L*	A	L	L	(+)A	H	A	(-)L	L*	L	L	H
Machinery	n.a.	H	(-)H	(-)H	H*	H	H	H	L*	L	L	L	(+)H	H	H	(-)A	L*	H	H	H
Transportation equipment	H	H	(+)H	(-)L	H	H	H	H	L	A	A	H	(+)H	H	H	(+)H	H	L	L	L
Electrical and electronic	(-)H	H	(-)H	(-)H	H	A	H	H	L	L	L	L	(-)H	H	H	(+)H	L	H	H	H
Non-metallic mineral	H	H	(+)H	(-)L	H	L	H	H	H	H	H	H	(-)H	(-)H	H	(+)L	L	L	L	L
Petroleum and coal	(-)H	A	(-)H	(-)H	H	A	A	L	H	H	H	H	(+)H	H	H	(+)H	H	H	H	H
Chemical	H	H	(-)H	(-)H	H	L	H	A	H	H	L	H	(+)H	H	H	(+)L	H	L	H	H

Notes:

H - Higher than Manufacturing Sector's Average

L - Lower than Manufacturing Sector's Average

A - Same as Manufacturing Sector's Average

* - 1961-77

n.a. - "Not Available"

(-) - Compounded Rate of Decrease

(+) - Compounded Rate of Increase

(O) - No Change

TABLE 4-3
EFFECTS OF ENERGY CRISIS ON COMPOUNDED ANNUAL RATES OF CHANGE IN SELECTED VARIABLES

	Capacity Utilization		Labour Productivity		Real Wages		Economies of Scale		Capital Intensity		Productivity of Capital		Technological Change (g)	
	1970-77	1973-77	1970-77	1973-77	1970-77	1973-77	1970-77	1973-77	1970-77	1973-77	1970-77	1973-77	1946-77	1970-77
Total manu.	(−)	(−)	(+)	(+)	(+)	(+)	(+)	(−)	(+)	(+)	(−)	(−)	(+)	(+)
Food and bev.	(−)H	(−)L	H	H	H	H	H	(−)L	H	H	(−)H	(−)L	L	L
Tobacco	(+)H	(+)H	H	H	L	H	H	(+)H	L	L	(+)H	(+)H	(−)H	(−)H
Rub. and plas.	(+)H	(+)H	H	H	H	H	H	(+)H	A	L	(+)H	(+)H	L	(−)L
Leather	(−)H	(−)L	H	H	H	H	H	(+)H	L	H	(−)H	(−)L	(−)L	L
Textile	(+)H	(−)L	H	H	H	H	H	(−)L	L	H	(+)H	(−)H	H	L
Knitting	(+)H	(−)L	H	H	H	H	H	(+)H	H	H	(O)	(O)	n.a.	(−)H
Clothing	(+)H	(+)H	H	H	H	H	H	(+)H	H	H	(O)	(−)H	L	(−)H
Wood	(+)H	(−)L	H	H	H	H	H	(+)H	H	H	(−)H	(−)L	(−)H	(−)H
Furn. and fix.	(−)H	(−)H	H	H	H	H	H	(+)L	H	L	(−)H	(−)L	n.a.	L
Print. and pub.	(+)H	(−)L	H	H	H	H	H	(+)H	L	L	(+)H	(+)H	L	L
Trans. equip.	(+)H	(−)L	H	H	A	H	H	(+)L	L	L	(+)H	(−)L	L	H
Electric. and electro.	(−)H	(−)H	H	H	L	L	H	H	H	H	(−)H	(O)	H	H
Non-met. min.	(+)H	(−)L	H	H	H	H	H	(+)L	L	H	(+)H	(−)L	(−)L	(−)L
Chemical	(−)H	(−)H	H	A	L	H	H	(+)L	H	H	(−)H	(−)H	(−)H	(−)H
Paper	(−)H	(−)L	L	L	H	H	H	(O)	L	L	(−)H	(−)L	L	L
Prim. metals	(−)H	(−)H	L	L	H	A	(−)H	(−)H	L	L	(−)H	(−)H	n.a.	(−)H
Metal fab.	(−)H	(−)H	L	L	L	H	A	(−)L	L	L	(−)H	(−)L	n.a.	(−)L
Machinery	(−)H	(−)H	H	L	L	L	H	(−)A	H	L	(O)	(−)H	n.a.	(−)H
Petrol. and coal	(−)H	(−)H	A	L	H	H	H	(+)H	H	L	(−)H	(−)H	(−)H	L

H - Higher than Manufacturing Sector's Average   (+) - Compounded Annual Rate of Increase   n.a. - "Not Available"

L - Lower than Manufacturing Sector's Average   (−) - Compounded Annual Rate of Decrease

A - Same as Manufacturing Sector's Average   (O) - "No Change"

industries adopted capital-using techniques at a faster rate than the sector in the 1970s.

The complexity of choosing winners without having clear objectives can now be appreciated. For example, if the government had a mix of policy objectives with the following priorities — first, increased employment; second, economic growth; and third, rising labour efficiency — then a series of steps should be taken.

- To increase employment the emphasis of industrial policy should in the first instance be on the following nine industries: food and beverage products, clothing, rubber and plastic products, transportation equipment, electrical and electronic products, non-metallic minerals, chemical and chemical products, machinery, and leather products. To promote regional employment, the leather products and clothing industries should assume top priority.
- The set of industry groups that would attain the economic growth objective could be selected in two ways. The first is to choose those industries that possess an absolute level of economies of scale, and all but five industry groups — leather products, textile, knitting, clothing, and machinery — seem to qualify. My preferred approach is to select those industries whose economies of scale have been growing at an increasing rate: rubber and plastic products, non-metallic minerals, transportation equipment, electrical and electronic products, chemicals and chemical products, food and beverage products, tobacco products, furniture and fixtures, paper and paper products, printing and publishing.
- The attainment of the third objective — labour efficiency — depends upon a high degree of complementarity between labour and capital in the production process, such that the introduction of technology has a large effect. Two groups of industries could be selected on this basis: a high-impact group, containing the leather products, wood products, primary metals, non-metallic minerals, petroleum and coal products, and chemicals and chemical products; and a medium impact group, including food and beverage products, rubber and plastic products, clothing, printing, publishing and allied industries, metal fabricating, and electrical and electronic products.
- The final task is to determine which industries fulfil all three of these objectives. Five industry groups — food and beverage products, clothing, non-metallic minerals, chemicals and chemical products, and electrical and electronic products — were "win-

ners'' in all three categories. Seven industry groups — clothing, transportation equipment, electrical and electronic products, non-metallic minerals, chemicals and chemical products, and leather products — are "winners" in terms of employment and growth objectives. In addition, textiles, wood, primary metals, petroleum and coal products, printing and publishing, and metal fabrication industries would all fulfil one of the three objectives.

Using this approach, policy-makers have a first test of whether their stated objectives are in conflict and whether any industry could ever meet them all simultaneously. Second, if the government decided to support an industry for social as well as economic reasons, a pure social objective could be inserted into this process. The economic tradeoffs would be explicit and could be estimated. Third, and most important, this study demonstrates that a "linear", or uni-dimensional, approach to policy-making is misleading because of the multidimensional reality that confronts governments. That is, no industry could be a true winner of the future if it meets only one objective among several stated in any government's socioeconomic policy. Thus a winner must be selected on the basis of several performance variables.

Another aspect of an economic policy for the manufacturing sector should be to promote competition and incentives for product rationalization through effective management in the public and the private sectors of our economy. It is obvious, however, that the point of maximum efficiency is somewhat distant for several industries for various geographic, economic, political, and historical reasons. Part of an industrial policy should be to rationalize the subsidy system and to ensure that it contributes to increased efficiency and market competition in the long term.

One way to approach such rationalization would be to subsidize output rather than inputs whenever possible. Such a subsidization policy would prevent the perpetuation of marginal producers in the economy. In the past there has been little incentive to become more efficient when labour and/or capital were continuously subsidized. If the government were to set a clear support policy of tariffs, quotas, and subsidies for a well-defined time period (say five years), producers would be forced to increase their rate of productivity growth while utilizing labour, materials, and capital at competitive market prices. This would be a superior approach, for it would guide production rather than "spoil" manufacturers by letting them habitually use subsidized labour and unrealistically priced capital and other inputs.

92

In sum, examination of the performance of the nineteen industries in the manufacturing sector has revealed that an overall sectoral policy based on average performance data is unlikely to be entirely appropriate. The application of the production function analysis shows that the performance variables were not consistent from industry to industry or over time. The research also demonstrated that the average figures mask underlying changes in behaviour that become clear in the analysis of rate of change and marginal data.

From this study, it should be apparent that an overall industrial strategy must be based on a stated set of long-term objectives that can be met through a mix of policies derived from the analysis of the behaviour of each manufacturing industry. A system of picking winners can be devised to promote the stated goals, supplemented by policies to encourage rationalization and competition through a temporary support system of tariffs, quotas, and subsidies. The advantage of such an approach is that it is flexible enough to meet changing economic and social conditions and still provide a framework for a consistent and constructive industrial strategy.

My hope and belief is that through such a policy, governments can foster more efficient use of labour and especially capital in Canada. With increased capital and technological efficiency, overall productivity in this country can be raised to enhance the competitiveness of Canada's manufacturing sector.

Appendix A: Methodology

The Variable Elasticity of Substitution (VES) Production Function[1]

To analyse productivity, neoclassical economics uses the concept of a production function, namely,

$$x_0 = f(x_1, x_2),\tag{1}$$

where x_i; $i = 0,1,2$, refers to the quantity of output, capital, and labour, respectively. The neoclassical production function satisfies certain constraints. We write f_i, f_{ii} for the partial derivatives of x_0 with respect to x_i ($i = 1,2$) of order one and two respectively, these constraints are:

(i) $f_i > 0$ ($i = 1,2$) and
(ii) $f_{ii} < 0$ ($i = 1,2$),

implying that marginal products of capital and labour are positive but diminishing. These two conditions ensure that the isoquants are convex to the origin. If, in addition to the neoclassical production function, we assume that both the market for the output and the two markets for capital and labour are perfect; and that the producers act rationally to maximize profits defined as total revenue minus total costs, or minimize total cost, then we can develop the marginal productivity theorem regarding the pricing of factors. The first-order equilibrium conditions ensure that:

$$(p_i / p_0) = cf_i \qquad i = (1,2),\tag{2}$$

where p_i ($i = 0,1,2$) refer to the price of output, capital, and labour

94

respectively. In common practice p_2 is the wage rate, p_1 the rate of return on capital,[2] and c is a constant, where under perfect markets $C \equiv 1$. Equation 2 implies that under perfect markets the factors are priced so that their price equals the value of their marginal products.

If we impose one further constraint on the production function 1 — namely, homogeneity of order one — then we can also obtain the result that the total output is exhausted by payment to two factors: labour and capital. In other words,

$$p_0 x_0 = p_1 x_1 + p_2 x_2 \qquad\qquad \text{or } S_1 + S_2 = 1, \qquad (3)$$

where $S_i = (p_i x_i / p_0 x_0)$ $\qquad\qquad\qquad$ $(i = 1,2)$.

The advantage of equation 3 is that from it we can develop information on p_1 given the information x_1, x_2, x_0, and p_2, assuming, of course, that $p_0 = 1$. The above is a standard neoclassical production and distribution theory. In this theory the production function is rather general.

In our analysis we need to give some form to this production function, particularly to use it for an econometric analysis. Four different forms of this production function have been suggested: Cobb-Douglas (CD), constant elasticity of substitution (CES), variable elasticity of substitution production function (VES), and translog production function.[3] All these four forms are based on different elasticities of factor substitution: Cobb-Douglas (CD) assumes a unitary elasticity of substitution; CES implies a particular constant volume of the elasticity of factor substitution; and in VES this elasticity itself is variable.

The Cobb-Douglas form may be written as

$$x_0 = A x_1^\alpha x_2^\beta, \qquad (4)$$

where A is a constant. To make equation 4 linear homogeneous, it may be assumed that $\alpha + \beta = 1$. As regard to A, it may be assumed that $A' = A(t)$, where t refers to time. In this case $A(t)$ is a variable that one can measure and interpret. Giving $A(t)$ a simple form, equation 4 may be written as

$$x_0 = A' x_1^\alpha x_2^\beta e^{\lambda t}, \qquad (4)'$$

where A' is a constant and A in equation 4 is equal to $A' e^{\lambda t}$ in equation 4'. λ has been interpreted as a measure of "neutral technical change," following Hicks or Harrod, because it shifts the isoquants without changing their shape. From 4', then one can find some explanation about the nature of the shifts; that is λ. It may, thus, provide us with an explanation of the differences in productivity.

The difficulty with CD is that it is a very simple case and implies unitary elasticity of substitution. Consequently, it is liable to overestimate the impact of technology, because λ is likely to contain "all other factors" unaccounted for by the variables of this function.[4] Furthermore, estimation of (4)' is relatively easy, where the interpretation of the parameters α and β is somewhat difficult unless and until these are close to expectations from theory.

It is quite common to find coefficient α and β with negative sign. Such results make no sense in theory. An improvement on this form may be made by choosing the CES form. The CES form may be written as

$$x_0 = A(ax_1^{-\rho} + (1 - a) x_2^{-\rho})^{-V\rho}. \qquad (5)$$

ρ is interpreted as a parameter of substitution, since it can be shown that

$$\sigma = 1/ (1 + \rho), \qquad (6)$$

where σ is the elasticity of substitution between capital and labour. In the case that $\sigma = 1$ or $\rho = 0$, equation 5 dissolves into the CD form:

$$x_0 = Ax_1^{\alpha} x_2^{1-\alpha} .$$

Equation 5 thus provides test of 4. It has further the advantage of providing information on the elasticity of substitution.

It should be remembered that the elasticity of substitution is the rate of change in the slope of the isoquant. Any explanation of productivity that is based on the production function would become all the more powerful if information on the elasticity of substitution were also obtained. Further, in case that elasticity of substitution is different from one, the parameter σ can then be interpreted as a measure of "non-neutral technical change."

Equation 5 is, however, nonlinear and it is not easy to estimate it directly. One of the methods to estimate its parameters is to formulate the marginal conditions as in equation 2. A manipulation of these conditions gives the relationship

$$(p_2/p_1) = A\left(x_1/x_2\right)^{\rho + 1} \qquad (7)$$

This is a stringent relationship for it follows from the assumption that *both* labour and capital markets are in equilibrium. The advantage of equation 7 is that from it one can estimate $(\rho + 1)$ directly given the estimate of $(\rho + 1)$. The remaining parameters can be easily estimated. Actually, in the simpler case of equation 5, where CES is also linear homogeneous, the constant term A in equation 7 is also made up of the parameter a, so that a can be easily unscrambled from the estimate of A.

Once one is involved in the estimation of the elasticity of substitution, one finds CES somewhat limited and frustrating. CES provides only a constant value, while the elasticity varies over the whole body of the isoquant. Also, technology is fundamentally dependent on, or interrelated with the elasticity of substitution. In addition, nowadays one can choose the VES form so that one can get a whole series of the elasticity and technical change instead of one number as in CES. Our analysis, therefore, automatically and somewhat naturally moves to the VES.

The main motivation in adapting the VES production function is that it provides one with a most general neoclassical form that produces three major measurements: an unconstant elasticity of factor substitution, of the biased type, a special elasticity coefficient representing technological impact on labour efficiency, and the bias of technological change, or a technological progress function.

Diwan's VES form is developed in the following manner: Postulate a general homogeneous production function

$$X_0^{-\rho} = (A_1 X_1)^{-\rho} + (A_2 X_2)^{-\rho} \qquad (8)$$

Where X_i ($i = 0, 1, 2$) refer to output, capital, and labour respectively. The inputs X_i ($i = 1, 2$) are assumed to be measured in physical and quantity terms. The A_i ($i = 1, 2$) are treated as variables instead of constants. One interpretation of these variables is that they define (or measure) capital and labour inputs in efficiency (or quality) units as contrasted with X_i ($i = 1, 2$), which measure the same inputs as physical (or quantity) units.

We hypothesize that labour input, measured in efficiency units, is a function of capital intensity of labour input measured in physical units.

97

That is

$$\frac{DA_2}{A_2} = f\left(\frac{Dk}{k}\right), \tag{9}$$

where $k = (x_1/x_2)$ and D refers to the operation dt. Diwan calls this "labor efficiency progress function." The function f has the general properties $f' > 0, f'' < 0, f' \to o$ as $Dk/k \to \infty$. For empirical purposes, we take the simple case of the preceding function and define

$$\frac{DA_2}{A_2} = m\frac{Dk}{k}, \tag{10}$$

where m is the elasticity of labour input measured in efficiency units with respect to capital intensity of labour input in physical units. Since k can be considered a measure of technology, m can be interpreted as a measure of the impact of technology on labour efficiency.

Equation 8 is similar to the CES production function. The difference is, and it is a major one, that A_i ($i = 1,2$) are variables and not constants. The production function in equation 8, thus takes into account not only the inputs in physical units but also in quality units, because m is defined from equation 10 as the elasticity of labour input measured in efficiency units with respect to capital intensity of labour input in physical units. Consider k as a measure of technology, then m measures the impact of technology on the efficiency of labour.[5]

Equation 10 is defined as a labour efficiency progress function, implying complementarity between labour efficiency and capital intensity. However, if m is negative, this complementarity is reversed so that capital intensity in that case is a hinderance to labour efficiency.

Since m is an elasticity, there are obvious implications to different values it assumes. If $m = 1$ the growth rate of labour efficiency and capital intensity are equal. If $m > 1$ labour efficiency grows at a faster rate than capital intensity. This implies that new or additional capital is complementary to labour efficiency.

Integrating equation 10 over time gives

$$\int \frac{DA_2}{A_2} = m\int \frac{Dk}{k} \tag{10}'$$

and

$$lnA_2 = m\, lnk + A_{20}.$$

98

Taking antilog, we have

$$A_2 = A_{20}\, k^m,$$ (11)

which is the labour efficiency progress function, where A_{20} is a constant of integration. Technical progress is thus expressed in terms directly usable in the production function.

The Properties of Technical Change

We now substitute the labour efficiency progress function (equation 11) into the production function 8 and get

$$X_0^{-\rho} = (A_1 X_1)^{-\rho} + (A_{20}\, k^m X_2)^{-\rho} \text{ and}$$

$$X_0^{-\rho} = (A_1 X_1)^{-\rho} + (A_{20} X_2)^{-\rho} (k)^{-m\rho}.$$ (12)

This substitution has implications for the production function, for capital-labour substitution, and for biases in technical change.

Equations 8, 10, and 12 are all non-operational in so far as they have quantities A_i ($i = 1,2$) for which no reliable data exist at present. To estimate ρ and m, therefore, we have to go to the marginal productivity conditions outlined in equation 2. If we assume the marginal productivity conditions; namely,

$$F_2 = cp_2,$$ (13)

where c is a constant and might reflect market imperfections, then equations 8, 10, and 13 can be reduced to

$$Z = \alpha_0 k^{\alpha_1}\, P_2^{\,\alpha_2},$$ (14)

which can be directly estimated. Z refers to labour productivity (x_0/x_2).

Equation 14 is basically an explanation of productivity in terms of the wage rate, capital intensity k, the elasticity of substitution, and the impact of technology on labour efficiency. The latter two influences follow because

$$\alpha_0 = \left(\frac{c}{1-m} A_{20}^\rho\right)^{1/1+\rho} \tag{15}$$

where

$$\alpha_1 = (m\rho)/(1 + \rho); \text{ and } \alpha_2 = 1/(1 + \rho) = \sigma_n.$$

The interesting thing about the function in equation 12 is that we can obtain a variable concept of elasticity of substitution of the biased type, which we call σ_b;

$$\sigma_b = 1/(1 + \rho - \frac{m\rho}{S_1}). \tag{16}$$

This is quite different from the elasticity of substitution in the CES of the Hick's neutral type, which we now write as σ_n so as to distinguish between the two elasticities.

Also, following Diwan, we can define a measure of technical change g as

$$g = 1 + \frac{m\rho(S_1 - S_2)}{m\rho S_2 - (\rho + 1)S_1}. \tag{17}$$

Both σ_b and g are variables since S_i ($i = 1,2$) are variables. These give us the nature of both the elasticity of substitution and technical change, so we can pursue the question regarding differences in productivity among industries examined.

A Note on Estimation Procedures

This short note intends to clarify the method by which the three production functions have been estimated. It is a common knowledge that various estimation methods embodied various biases, and these provided different results.[6]

The VES function was estimated directly in one step by the least

100

squares method. The estimation procedure of the CES requires several steps, as pointed out by most writers on this subject. A two-step estimation procedure was thus implemented as follows. From the initial form of the CES we have

$$Q = A \, [\delta K^{-\rho} + (1 - \delta) L^{-\rho}]^{-\, V/\rho} e^{\lambda t}, \qquad (1)$$

where $\qquad\qquad$ V represents economies of scale;

$\qquad\qquad$ δ, a distribution parameter; and

$\dfrac{1}{(1 + \rho)}$, elasticity of substitution (σ_n).

First, the estimated values of δ and ρ are obtained from

$$w/r = \frac{(1 - \delta)}{\delta} \, (K/L)^{1 + \rho.} \qquad (2)$$

Then the following estimating equation

$$ln \, (w/r) = lnM + Nln \, (K/L) \qquad (3)$$

is used, where $\quad M = \dfrac{1 - \delta}{\delta}$ and $N = 1 + \rho.$

Estimates of M and N give the values of δ and $\hat{1} + \hat{\rho}$. Given the estimated values of δ and ρ, we estimated the parameter V, and then computed the value of σ_n. Thus

$$lnQ = lnA + V \, [-\frac{1}{\rho} ln \, (\hat{\delta} K^{-\hat{\rho}} + (1 - \hat{\delta}) L^{-\hat{\rho}}) + \lambda t. \qquad (4)$$

This gives a value of V, which is an average of the magnitude of economies of scale over thirty-two years. Our preference, however, is to obtain a calculated figure for economies of scale for each year, which would provide us with factual evidence regarding dynamic changes (if any) of scale as they deviate from an average regression line.

Thus, from the estimated value of V (a point estimate), we generate a vector of unique Vs for each year in the entire time series by the following computations:

$$\text{Let } D_0 = lnQ$$

$$C = lnA, \text{ and } XC = A$$

$$D_2 = [-\frac{1}{\rho} ln(\delta K^{-\rho} + (1 - \delta)L^{-\rho})].$$

Such a derivation has not been proposed so far in the literature, but it provides a way to evaluate dynamic changes of economies of scale in the CES and the CD functions.

$$\text{Then } \hat{D}_0 = D_2 V + C$$

$$\text{and } (D_0 - C)/ D_2 = V.$$

$$\text{Similarly } (D_0 - XC)/ D_2 = VC,$$

where VC stands for calculated V, which simply shows that diagramatically:

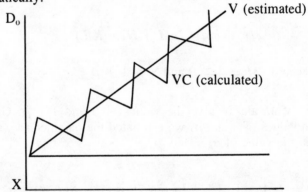

By these calculations we capture the yearly "deviation" or changes of economies of scale by our VC. Evidence of such changes is demonstrated in the empirical part of this study.

The Cobb-Douglas equation was estimated in stages as well, following Diwan's methodology, which has clearly shown preference to estimation by stages, in order to reduce the bias resulting from direct estimation.[7] This very bias was demonstrated, by Dhrymes when he used Klein's method.[8] Our estimation procedure is as follows.

Given the usual Cobb-Douglas function,

$$Q = AL^{\alpha} K^{\beta} e^{qt}, \qquad (1)$$

we first compute the ratio of capital and wage income, or the ratio of income shares,

$$rK/wL = \beta/\alpha, \qquad (2)$$

where r denotes the "rate of return on capital" and w denotes the wage rate. Second, denoting β/α by h, we compute

$$Y = lnL + hlnK. \qquad (3)$$

Since h is computed independently, Y is determined by equation 3. What is left now is the estimation of α. Thus

$$lnQ = lnA + \alpha Y + qt \qquad (4)$$

becomes the estimating equation for α. Given the values of h, β is determined by the simple relations $\beta = \alpha h$.

From the values of β, $\hat{\alpha}$ using equation 4, we generate the vector of unique value of α and β for each year:

$\alpha c = (lnQ - \alpha_0)/Y$, where α_0 is the value of the intercept of the production function, or an efficiency parameter, and where the calculated α for each year is denoted by αc, in order to differentiate it from $\hat{\alpha}$. The method of calculating unique values for α and β and thus examining changes of returns to scale over time ($\alpha + \beta$) is identical to that described in the CES case.

Capacity Utilization

Our methodology in deriving capacity utilization follows that of Statistics Canada Construction Division. It is stated in detail in its publication, *Capacity Utilization Rates in Canadian Manufacturing*, Catalogue 31-003 Quarterly, First Quarter 1979 (Ottawa, July 1979), Vol. 4, No. 1. This method of deriving utilization rates follows Daniel Creamer, "Capital Expansion and Capacity in Post-War Manufacturing", *Studies in Business Economics*, No. 72, National Industrial Conference Board (New York 1961).

To be consistent with Statistics Canada we selected a method that would produce a comparable set of measurements. It should be noted, however, that since the determination of the full capacity year is sensitive to the length of the time series, our figures differ somewhat because of the longer period we computed (1946-77 compared with 1961-79).

In short, the measurements of capacity output are based on two variables: gross capital stock; actual output (all in 1971 constant dollars). First we set up a series of capital-output ratios for each year of the series. The year in which such ratios reached a relatively minimum value is considered taken to be the historical maximum output year of the series. Let B equal that minimum value of capital-output ratio, and KG be the gross capital stock series. We then divide KG by B and potential capacity output results for each year. Next a capacity utilization index is derived for that time series, simply by dividing *actual* value added output by the above potential capacity index to yield a series of capacity utilization for each year. In order to convert such index to percentages, we multiply this index by 100.

The Translog Production Function

The formulation and estimation procedures of this function follows the Griliches and Ringstud methodology.[9]

The basic estimation and computational procedures are as follows: starting with their initial functional form of a CES production function

$$Q/L = BL^h[\delta + (1 - \delta)(K/L)^{-\rho}]^{-\mu/\rho}$$

where $h = \mu - 1$

then $ln\ Q/L = lnB + h\ ln\ L - (\mu/\rho)\ ln\ [\delta + (1 - \delta)(K/L)^{-\rho}]$.

Expansion of the last term around the value $\rho = 0$, using Taylor's theorem, yields a logarithmic approximation of the CES production function

$$ln\ Q/L \simeq ln\ B + h\ ln\ L + \mu(1 - \delta)\ ln\ (K/L)$$

$$- \tfrac{1}{2}\ \rho\mu\delta(1 - \delta)\ [ln\ (K/L)]^2$$

or ln $Q/L \simeq \alpha_0 + \alpha_1$ ln $L + \alpha_2$ ln $(K/L) + \alpha_3$ $[ln(K/L)]^2$.

Given this Griliches form, we would like to know the content of each α coefficient. One way of conducting such an exercise is to assume given estimated values of $\hat{\alpha}_0, \hat{\alpha}_1, \hat{\alpha}_2$ and $\hat{\alpha}_3$ and to find $\hat{\beta}_0, \hat{\beta}_1, \hat{\beta}_2, \hat{\beta}_3$. This is because the parameter estimates of α_1 and α_2 (and by implication $[1 - \delta]$, α_0 and σ] are not independent of the units by which K and L are measured. Following Griliches we evaluate the elasticities at the geometric mean levels of the inputs, and in particular, at a level where the geometric means of the sample are equal. This is, $\overline{K} = \overline{L}$ and ln $(\overline{K}/\overline{L} = ln$ $1 = 0$. Following the latter we have

$$ln \ Q/L = \beta_0 + \beta_1 \ ln \ L + \beta_2 \ [ln \ K/L - ln \ \overline{K}/L]$$
$$+ \beta_3 \ [(ln \ K/L - ln \ K/L)^2]$$
$$= \beta_0 + \beta_1 \ ln \ L + \beta_2 \ ln \ K/L - \beta_2 \ ln \ \overline{K}/L$$
$$+ \beta_3 \ (ln \ K/L)^2 - 2\beta_3 \ ln \ K/L \ ln \ \overline{K}/L + \beta_3 \ (ln \ \overline{K}/L)^2$$
$$= \beta_0 - \beta_2 \ ln \ \overline{K}/L + \beta_3 \ (ln \ \overline{K}/L)^2 + \beta_1 \ ln \ L + \beta_2 \ ln \ K/L$$
$$- 2 \ \beta_3 \ ln \ K/L \ ln \ \overline{K}/L + \beta_3 \ (ln \ \overline{K}/L)^2$$

We can now state the content of the estimated α coefficients

$$\hat{\alpha}_0 = \hat{\beta}_0 - \hat{\beta}_2 \ ln \ \overline{K}/L + \hat{\beta}_3 \ (\ ln \ \overline{K}/L)^2$$

$$\hat{\alpha}_1 = \hat{\beta}_1$$

$$\hat{\alpha}_2 = \hat{\beta}_2 - 2\hat{\beta}_3 \ ln \ \overline{K}/L$$

$$\hat{\alpha}_3 = \hat{\beta}_3 \ .$$

The computation of elasticity of substitution proceeds as follows:

$$\alpha_1 = h = \mu - 1 \text{ which is scale elasticity}$$

$$\alpha_2 = \mu \ (1 - \delta)$$
$$\alpha_3 = -\tfrac{1}{2} \rho\mu\delta \ (1 - \delta)$$

105

$$\alpha_2 = (h + 1)(1 - \delta)$$

$$= (\alpha_1 + 1)(1 - \delta)$$

$$(1 - \delta) = \frac{\alpha_2}{\alpha_1 + 1}$$

$\delta = 1 - \alpha_2/\alpha_1 + 1$ which is our CES distributive parameter

$\alpha_3 = -\frac{1}{2} \rho\mu\delta (1 - \delta)$

$\quad = -\frac{1}{2} \rho(\alpha_1 + 1)(1 - \alpha_2/\alpha_1 + 1) \; \alpha_2/\alpha_1 + 1$

$\rho = -2 \alpha_3 (\alpha_1 + 1/\alpha_2 (\alpha_1 + 1 - \alpha_2)$ substitution parameter

and our elasticity of substitution is:

$$\sigma = \frac{1}{1 + \rho}$$

There are several problems associated with this approach and which were noted by Griliches.

First, since the expansion was carried out around $\rho = 0$, implying $\sigma = 1$, the approximation is better the closer the elasticity of substitution is to unity.

A second problem relates to the small size of α_3, since it is a product of three parameters all of which are less than unity. This implies that we need large samples with adequate dispersion of (K/L) to say something about the sign and magnitude of α_3.

Third, the function collapses to a Cobb-Douglas form when α_3 is insignificantly different from zero. In the case that $\alpha_3 \neq 0$ it may imply a production function outside the CES class.

Appendix B: Data Sources

Value Added Output, Total Activity in Current Prices — *Manufacturing Industries of Canada; National and Provincial Areas*, Statistics Canada, Catalogue No. 31 — 203 (Various issues).

Real Domestic Product Implicit Deflater 1971=100 — CANSIM Matrix 1124 "Annual Historical Indexes of Real Domestic Product by Industry," 1971 Reference Base, 1970 SIC.

Wages and Salaries, Total Activity — *Manufacturing Industries of Canada; National and Provincial Areas*, Statistics Canada, Catalogue No. 31 — 203 (Various issues).

Average Weekly Hours Paid — *Employment Earnings and Hours*, Statistics Canada, Catalogue No. 72 — 204, 72 — 002 (Various issues).

Total Employees — Manufacturing Industries of Canada: National and Provincial Areas, Catalogue No. 31 — 203.

Consumer Price Index — Consumer Price Index for Canada, Statistics Canada, Catalogue No. 62 — 001, 1971=100, Annually 1914-1976.

Net Capital Stock (Mid-Year) — *Fixed Capital Flows and Stocks 1926-1978*, Statistics Canada, Catalogue No. 13 — 568 (at 1971 constant dollars).

Gross Capital Stock (Mid-Year) — *Fixed Capital Flows and Stocks 1926-1978*, Statistics Canada, Catalogue No. 13 — 568 (at 1971 constant dollars).

TABLE B-1
SELECTED DATA, TOTAL MANUFACTURING INDUSTRIES
(1971 dollars)

	Value Added Output	Gross Capital Stock	Wages & Salaries (Current Prices)	Weekly Hours Paid	Total Person-Days Paid	Net Capital Stock	CPI
			(millions $)				
1946	6307.1	14371.8	1741	42.7	1058	7629	45.0
1947	7002.7	14767.9	2086	42.5	1132	8040	49.2
1948	7304.2	15406.0	2409	42.3	1152	8630	56.3
1949	7512.9	16018.0	2592	42.2	1171	9129	58.0
1950	7999.8	16428.0	2771	42.3	1183	9494	59.7
1951	8695.5	17028.0	3276	41.7	1258	10008	66.0
1952	9020.1	18028.0	3637	41.5	1288	10838	67.6
1953	9669.4	19126.0	3957	41.3	1327	11743	67.0
1954	9460.7	20140.0	3897	40.7	1268	12458	67.4
1955	10365.0	20160.0	4142	41.0	1298	13086	67.5
1956	11338.9	22548.0	4571	41.0	1353	14046	68.5
1957	11315.7	24163.0	4778	40.4	1341	15261	70.7
1958	11107.0	25438.0	4759	40.2	1273	16125	72.7
1959	12034.5	26463.0	5030	40.7	1288	16676	73.4
1960	12127.3	27589.0	5150	40.4	1275	17224	74.3
1961	12614.2	28646.0	5702	40.6	1353	17708	75.0
1962	13773.6	29589.0	6096	40.7	1389	18160	75.9
1963	13701.1	30532.0	6495	40.8	1425	18710	77.2
1964	16115.6	31758.0	7081	41.0	1491	19485	78.6
1965	17576.4	33569.0	7823	41.1	1570	20675	80.5
1966	18898.1	35959.0	8696	40.8	1646	22283	83.5
1967	19454.6	38385.0	9254	40.3	1653	23860	86.6
1968	20660.4	40362.0	9905	40.2	1642	24969	90.0
1969	22214.0	42219.0	10848	40.0	1675	25992	94.1
1970	21912.6	44400.0	11364	39.7	1637	27369	97.2
1971	23187.9	46634.0	12130	39.7	1628	28737	100.0
1972	24857.4	48614.0	13415	40.0	1676	29767	104.8
1973	27083.5	50678.0	15220	39.6	1751	30885	112.7
1974	28011.0	63078.0	17557	38.9	1786	32411	125.0
1975	26457.4	55578.0	19161	38.6	1741	34051	138.5
1976	27871.9	57919.0	20923	38.7	1766	35382	148.9
1977	28938.5	60116.0	22850	38.7	1741	36512	160.8

TABLE B-2
SELECTED DATA, FOOD AND BEVERAGE PRODUCTS INDUSTRIES
(1971 dollars)

	Value Added Output	Gross Capital Stock	Wages & Salaries (Current Prices)	Weekly Hours Paid	Total Person- Days Paid	Net Capital Stock	CPI
	(000s $)	(000,000 $)	(000s $)			(000s $)	
1946	1304184	1794.7	241770	43.9	160821	995400	45.0
1947	1294101	1919.3	276245	44.1	167865	1099800	49.2
1948	1324352	2076.3	311236	44.0	168893	1227000	56.3
1949	1334436	2205.7	332536	44.3	170024	1331800	58.0
1950	1371410	2285.9	346715	43.8	167664	1412600	59.7
1951	1425191	2362.0	392859	43.4	172493	1485300	66.0
1952	1512585	2444.5	439650	43.1	175552	1552600	67.6
1953	1556282	2530.2	455281	42.6	176649	1620400	67.0
1954	1616785	2646.7	477059	41.8	177883	1705200	67.4
1955	1677289	2778.4	498787	42.0	180085	1798300	67.5
1956	1778128	2906.2	531634	41.8	183008	1887800	68.5
1957	1852076	3037.2	483200	40.8	189081	1977800	70.7
1958	1939470	3168.9	616154	41.6	187720	2071100	72.6
1959	2036948	3306.9	655019	41.4	189154	2169600	73.4
1960	2080645	3469.6	681244	41.0	190946	2278600	74.3
1961	2161316	3660.3	783737	40.4	210762	2400400	75.0
1962	2275600	3861.6	817723	40.3	210312	2523000	75.9
1963	2376439	4052.0	848348	40.3	210119	2630100	77.2
1964	2527698	4234.9	905641	40.6	214986	2727000	78.6
1965	2611730	4430.7	971700	40.6	220700	2830400	80.5
1966	2769711	4648.1	1057994	40.4	227221	2956300	83.5
1967	2934415	4886.5	1140377	40.0	228748	3105200	86.0
1968	3011725	5126.1	1211043	39.7	226470	3248700	90.0
1969	3119286	5364.1	1293546	39.4	224111	3381000	94.1
1970	3220125	5618.9	1383910	39.4	221768	3528100	97.2
1971	3361300	5871.1	1471184	39.0	218315	3670200	100.0
1972	3492391	6108.0	1595889	38.7	220483	3783600	104.8
1973	3579785	6367.0	1756091	38.0	222512	3910800	112.7
1974	3579785	6643.6	1998817	38.0	220932	4054600	125.0
1975	3613398	6868.2	2312018	38.1	220415	4157600	138.5
1976	3727682	7020.4	2624689	37.7	219646	4217100	148.9
1977	3774740	7153.1	2889594	37.1	222858	4277200	160.8

TABLE B-3
SELECTED DATA, TOBACCO PRODUCTS INDUSTRIES
(1971 dollars)

	Value Added Output	Gross Capital Stock	Wages & Salaries (Current Prices)	Weekly Hours Paid	Total Person-Days Paid	Net Capital Stock	CPI
	(000s $)	(000,000 $)	(000s $)			(000s $)	
1957	134413	126.1	33323	38.6	19881.3	70700	70.7
1958	146183	140.4	37144	39.6	21248.9	72600	72.6
1959	154658	153.2	38078	40.4	21610.9	73400	73.4
1960	165015	161.9	38355	40.0	20240.5	74300	74.3
1961	171842	170.1	43853	39.5	21345.2	75000	75.0
1962	177727	175.6	47586	39.4	22817.5	75900	75.9
1963	184318	178.8	48039	38.7	22158.5	77200	77.2
1964	191145	184.3	49634	37.9	21416.7	78600	78.6
1965	199148	192.6	50806	37.6	20046.7	80500	80.5
1966	206210	204.3	53489	37.7	19951.0	83500	83.5
1967	218216	217.1	59779	37.6	20637.1	86000	86.0
1968	213037	228.8	63901	37.6	19902.0	90000	90.0
1969	220099	238.1	66871	37.0	19334.3	94100	94.1
1970	233752	245.5	74054	37.5	19588.3	97200	97.2
1971	235400	251.7	77504	36.8	18523.7	100000	100.0
1972	241991	254.9	82504	36.6	18128.0	104800	104.8
1973	249289	255.4	89027	36.6	17895.8	112700	112.7
1974	266473	261.8	98528	36.8	18362.9	125000	125.0
1975	266237	271.9	117332	36.6	18434.4	138500	138.5
1976	272122	274.7	125744	36.5	17196.1	148900	148.9
1977	283892	276.4	138976	36.4	16908.4	160800	160.8

TABLE B-4
SELECTED DATA, RUBBER AND PLASTIC PRODUCTS INDUSTRIES
(1971 dollars)

	Value Added Output	Gross Capital Stock	Wages & Salaries (Current Prices)	Weekly Hours Paid	Total Person-Days Paid	Net Capital Stock	CPI
	(000s $)	*(000,000 $)*	*(000s $)*			*(000s $)*	
1946	153258	173.4	37813	44.8	22055	100300	45.0
1947	217549	194.2	46614	43.7	23475	117000	49.2
1948	198716	213.1	48273	43.4	21703	131200	56.3
1949	237680	225.7	48172	42.3	20729	138000	58.0
1950	200665	234.0	54263	43.6	21812	141400	59.7
1951	213003	243.2	64358	41.4	23054	148100	66.0
1952	200015	256.5	65478	42.3	21582	158400	67.6
1953	229888	274.8	70995	41.4	22600	171700	67.0
1954	200665	299.1	67476	41.6	20894	188000	67.4
1955	237680	323.3	73775	43.0	21913	202400	67.5
1956	270800	346.8	82155	42.4	23136	213800	68.5
1957	256513	372.5	83215	40.8	22181	226300	70.7
1958	258461	393.2	76497	41.9	19948	233200	72.6
1959	299373	411.6	86884	42.4	21082	237500	73.4
1960	258461	441.1	84531	41.3	20298	254700	74.3
1961	252617	466.6	95737	41.3	21821	270600	75.0
1962	326648	477.1	104203	41.7	22788	278200	75.9
1963	342883	487.6	110974	41.2	24162	286200	77.2
1964	377951	508.6	122530	41.9	24972	298100	78.6
1965	403927	538.5	134151	41.8	26206	316200	80.5
1966	459775	584.6	148753	41.5	27821	350100	83.5
1967	505883	629.6	155953	41.2	26906	383200	86.0
1968	546145	665.0	154959	41.0	24833	407000	90.0
1969	602643	718.1	171187	41.1	25259	448200	94.1
1970	611735	780.7	289648	40.7	44189	495900	97.2
1971	649400	859.7	313461	40.6	44672	557700	100.0
1972	739667	949.0	372587	40.9	49100	620000	104.8
1973	848766	1032.9	442123	41.0	54377	676600	112.7
1974	864351	1129.2	489949	39.9	54173	737000	125.0
1975	800061	1199.9	531854	39.3	52963	775900	138.5
1976	944228	1241.1	622455	39.7	55309	785700	148.9
1977	1071510	1272.2	681842	39.4	55699	781700	160.8

TABLE B-5
SELECTED DATA, LEATHER PRODUCTS INDUSTRIES
(1971 dollars)

	Value Added Output	Gross Capital Stock	Wages & Salaries (Current Prices)	Weekly Hours Paid	Total Person-Days Paid	Net Capital Stock	CPI
	(000s $)	(000,000 $)	(000s $)			(000s $)	
1957	176237	152.1	78773	38.2	31573	86200	70.7
1958	177990	154.0	80311	39.8	30784	85300	72.6
1959	186978	155.1	83539	39.6	31415	83900	73.4
1960	178429	156.4	83448	39.4	30266	83500	74.3
1961	197280	156.5	97442	40.4	33283	83500	75.0
1962	203856	156.2	100425	40.1	32960	83000	75.9
1963	204952	156.5	102140	39.9	32647	83800	77.2
1964	212405	157.2	105673	39.9	32404	84900	78.6
1965	215693	157.9	109806	39.5	32585	85000	80.5
1966	217885	160.7	117671	39.3	32589	86500	83.5
1967	211747	164.8	121760	38.9	31496	88900	86.0
1968	224242	169.1	131879	39.3	31741	91200	90.0
1969	224242	174.2	137530	38.4	31192	94100	94.1
1970	211528	178.3	131433	38.2	28286	95300	97.2
1971	219200	181.3	140015	38.5	27930	95400	100.0
1972	221173	187.9	145892	38.5	27279	99500	104.8
1973	226214	195.3	158581	37.9	27251	103800	112.7
1974	229283	201.0	177296	37.3	26444	105700	125.0
1975	225557	206.7	200819	36.7	26834	107300	138.5
1976	214158	210.4	226831	36.7	26461	107300	148.9
1977	222926	212.2	219698	36.5	23456	106400	160.8

TABLE B-6
SELECTED DATA, TEXTILE INDUSTRIES
(1971 dollars)

	Value Added Output	Gross Capital Stock	Wages & Salaries (Current Prices)	Weekly Hours Paid	Total Person-Days Paid	Net Capital Stock	CPI
	(000s $)	(000,000 $)	(000s $)			(000s of $)	
1961	389821	1360.3	224645	42.0	64969	739800	75.0
1962	434136	1360.0	243021	42.1	67918	735600	75.9
1963	473944	1382.9	263380	42.1	70276	744100	77.2
1964	522015	1444.5	291933	42.2	74455	783500	78.6
1965	543796	1539.1	315082	41.9	76676	852200	80.5

112

TABLE B-6 (continued)

	Value Added Output	Gross Capital Stock	Wages & Salaries (Current Prices)	Weekly Hours Paid	Total Person Hours Paid	Net Capital Stock	CPI
1966	551307	1628.6	341414	41.6	77248	918800	83.5
1967	565578	1690.3	359553	41.2	77360	959400	86.0
1968	630173	1734.4	364097	41.1	73234	972900	90.0
1969	715047	1788.7	399543	40.8	75351	986900	94.1
1970	686505	1850.9	393047	40.4	69719	1009500	97.2
1971	751100	1897.4	422780	40.5	69350	1025100	100.0
1972	850996	1925.4	480835	40.7	74242	1042900	104.8
1973	906578	1952.5	537423	40.4	76863	1075900	112.7
1974	883294	1986.6	589296	39.3	75647	1119200	125.0
1975	847241	2021.9	614644	38.9	71050	1164900	138.5
1976	860010	2047.7	682746	39.1	68209	1186300	148.9
1977	883294	2942.9	727668	39.0	65508	1171500	160.8

TABLE B-7
SELECTED DATA, KNITTING MILLS
(1971 dollars)

	Value Added Output	Gross Capital Stock	Wages & Salaries (Current Prices)	Weekly Hours Paid	Total Person-Days Paid	Net Capital Stock	CPI
	(000s $)	(000,000 $)	(000s $)			(000s $)	
1961	100233	176.2	62189	40.8	22691	94300	75.0
1962	108754	180.4	63730	40.8	22816	95100	75.9
1963	122349	186.0	66551	41.0	22573	95900	77.2
1964	130465	193.6	72383	41.5	22972	96400	78.6
1965	136349	201.2	78661	41.1	24070	96600	80.5
1966	138175	208.3	82478	40.8	23609	98600	83.5
1967	186958	211.5	85434	40.3	22814	100000	86.0
1968	160088	211.0	94334	40.6	23845	101000	90.0
1969	174494	214.9	104850	40.2	24704	107400	94.1
1970	184639	221.0	106985	40.2	23735	115900	97.2
1971	202900	225.0	116331	41.0	23919	122700	100.0
1972	216697	232.0	127626	40.4	24732	128600	104.8
1973	232118	242.6	143058	39.5	25879	138000	112.7
1974	222784	249.5	163883	38.6	25540	143700	125.0
1975	219538	249.5	182833	38.1	24682	143100	138.5
1976	218320	247.6	192949	37.7	23525	139100	148.9
1977	228465	246.0	186233	38.2	20625	134200	160.8

113

TABLE B-8
SELECTED DATA, CLOTHING INDUSTRIES
(1971 dollars)

	Value Added Output	Gross Capital Stock	Wages & Salaries (Current Prices)	Weekly Hours Paid	Total Person-Days Paid	Net Capital Stock	CPI
	(000s $)	(000,000 $)	(000s $)			(000s $)	
1957	497759	259.3	213478	37.8	89425	135300	70.7
1958	492746	253.3	213296	38.9	86208	132300	72.6
1959	502056	246.2	222595	38.9	86181	129700	73.4
1960	507786	246.6	225632	39.0	86367	128500	74.3
1961	530704	250.8	256123	37.5	93306	127500	75.0
1962	556487	254.6	265140	37.4	91652	125800	75.9
1963	583703	259.6	277089	37.7	92305	124600	77.2
1964	612351	266.8	299938	37.2	96408	124800	78.6
1965	633121	276.5	321730	37.1	98659	125300	80.5
1966	651742	284.6	342044	36.5	99708	126100	83.5
1967	640999	287.5	356027	36.7	98263	125600	86.0
1968	663917	287.7	378694	36.5	97596	124500	90.0
1969	675377	288.6	412543	36.0	99091	125200	94.1
1970	674660	287.2	425673	36.3	97418	124900	97.2
1971	716200	274.2	461021	36.4	98457	124100	100.0
1972	755591	265.6	514502	36.0	102043	128100	104.8
1973	800712	273.2	569612	35.7	104300	137400	112.7
1974	799279	280.3	634746	35.4	101704	145100	125.0
1975	802144	278.4	722130	35.0	100528	149800	138.5
1976	838670	278.1	827113	34.8	101719	154700	148.9
1977	835089	282.3	849755	34.7	94939	158800	160.8

TABLE B-9
SELECTED DATA, WOOD INDUSTRIES
(1971 dollars)

	Value Added Output	Gross Capital Stock	Wages & Salaries (Current Prices)	Weekly Hours Paid	Total Person-Days Paid	Net Capital Stock	CPI
	(000s $)	(000,000 $)	(000s $)			(000s $)	
1957	580707	1009.1	259610	41.8	88163	604900	70.7
1958	592911	1021.6	261026	42.9	83782	610700	72.6
1959	621387	1046.3	271219	42.9	86181	623100	73.4
1960	637659	1081.8	278189	42.3	82734	645700	74.3
1961	652914	1128.4	292700	40.6	82085	666800	75.0
1962	703764	1174.2	311975	40.6	83466	684700	75.9
1963	754614	1216.4	340750	40.5	86888	703100	77.2
1964	817668	1269.6	367005	40.7	89407	730600	78.6
1965	843093	1343.3	398939	40.8	91589	769300	80.5

TABLE B-9 (continued)

	Value Added Output	Gross Capital Stock	Wages & Salaries (Current Prices)	Weekly Hours Paid	Total Person Hours Paid	Net Capital Stock	CPI
1966	864450	1421.7	429116	40.1	91937	809800	83.5
1967	878688	1469.4	451192	40.1	89873	836600	86.0
1968	905130	1516.4	490721	40.1	90309	860300	90.0
1969	951912	1631.1	541323	39.3	92524	933000	94.1
1970	916317	1779.4	551880	38.7	87829	1039300	97.2
1971	1017000	1913.3	638202	39.1	91846	1133000	100.0
1972	1093275	2044.0	770902	39.6	102699	1230400	104.8
1973	1214298	2209.0	938843	39.2	111600	1376700	112.7
1974	1163448	2409.3	1038109	37.9	106620	1545900	125.0
1975	1090224	2586.2	1070932	38.0	97717	1668900	138.5
1976	1324134	2715.6	1352849	38.1	106178	1747800	148.9
1977	1454310	2811.2	1557889	39.9	108660	1804300	160.8

TABLE B-10
SELECTED DATA, FURNITURE & FIXTURES INDUSTRIES
(1971 dollars)

	Value Added Output	Gross Capital Stock	Wages & Salaries (Current Prices)	Weekly Hours Paid	Total Person- Days Paid	Net Capital Stock	CPI
	(000s $)	(000,000 $)	(000s $)			(000s $)	
1961	242360	192.0	117119	42.6	33475	104700	75.0
1962	259375	193.0	125172	42.6	34362	105700	75.9
1963	277635	193.7	134442	42.6	35916	110500	77.2
1964	299215	197.1	148201	42.5	37986	118300	78.6
1965	340715	208.1	164112	42.7	40374	128600	80.5
1966	383875	228.2	89781	42.1	43598	142100	83.5
1967	391760	248.9	201833	41.8	43895	156800	86.0
1968	405455	268.8	211140	41.5	43171	170100	90.0
1969	425790	282.5	232847	41.5	44248	178100	94.1
1970	398400	293.1	235186	40.5	42238	183100	97.2
1971	415000	304.5	253530	41.3	43021	187900	100.0
1972	475175	315.7	299296	41.7	46942	193100	104.8
1973	512110	333.8	340706	40.6	49051	206500	112.7
1974	525805	359.7	402267	39.8	51441	226900	125.0
1975	477665	383.0	431897	39.0	49688	241600	138.5
1976	511695	394.9	474151	39.2	47847	244600	148.9
1977	511695	400.2	467400	39.1	43651	242000	160.8

115

TABLE B-11
SELECTED DATA, PAPER AND PAPER PRODUCTS INDUSTRIES
(1971 dollars)

	Value Added Output	Gross Capital Stock	Wages & Salaries (Current Prices)	Weekly Hours Paid	Total Person-Days Paid	Net Capital Stock	CPI
	(000s $)	(000,000 $)	(000s $)			(000s $)	
1946	615062	2219.3	134321	47.1	67442	1041100	45.0
1947	674584	2297.2	168632	47.2	73445	1135300	49.2
1948	719676	2397.9	197398	47.2	75980	1256000	56.3
1949	757554	2481.3	208349	47.1	76471	1361300	58.0
1950	820684	2536.5	225198	47.5	77519	1442900	59.7
1951	885617	2652.5	276521	46.5	82889	1552700	66.0
1952	851346	2811.9	292682	45.1	82965	1696200	67.6
1953	896439	2957.0	310108	43.6	84436	1810100	67.0
1954	927102	3097.1	331556	42.7	87370	1877400	67.4
1955	964980	3264.8	349777	43.0	89750	1963500	67.5
1956	1037128	3554.2	386887	42.4	93705	2168800	68.5
1957	1017287	3923.9	406021	41.0	95067	2449900	70.7
1958	1011876	4182.5	410855	41.5	93227	2607600	72.6
1959	1085827	4324.1	431800	41.9	94435	2642500	73.4
1960	1134527	4483.5	458224	41.8	95281	2694800	74.3
1961	1143546	4653.0	493444	41.2	98292	2761900	75.0
1962	1183227	4798.8	518784	41.1	100075	2827200	75.9
1963	1246357	4966.7	541195	41.3	101556	2911700	77.2
1964	1376223	5238.5	588358	41.7	106309	3072300	78.6
1965	1451979	5640.3	634425	41.8	110180	3336800	80.5
1966	1567415	6165.6	727120	41.8	116840	3703300	83.5
1967	1554789	6704.7	781885	41.3	118609	4071800	86.0
1968	1625134	7075.8	836084	41.2	117595	4268100	90.0
1969	1805504	7335.3	926270	41.1	121877	4388500	94.1
1970	1801896	7661.6	973114	40.9	121080	4617400	97.2
1971	1803700	8055.9	1039306	40.4	119709	4896700	100.0
1972	1962426	8398.5	1135298	40.8	120758	5092900	104.8
1973	2085077	8619.8	1248340	40.4	123138	5187800	112.7
1974	2213140	8830.6	1525816	40.0	131275	5273800	125.0
1975	1758608	9034.8	1553080	39.6	127342	5367200	138.5
1976	2002107	9255.5	1937848	39.7	130207	5447900	148.9
1977	2121151	9497.2	2080169	39.2	124463	5552900	160.8

TABLE B-12
SELECTED DATA, PRINTING, PUBLISHING AND ALLIED INDUSTRIES
(1971 dollars)

	Value Added Output	Gross Capital Stock	Wages & Salaries (Current Prices)	Weekly Hours Paid	Total Person- Days Paid	Net Capital Stock	CPI
	(000s $)	(000,000 $)	(000s $)			(000s $)	
1946	339841	589.2	86434	42.0	48950	274100	45.0
1947	369098	597.0	101612	41.1	52096	281700	49.2
1948	409609	619.2	119088	40.9	54541	301000	56.3
1949	441118	646.6	141490	41.0	61834	324000	58.0
1950	485004	668.2	154370	40.4	63125	343700	59.7
1951	498508	694.8	170829	40.0	64694	364800	66.0
1952	506385	717.0	186251	40.0	64485	379900	67.6
1953	555898	719.4	205627	40.0	66530	387100	67.0
1954	598660	737.9	220276	40.2	68614	407400	67.4
1955	629043	768.4	234580	40.1	69602	432100	67.5
1956	695435	790.4	254372	40.3	72361	449900	68.5
1957	706688	823.1	269169	39.5	70944	475900	70.7
1958	694310	855.7	284158	39.6	69738	505600	72.6
1959	749450	878.7	304828	39.7	71622	533900	73.4
1960	765204	901.1	320281	39.3	73049	558300	74.3
1961	785459	924.2	343620	38.8	75193	574500	75.0
1962	805715	953.5	356096	38.7	74544	593500	75.9
1963	822594	994.0	371074	38.6	75166	619800	77.2
1964	836098	1048.3	385687	38.9	75448	655500	78.6
1965	893488	1095.7	422225	39.0	78737	689200	80.5
1966	958756	1138.6	463662	38.9	81996	718200	83.5
1967	991389	1182.1	497916	38.6	83594	741800	86.0
1968	1012770	1221.4	535237	38.1	84143	760600	90.0
1969	1061158	1261.6	576928	37.9	84654	782600	94.1
1970	1075787	1306.8	606958	37.2	84045	812300	97.2
1971	1125300	1365.0	649508	37.2	84110	845600	100.0
1972	1208572	1424.0	712463	37.7	86071	875200	104.8
1973	1288469	1481.0	811834	37.2	90593	903300	112.7
1974	1336856	1543.4	961638	36.1	92939	933900	125.0
1975	1352611	1607.6	1042556	35.5	92912	963100	138.5
1976	1410001	1670.7	1171015	35.7	93487	992100	148.9
1977	1435883	1727.8	1253583	35.3	91760	1018900	160.8

TABLE B-13
SELECTED DATA, PRIMARY METAL INDUSTRIES
(1971 dollars)

	Value Added Output	Gross Capital Stock	Wages & Salaries (Current Prices)	Weekly Hours Paid	Total Person- Days Paid	Net Capital Stock	CPI
	(000s $)	(000,000 $)	(000s $)			(000s $)	
1961	1089872	4170.1	475320	40.3	89956	2605900	75.0
1962	1176399	4342.9	496878	40.5	91713	2684000	75.9
1963	1259244	4494.8	528422	40.6	94107	2789100	77.2
1964	1413888	4643.2	583191	40.9	100407	2911800	78.6
1965	1553804	4858.2	651267	41.2	107504	3066600	80.5
1966	1618239	5168.5	716557	40.8	113645	3262500	83.5
1967	1555645	5511.7	754681	40.5	112945	3453500	86.0
1968	1710289	5762.6	803456	40.8	113023	3546300	90.0
1969	1747109	5986.2	839046	40.7	110953	3628000	94.1
1970	1857569	6288.7	958507	40.6	116545	3793600	97.2
1971	1841000	6641.2	1017713	40.2	114314	3992700	100.0
1972	1905435	6972.3	1108809	40.4	113958	4135500	104.8
1973	2063761	7288.8	1237900	40.4	116462	4247800	112.7
1974	2223928	7641.4	1455671	40.1	122219	4443300	125.0
1975	2026941	8048.9	1612991	39.4	120335	4717600	138.5
1976	1988280	8400.2	1753128	39.9	117041	4896200	148.9
1977	2148447	8681.9	1945347	40.1	119219	4988800	160.8

TABLE B-14
SELECTED DATA, METAL FABRICATING INDUSTRIES
(1971 dollars)

	Value Added Output	Gross Capital Stock	Wages & Salaries (Current Prices)	Weekly Hours Paid	Total Person- Days Paid	Net Capital Stock	CPI
	(000s $)	(000,000 $)	(000s $)			(000s $)	
1961	1023838	1606.3	457886	41.2	101054	875900	75.0
1962	1127733	1592.8	509582	41.6	109575	877300	75.9
1963	1214627	1553.5	543982	41.6	113278	888800	77.2
1964	1343079	1550.1	602707	42.0	121021	912400	78.6
1965	1533868	1610.3	691525	42.0	133992	966200	80.5
1966	1698211	1729.7	794770	41.8	143311	1048200	83.5

118

TABLE B-14 (continued)

	(000s $)	(000,000 $)	(000s $)			(000s $)	
1967	1696322	1845.2	817639	41.1	139232	1126100	86.0
1968	1709545	1936.6	684199	41.0	137559	1185900	90.0
1969	1847442	2037.5	957930	40.8	141417	1249100	94.1
1970	1845553	2152.8	1011060	40.5	139471	1316600	97.2
1971	1889000	2251.0	1060181	40.4	137015	1362200	100.0
1972	1955115	2331.5	1150517	40.8	138309	1392900	104.8
1973	2157238	2424.1	1313501	40.5	144921	1438700	112.7
1974	2327248	2533.4	1568346	39.4	153745	1502700	125.0
1975	2117569	2638.3	1727946	38.9	150899	1556400	138.5
1976	2213908	2724.3	1926231	39.5	152127	1585000	148.9
1977	2189351	2782.1	2135200	39.4	146735	1591000	160.8

TABLE B-15
SELECTED DATA, MACHINERY INDUSTRIES
(1971 dollars)

	Value Added Output	Gross Capital Stock	Wages & Salaries (Current Prices)	Weekly Hours Paid	Total Person- Days Paid	Net Capital Stock	CPI
	(000s $)	(000,000 $)	(000s $)			(000s $)	
1961	461570	582.2	243436	40.7	50639	369200	75.0
1962	516110	599.5	271661	41.3	54439	379200	75.9
1963	560550	629.8	305715	41.5	58912	397800	77.2
1964	661550	680.4	346553	42.1	63912	433600	78.6
1965	740330	736.4	399342	42.5	70683	471000	80.5
1966	844360	793.0	455083	42.1	75451	506400	83.5
1967	864560	855.6	505095	41.1	79171	545600	86.0
1968	866580	908.6	520131	41.1	76350	575400	90.0
1969	987780	952.4	602881	40.9	81747	601300	94.1
1970	981720	1003.3	636243	40.7	79725	635000	97.2
1971	1010000	1050.5	584534	40.2	71062	660500	100.0
1972	1117060	1085.7	676016	40.5	77437	674500	104.8
1973	1244320	1132.7	772468	40.7	81640	703200	112.7
1974	1407940	1198.1	943565	39.7	89155	750400	125.0
1975	1395820	1274.0	1073613	39.3	92290	804300	138.5
1976	1344310	1346.5	1151828	39.6	89201	847500	148.9
1977	1343300	1453.5	1238612	39.4	87657	876200	160.8

119

SELECTED DATA, TRANSPORTATION EQUIPMENT
INDUSTRIES (1971 dollars)

	Value Added Output	Gross Capital Stock	Wages & Salaries (Current Prices)	Weekly Hours Paid	Total Person-Days Paid	Net Capital Stock	CPI
	(000s $)	(000,000 $)	(000s $)			(000s $)	
1946	526511	1364.5	200098	42.3	100745	655200	45.0
1947	647801	1318.7	230899	43.6	104348	640900	49.2
1948	661584	1275.8	255505	43.2	101816	627400	56.3
1949	680880	1271.8	270852	42.9	104750	625000	58.0
1950	736012	1282.5	290436	43.8	104176	635900	59.7
1951	887625	1306.0	368106	42.1	122517	669300	66.0
1952	1017185	1354.8	473119	42.3	146360	728900	67.6
1953	1146746	1436.9	555411	41.6	156059	827200	67.0
1954	940001	1530.2	479080	41.3	133432	928000	67.4
1955	1006159	1590.1	490435	40.5	131789	985500	67.5
1956	1083344	1640.1	553572	40.8	141257	1031500	68.5
1957	1061291	1687.9	592253	40.1	144824	1078900	70.7
1958	931731	1720.9	554565	40.3	126209	1116900	72.6
1959	923461	1765.8	532266	40.6	113706	1154700	73.4
1960	893138	1821.8	519733	40.5	109160	1185500	74.3
1961	882112	1867.3	494028	40.7	99280	1198000	75.0
1962	1050265	1913.8	550155	41.1	104931	1207100	75.9
1963	1212904	1982.6	619685	42.1	111822	1235300	77.2
1964	1334194	2109.1	708833	42.1	123767	1315300	78.6
1965	1656717	2314.6	830251	42.0	135481	1417800	80.5
1966	1797303	2577.9	922729	41.2	146932	1675400	83.5
1967	2089503	2815.6	979333	40.8	150215	1848000	86.0
1968	2409268	2973.9	1102226	40.9	149379	1948600	90.0
1969	2687685	3112.6	1228156	40.6	157755	2029900	94.1
1970	2359650	3310.4	1208545	40.3	146979	2165600	97.2
1971	2756600	3482.9	1337495	39.9	150155	2267500	100.0
1972	3018477	3576.5	1517008	40.8	158105	2294700	104.8
1973	3476073	3683.5	1800378	40.6	173358	2337600	112.7
1974	3445750	3857.1	1975402	39.8	171970	2429400	125.0
1975	3307920	4032.4	2033079	39.3	159642	2518400	138.5
1976	3580823	4148.4	2360557	40.2	162226	2547400	148.9
1977	3820648	4278.2	2671795	40.6	165287	2584900	160.8

TABLE B-17
SELECTED DATA, ELECTRICAL AND ELECTRONIC PRODUCTS INDUSTRIES
(1971 dollars)

	Value Added Output	Gross Capital Stock	Wages & Salaries (Current Prices)	Weekly Hours Paid	Total Person-Days Paid	Net Capital Stock	CPI
	(000s $)	*(000,000 $)*	*(000s $)*			*(000s $)*	
1946	243043	238.1	74511	41.9	43998	119600	45.0
1947	321953	249.5	103891	42.6	52736	131100	49.2
1948	328266	277.8	122114	41.8	53873	157300	56.3
1949	358251	316.7	137279	42.1	55916	192700	58.0
1950	404019	348.4	155337	42.4	60262	222200	59.7
1951	434005	387.4	194749	41.5	67626	258100	66.0
1952	448209	442.7	217565	42.1	69200	308600	67.6
1953	541323	497.7	250647	41.8	76856	359000	67.0
1954	544479	549.0	258510	40.9	75075	402000	67.4
1955	628124	598.0	264032	42.3	76244	436300	67.5
1956	552370	650.7	310523	41.7	83296	472800	68.5
1957	659688	712.6	351229	40.3	89962	516100	70.7
1958	645484	762.7	343221	40.8	82290	544400	72.6
1959	684939	801.8	347240	41.3	81729	558700	73.4
1960	710190	839.8	349171	40.7	78827	572500	74.3
1961	755958	874.8	409559	40.7	89360	582900	75.0
1962	897996	916.4	453357	40.8	96595	596900	75.9
1963	975328	963.4	487770	40.6	101235	616300	77.2
1964	1088958	1013.2	527084	40.9	105414	637100	78.6
1965	1221527	1077.6	584665	40.9	113463	667500	80.5
1966	1379347	1172.1	670340	40.8	124498	725500	83.5
1967	1393551	1279.6	718584	39.9	127561	796000	86.0
1968	1453522	1363.7	747909	40.1	124215	841000	90.0
1969	1570309	1435.4	813227	40.1	126986	875700	94.1
1970	1504025	1506.5	840938	39.3	120112	919200	97.2
1971	1578200	1575.7	920010	39.2	123181	965600	100.0
1972	1704456	1641.7	965915	39.7	121135	1002600	104.8
1973	1896996	1714.4	1087096	39.7	127928	1041800	112.7
1974	2004314	1794.1	1273787	39.0	133204	1089400	125.0
1975	1843338	1857.1	1364138	38.8	125868	1121900	138.5
1976	1934873	1909.7	1481756	38.8	121274	1143000	148.9
1977	1870167	1955.6	1484638	38.9	110813	1154400	160.8

TABLE B-18
SELECTED DATA, NON-METALLIC MINERAL PRODUCTS
INDUSTRIES
(1971 dollars)

	Value Added Output	Gross Capital Stock	Wages & Salaries (Current Prices)	Weekly Hours Paid	Total Person-Days Paid	Net Capital Stock	CPI
	(000s $)	(000,000 $)	(000s $)			(000s $)	
1946	172524	672.5	39651	46.1	24387	331800	45.0
1947	207207	687.7	50456	46.4	26443	344400	49.2
1948	221436	725.2	58816	46.4	27278	376400	56.3
1949	240111	751.8	64594	46.0	28139	400900	58.0
1950	266790	761.0	72381	46.4	29603	411400	59.7
1951	293469	784.0	86079	45.0	31522	428100	66.0
1952	307698	823.1	92819	45.1	31422	457600	67.6
1953	338823	861.4	107275	44.4	34352	486400	67.0
1954	353052	905.7	114849	44.7	35229	518100	67.4
1955	402853	960.5	131007	45.0	38949	558000	67.5
1956	457100	1075.3	143223	44.2	40165	654400	68.5
1957	465993	1214.5	145710	43.0	38879	768500	70.7
1958	483779	1282.3	156459	44.1	39463	811200	72.6
1959	522019	1342.8	172643	44.4	41886	843900	73.4
1960	505122	1419.7	172425	42.9	41308	883100	74.3
1961	527355	1472.1	191818	42.4	43320	900400	75.0
1962	604724	1521.1	210094	42.9	45471	917300	75.9
1963	608281	1553.0	218356	42.9	46043	936400	77.2
1964	675868	1576.5	240129	43.3	48501	970400	78.6
1965	740787	1635.2	268819	43.4	51218	1033200	80.5
1966	764798	1756.5	294931	43.3	53189	1133600	83.5
1967	717665	1902.6	301482	42.7	51276	1232700	86.0
1968	774580	2007.2	326042	42.7	51670	1284200	90.0
1969	804817	2104.3	357764	42.4	51888	1330100	94.1
1970	770134	2223.3	364661	41.7	49963	1394600	97.2
1971	889300	2316.8	405131	41.9	51291	1428300	100.0
1972	959555	2399.2	458227	42.2	53087	1451700	104.8
1973	1081389	2522.9	522112	41.6	55949	1521700	112.7
1974	1112514	2642.0	604898	40.7	57566	1592800	125.0
1975	1076942	2739.1	669350	40.4	55932	1639100	138.5
1976	1104511	2852.0	747428	40.4	55021	1688600	148.9
1977	1186326	2979.4	794428	40.2	52518	1748700	160.8

TABLE B-19
SELECTED DATA, PETROLEUM & COAL PRODUCTS
INDUSTRIES (1971 dollars)

	Value Added Output	Gross Capital Stock	Wages & Salaries (Current Prices)	Weekly Hours Paid	Total Person-Days Paid	Net Capital Stock	CPI
	(000s $)	*(000,000 $)*	*(000s $)*			*(000s $)*	
1957	220262	1532.7	76800	41.4	15131	1160000	70.7
1958	222438	1671.6	83820	40.8	15860	1265000	72.6
1959	243768	1817.5	81544	41.4	14252	1370400	73.4
1960	254215	1913.1	84246	41.1	14315	1438400	74.3
1961	269886	1995.6	100310	41.2	16392	1452500	75.0
1962	292086	2066.2	104410	41.3	16277	1469500	75.9
1963	315157	2137.4	101042	41.9	15398	1494100	77.2
1964	317769	2171.6	102598	41.9	15009	1485200	78.6
1965	329522	2207.4	102825	42.1	14330	1468700	80.5
1966	344758	2268.5	119653	42.9	15403	1476500	83.5
1967	347805	2362.5	128781	42.5	15662	1518100	86.0
1968	386111	2482.3	138470	43.0	15631	1594000	90.0
1969	400911	2604.9	151653	42.9	15633	1680900	94.1
1970	410923	2781.5	160653	42.2	15647	1815800	97.2
1971	435300	3004.9	172593	41.9	15517	1984000	100.0
1972	470559	3220.4	186037	42.5	15409	2131200	104.8
1973	537160	3457.8	210443	43.2	16087	2300800	112.7
1974	553266	3737.4	254539	41.6	17435	2513500	125.0
1975	546302	4030.0	298040	41.6	17264	2727500	138.5
1976	556749	4259.0	320316	40.8	16689	2872700	148.9
1977	581996	4416.8	375098	41.0	17849	2965100	160.8

123

TABLE B-20
SELECTED DATA, CHEMICAL & CHEMICAL PRODUCTS INDUSTRIES
(1971 dollars)

	Value Added Output	Gross Capital Stock	Wages & Salaries (Current Prices)	Weekly Hours Paid	Total Person- Days Paid	Net Capital Stock	CPI
	(000s $)	(000,000 $)	(000s $)			(000s $)	
1946	261113	950.7	67842	44.4	38012	467300	45.0
1947	273772	999.9	78994	43.8	39237	502800	49.2
1948	283267	1072.3	89326	44.0	39548	555900	56.3
1949	299092	1142.4	100691	44.3	41328	605200	58.0
1950	327577	1189.6	106794	43.4	41475	634700	59.7
1951	370305	1243.4	131310	42.7	45664	671400	66.0
1952	403538	1389.0	148076	42.3	47694	796200	67.6
1953	447847	1593.5	164591	42.3	50207	970200	67.0
1954	487410	1716.5	177312	41.6	51603	1052000	67.4
1955	530138	1780.1	185268	41.5	51856	1070900	67.5
1956	580777	1918.9	200743	41.5	52821	1163800	68.5
1957	629835	2120.5	218136	40.9	53536	1317800	70.7
1958	669397	2290.6	231089	41.3	53576	1439500	72.6
1959	689970	2410.3	239127	41.1	53630	1501100	73.4
1960	724785	2519.3	251909	40.8	53840	1550500	74.3
1961	772260	2643.0	318709	40.8	63357	1628200	75.0
1962	827647	2740.5	332577	41.0	63905	1693500	75.9
1963	883035	2814.4	355064	40.8	65494	1745900	77.2
1964	1012800	2920.8	377408	41.1	67433	1817400	78.6
1965	1112497	3132.7	412402	41.1	70975	1971000	80.6
1966	1215360	3415.9	451833	41.2	73317	2187900	83.5
1967	1251757	3682.1	488652	40.8	75245	2382200	86.0
1968	1348290	3953.7	537992	40.7	77027	2574800	90.0
1969	1484385	4189.6	592574	40.7	78441	2735100	94.1
1970	1503375	4382.3	673159	40.6	79070	2854400	97.2
1971	1582500	4560.6	669314	40.2	77377	2952500	100.0
1972	1685363	4719.9	694117	40.8	74731	3018500	104.8
1973	1881592	4900.4	775242	40.8	77328	3105500	112.7
1974	1971795	5157.8	893309	40.0	79795	3320600	125.0
1975	1854690	5632.9	1003909	39.8	78025	3736800	138.5
1976	1938563	6300.0	1130381	39.5	79397	4295500	148.9
1977	2122132	7069.9	1289431	39.8	81105	4880400	160.8

Appendix C: Productivity and Technical Change: Detailed Data

TABLE C-1
RATIO OF PRODUCTIVITY AND CAPITAL INTENSITY,
NET CAPITAL STOCK
(1961 dollars)

	Total Activity		Production Activity	
	Output/ Labour	Capital/ Labour	Output/ Labour	Capital/ Labour
1946	2.33	2.34	2.68	2.82
1947	2.43	2.32	2.79	2.79
1948	2.50	2.46	2.87	2.96
1949	2.53	2.57	2.98	3.17
1950	2.66	2.64	3.16	3.28
1951	2.76	2.66	3.28	3.31
1952	2.81	2.83	3.37	3.55
1953	2.94	2.99	3.60	3.83
1954	3.06	3.37	3.74	4.32
1955	3.25	3.43	3.98	4.41
1956	3.41	3.53	4.18	4.55
1957	3.48	3.93	4.31	5.10
1958	3.62	4.40	4.52	5.76
1959	3.83	4.44	4.76	5.78
1960	3.92	4.67	4.91	6.13
1961	3.83	4.50	5.10	6.28
1962	4.06	4.48	5.73	6.63
1963	4.21	4.49	5.89	6.58
1964	4.39	4.45	6.23	6.61
1965	4.54	4.48	6.44	6.65
1966	4.69	4.64	6.60	6.85
1967	4.87	5.01	6.55	7.06
1968	5.22	5.29	6.99	7.43
1969	5.53	5.42	7.62	7.83
1970	5.62	5.89	7.38	8.10
1971	5.98	6.21	7.96	8.66
1972	6.18	6.20	8.46	8.90
1973	6.51	6.22	8.97	8.98
1974	6.72	6.52	8.98	9.13
1975	6.56	7.09	8.38	9.48
1976	6.80	7.25	8.70	9.72
1977	7.16	7.59	9.14	10.16

TABLE C-2
PRODUCTIVITY AND CAPITAL INTENSITY,
GROSS CAPITAL STOCK
(1961 dollars)

| | Total Activity | | Production Activity | |
	Output Per Man-Hour	Gross Capital Stock Per Man-Hour	Output Per Man-Hour	Gross Capital Stock Per Man-Hour
1946	2.33	4.41	2.68	5.32
1947	2.43	4.26	2.79	5.12
1948	2.50	4.39	2.87	5.28
1949	2.53	4.50	2.98	5.55
1950	2.66	4.56	3.16	5.67
1951	2.76	4.51	3.28	5.61
1952	2.81	4.69	3.37	5.89
1953	2.94	4.86	3.60	6.22
1954	3.06	5.43	3.74	6.97
1955	3.25	5.54	3.98	7.11
1956	3.41	5.66	4.18	7.28
1957	3.48	6.22	4.31	8.06
1958	3.62	6.93	4.52	9.08
1959	3.83	7.04	4.76	9.17
1960	3.92	7.47	4.91	9.80
1961	3.83	7.28	5.10	10.16
1962	4.06	7.31	5.73	10.81
1963	4.21	7.34	5.89	10.73
1964	4.39	7.26	6.22	10.79
1965	4.54	7.28	6.43	10.81
1966	4.69	7.50	6.60	11.06
1967	4.87	8.07	6.55	11.38
1968	5.22	8.57	6.99	12.04
1969	5.53	8.83	7.62	12.75
1970	5.62	9.57	7.38	13.17
1971	5.98	10.11	7.96	14.10
1972	6.18	10.16	8.46	14.58
1973	6.51	10.24	8.97	14.78
1974	6.72	10.71	8.98	14.99
1975	6.56	11.59	8.38	15.52
1976	6.80	11.88	8.70	15.94
1977	7.16	12.52	9.14	16.75

TABLE C-3
PRODUCTIVITY AND CAPITAL INTENSITY,
GROSS CAPITAL STOCK
(1971 dollars)

| | Total Activity | | Production Activity | |
	Outper Per Man-Hour	Gross Capital Stock Per Man-Hour	Output Per Man-Hour	Gross Capital Stock Per Man-Hour
1946	2.69	6.12	3.04	7.38
1947	2.80	5.90	3.16	7.10
1948	2.88	6.08	3.25	7.32
1949	2.92	6.23	3.38	7.68
1950	3.07	6.31	3.58	7.85
1951	3.19	6.24	3.72	7.77
1952	3.25	6.49	3.82	8.15
1953	3.39	6.71	4.08	8.60
1954	3.53	7.50	4.24	9.62
1955	3.75	7.28	4.51	9.35
1956	3.93	7.82	4.74	10.05
1957	4.02	8.58	4.88	11.11
1958	4.17	9.56	5.12	12.52
1959	4.41	9.71	5.39	12.64
1960	4.53	10.30	5.57	13.51
1961	4.42	10.03	5.78	14.00
1962	4.69	10.07	6.50	14.89
1963	4.86	10.10	6.67	14.78
1964	5.07	9.99	7.06	14.84
1965	5.24	10.00	7.29	14.86
1966	5.41	10.30	7.48	15.19
1967	5.62	11.08	7.42	15.62
1968	6.02	11.76	7.93	16.52
1969	6.38	12.12	8.63	17.50
1970	6.48	13.14	8.36	18.07
1971	6.90	13.88	9.02	19.36
1972	7.13	13.95	9.59	20.01
1973	7.51	14.06	10.16	20.29
1974	7.75	17.46	10.17	24.44
1975	7.57	15.90	9.50	21.28
1976	7.84	16.30	9.86	21.85
1977	8.26	17.16	10.36	22.96

TABLE C-4
EARNINGS RATE AND SHARE OF VALUE ADDED,
NET CAPITAL STOCK
(1961 dollars)

	Total Activity		Production Activity	
	Hourly Earnings	Wage Share of Value Added	Hourly Earnings	Wage Share of Value Added
1946	1.23	0.5306	1.14	0.425
1947	1.27	0.5237	1.18	0.424
1948	1.27	0.5067	1.19	0.414
1949	1.30	0.5145	1.22	0.408
1950	1.33	0.5019	1.25	0.394
1951	1.36	0.4938	1.27	0.388
1952	1.45	0.5159	1.36	0.403
1953	1.55	0.5283	1.48	0.411
1954	1.62	0.5286	1.50	0.401
1955	1.66	0.5120	1.54	0.388
1956	1.73	0.5090	1.61	0.384
1957	1.80	0.5166	1.65	0.384
1958	1.84	0.5098	1.68	0.371
1959	1.89	0.4925	1.72	0.361
1960	1.94	0.4944	1.76	0.359
1961	2.00	0.5213	1.73	0.338
1962	2.05	0.5044	1.91	0.332
1963	2.09	0.4950	1.92	0.327
1964	2.12	0.4835	2.01	0.323
1965	2.17	0.4782	2.07	0.321
1966	2.24	0.4766	2.11	0.320
1967	2.32	0.4757	2.07	0.316
1968	2.40	0.4608	2.14	0.306
1969	2.48	0.4489	2.29	0.300
1970	2.59	0.4615	2.27	0.308
1971	2.71	0.4525	2.43	0.306
1972	2.81	0.4454	2.58	0.305
1973	2.91	0.4313	2.68	0.299
1974	2.97	0.4337	2.70	0.301
1975	2.96	0.4523	2.63	0.313
1976	3.04	0.4361	2.50	0.286
1977		0.4247	2.42	0.264

TABLE C-5
EARNINGS RATE AND SHARE OF VALUE ADDED,
GROSS CAPITAL STOCK
(1961 dollars)

	Total Activity		Production Activity	
	Hourly Earnings	Wage Share of Value Added	Hourly Earnings	Wage Share of Value Added
1946	1.23	0.530	1.14	0.425
1947	1.27	0.524	1.18	0.424
1948	1.26	0.507	1.19	0.414
1949	1.30	0.515	1.22	0.408
1950	1.34	0.502	1.25	0.394
1951	1.36	0.494	1.27	0.388
1952	1.45	0.516	1.36	0.403
1953	1.55	0.528	1.48	0.411
1954	1.62	0.529	1.50	0.401
1955	1.66	0.512	1.54	0.388
1956	1.73	0.509	1.61	0.385
1957	1.80	0.517	1.65	0.384
1958	1.84	0.510	1.68	0.371
1959	1.88	0.493	1.72	0.361
1960	1.94	0.494	1.76	0.359
1961	1.99	0.521	1.73	0.338
1962	2.05	0.504	1.91	0.332
1963	2.09	0.495	1.92	0.327
1964	2.12	0.484	2.01	0.323
1965	2.17	0.478	2.07	0.321
1966	2.24	0.477	2.11	0.320
1967	2.32	0.476	2.07	0.316
1968	2.40	0.461	2.14	0.305
1969	2.48	0.449	2.29	0.300
1970	2.59	0.462	2.27	0.308
1971	2.71	0.452	2.43	0.305
1972	2.75	0.445	2.58	0.304
1973	2.81	0.431	2.68	0.299
1974	2.91	0.434	2.70	0.301
1975	2.96	0.452	2.63	0.313
1976	3.04	0.436	2.50	0.288
1977		0.425	2.42	0.264

TABLE C-6
EARNINGS RATE AND SHARE OF VALUE ADDED,
GROSS CAPITAL STOCK
(1971 dollars)

	Total Activity		Production Activity	
	Hourly Earnings	Wage Share of Value Added	Hourly Earnings	Wage Share of Value Added
1946	1.65	0.613	1.52	0.500
1947	1.69	0.605	1.57	0.499
1948	1.69	0.586	1.58	0.487
1949	1.74	0.595	1.62	0.481
1950	1.78	0.580	1.66	0.464
1951	1.82	0.571	1.70	0.457
1952	1.94	0.596	1.82	0.474
1953	2.07	0.611	1.97	0.484
1954	2.15	0.611	2.00	0.472
1955	2.22	0.592	2.06	0.457
1956	2.31	0.588	2.15	0.453
1957	2.40	0.597	2.21	0.452
1958	2.46	0.589	2.24	0.437
1959	2.51	0.569	2.29	0.425
1960	2.59	0.572	2.35	0.422
1961	2.66	0.603	2.30	0.398
1962	2.73	0.583	2.54	0.391
1963	2.78	0.572	2.57	0.385
1964	2.83	0.559	2.68	0.380
1965	2.90	0.552	2.76	0.378
1966	2.98	0.551	2.82	0.377
1967	3.09	0.550	2.76	0.372
1968	3.21	0.533	2.85	0.360
1969	3.31	0.519	3.05	0.353
1970	3.46	0.534	3.03	0.362
1971	3.61	0.523	3.25	0.360
1972	3.67	0.515	3.44	0.359
1973	3.75	0.499	3.57	0.352
1974	3.89	0.501	3.61	0.354
1975	3.96	0.523	3.50	0.368
1976	3.95	0.504	3.34	0.338
1977	4.06	0.491	3.22	0.311

TABLE C-7
ELASTICITY OF SUBSTITUTION AND TECHNICAL CHANGE,
NET CAPITAL STOCK
(1961 dollars)

| | Total Activity | | Production Activity | |
	Elasticity of Substitution of the Biased Type	Technical Progress Function	Elasticity of Substitution of the Biased Type	Technical Progress Function
1946	1.040	0.981	2.115	0.9014
1947	1.044	0.986	2.111	0.9005
1948	1.054	0.996	2.074	0.8905
1949	1.049	0.991	2.055	0.8853
1950	1.056	0.999	2.010	0.8730
1951	1.061	1.004	1.991	0.8678
1952	1.049	0.991	2.038	0.8808
1953	1.042	0.983	2.065	0.8882
1954	1.041	0.983	2.031	0.8788
1955	1.051	0.983	1.989	0.8674
1956	1.052	0.995	1.980	0.8648
1957	1.048	0.990	1.978	0.8643
1958	1.052	0.994	1.941	0.8537
1959	1.061	1.004	1.914	0.8461
1960	1.060	1.003	1.908	0.8444
1961	1.046	0.987	1.860	0.8306
1962	1.055	0.997	1.847	0.8267
1963	1.060	1.003	1.835	0.8233
1964	1.066	1.009	1.827	0.8208
1965	1.069	1.012	1.823	0.8196
1966	1.069	1.013	1.821	0.8191
1967	1.070	1.014	1.813	0.8166
1968	1.077	1.022	1.793	0.8107
1969	1.083	1.028	1.782	0.8074
1970	1.077	1.021	1.796	0.8117
1971	1.081	1.026	1.792	0.8105
1972	1.084	1.029	1.991	0.8101
1973	1.090	1.036	1.779	0.8066
1974	1.089	1.035	1.784	0.8080
1975	1.081	1.026	1.807	0.8150
1976	1.089	1.034	1.759	0.8006
1977	1.094	1.039	1.721	0.7889

TABLE C-8
ELASTICITY OF SUBSTITUTION AND TECHNICAL CHANGE,
GROSS CAPITAL STOCK
(1961 dollars)

	Total Activity		Production Activity	
	Elasticity of Substitution of the Biased Type	Technical Progress Function	Elasticity of Substitution of the Biased Type	Technical Progress Function
1946	1.43	1.02	3.489	0.834
1947	1.42	1.01	3.472	0.832
1948	1.41	1.00	3.302	0.816
1949	1.41	1.01	3.219	0.808
1950	1.40	1.00	3.032	0.790
1951	1.396	0.996	2.959	0.783
1952	1.41	1.01	3.149	0.802
1953	1.43	1.02	3.265	0.813
1954	1.43	1.02	3.118	0.799
1955	1.41	1.01	2.953	0.782
1956	1.409	1.00	2.919	0.778
1957	1.42	1.01	2.911	0.777
1958	1.41	1.01	2.773	0.762
1959	1.40	0.996	2.679	0.751
1960	1.40	0.997	2.660	0.749
1961	1.42	1.01	2.503	0.729
1962	1.41	1.00	2.461	0.723
1963	1.40	0.997	2.426	0.719
1964	1.39	0.99	2.399	0.715
1965	1.38	0.989	2.387	0.713
1966	1.38	0.988	2.382	0.713
1967	1.38	0.987	2.357	0.709
1968	1.37	0.981	2.300	0.701
1969	1.36	0.976	2.269	0.697
1970	1.37	0.981	2.309	0.703
1971	1.365	0.978	2.298	0.701
1972	1.36	0.975	2.293	0.700
1973	1.35	0.969	2.261	0.696
1974	1.35	0.970	2.274	0.698
1975	1.37	0.977	2.342	0.707
1976	1.35	0.971	2.206	0.688
1977	1.348	0.966	2.104	0.672

TABLE C-9
ELASTICITY OF SUBSTITUTION AND TECHNICAL CHANGE,
GROSS CAPITAL STOCK,
(1971 dollars)

	Total Activity		Production Activity	
	Elasticity of Substitution of the Biased Type	Technical Progress Function	Elasticity of Substitution of the Biased Type	Technical Progress Function
1946	1.685	1.114	3.866	1.000
1947	1.663	1.103	3.840	0.997
1948	1.617	1.078	3.581	0.970
1949	1.637	1.089	3.461	0.956
1950	1.605	1.072	3.199	0.925
1951	1.586	1.061	3.101	0.912
1952	1.641	1.091	3.362	0.945
1953	1.677	1.111	3.527	0.937
1954	1.678	1.111	3.317	0.939
1955	1.631	1.086	3.093	0.911
1956	1.623	1.082	3.047	0.905
1957	1.643	1.092	3.037	0.904
1958	1.625	1.083	2.857	0.879
1959	1.583	1.060	2.740	0.862
1960	1.587	1.062	2.716	0.858
1961	1.656	1.100	2.526	0.829
1962	1.611	1.075	2.477	0.821
1963	1.589	1.063	2.436	0.814
1964	1.563	1.049	2.405	0.809
1965	1.553	1.043	2.391	0.806
1966	1.549	1.042	2.385	0.805
1967	1.547	1.040	2.357	0.800
1968	1.520	1.025	2.292	0.789
1969	1.500	1.014	2.257	0.783
1970	1.521	1.026	2.303	0.791
1971	1.505	1.017	2.290	0.789
1972	1.494	1.011	2.285	0.788
1973	1.473	0.999	2.249	0.781
1974	1.476	1.001	2.264	0.784
1975	1.505	1.017	2.340	0.797
1976	1.480	1.002	2.188	0.770
1977	1.464	0.993	2.077	0.749

Appendix D: Production Function Estimations

TABLE D-1
COBB-DOUGLAS PRODUCTION FUNCTION, MARGINAL CONDITION
(1971 dollars)

$$\ln Q = A + \alpha \ln L + \beta \ln K + \lambda T$$

	A	α	β	λ	$\bar{R}^2$	D.W.	ρ
Total manu.	−5.8376 (12.3937)	0.9799 (32.9867)	0.7709		0.9974	1.8550	0.685
	−5.1384 (2.3456)	0.9329 (6.3446)	0.7339	0.00239 (0.3204)	0.9974	1.8645	0.680
Food & beverages	−6.6607 (12.8474)	0.6776 (41.1898)	0.8505		0.9975	1.5376	0.612
	2.7981 (1.4694)	0.3668 (5.8603)	0.4604	0.0182 (4.9069)	0.9986	1.5910	0.562
Tobacco	−9.6913 (10.7312)	0.7005 (23.9671)	1.2816		0.9504	0.3706	
	1.6853 (1.0129)	0.3177 (5.6996)	0.5814	0.0271 (7.2416)	0.9586	0.4509	
Rubber & plastic	−0.5941 (0.7176)	0.4828 (16.2969)	0.6440		0.9639	1.8314	0.424
	3.4126 (1.2983)	0.3265 (3.2081)	0.4355	0.0202 (1.6016)	0.9669	1.8159	0.406
Leather	1.1824 (0.4387)	0.6635 (4.1804)	0.3747		0.9182	1.5008	0.978
	0.5963 (0.2595)	0.6395 (4.9003)	0.3611	0.0219 (13.5441)	0.9549	1.6789	0.450
Textile	4.3446 (1.4726)	0.6447 (3.8464)	0.2367		0.9866	2.1937	0.983
	−2.2163 (0.9246)	0.8494 (5.9942)	0.3118	0.0486 (24.1363)	0.9917	2.1693	0.549
Knitting mills	0.1643 (0.0450)	0.5776 (2.7622)	0.3281		0.9689	1.3273	1.020
	1.2263 (0.4299)	0.5632 (3.3988)	0.3199	0.0418 (8.8534)	0.9806	1.5036	0.538
Clothing	1.2386 (0.3652)	0.6588 (3.7069)	0.3857		0.9876	1.8250	0.946
	1.6061 (0.4692)	0.6047 (3.3437)	0.3541	0.0245 (10.7599)	0.9907	1.6939	0.619
Wood	−2.8344 (1.4606)	0.8082 (8.6107)	0.4909		0.9807	1.4567	0.78
	−2.2759 (0.6549)	0.7790 (4.4409)	0.4732	0.0269 (0.2238)	0.9808	1.4869	0.77
Furniture & fixtures	−3.4059 (4.1507)	0.8499 (19.8938)	0.5474		0.9745	1.5063	0.12
	−0.9051 (0.4114)	0.7095 (5.8063)	0.4570	0.00798 (1.2218)	0.9770	1.6410	0.22

TABLE D-1 (continued)

Industry	A	α	β	λ			
Paper	−2.2303	0.6545	0.5525		0.9829	1.7570	0.3069
	(3.8597)	(28.2036)					
	1.9234	0.4804	0.4056	0.01032	0.9836	1.8407	0.2514
	(0.5352)	(3.1916)		(1.1610)			
Printing & publishing	−6.8375	0.9152	0.7176		0.9951	2.1254	0.7720
	(5.2024)	(15.6609)					
	4.1075	0.4079	0.3199	0.0225	0.9968	2.1353	0.6839
	(1.4098)	(3.0325)		(3.9928)			
Primary metal	−4.3922	0.7502	0.6268		0.9627	1.6633	0.3548
	(2.7075)	(11.5759)					
	−6.2041	0.8264	0.6905	−0.0038	0.9629	1.6299	0.3493
	(1.0524)	(3.3464)		(0.3188)			
Metal fabricating	−7.0545	0.9215	0.7026		0.9887	1.8928	0.2711
	(7.9498)	(24.1816)					
	−7.9856	0.9637	0.7348	−0.0021	0.9888	1.8655	0.2638
	(3.1483)	(8.4303)		(0.3888)			
Machinery	1.6449	0.6157	0.3715		0.9840	2.1950	0.8883
	(0.4158)	(3.1929)					
	−0.0715	0.6624	0.3997	0.0236	0.9851	1.8313	0.6137
	(0.01945)	(3.4137)		(2.2332)			
Transporation equipment	−6.7443	0.9816	0.6317		0.9879	1.8733	0.9359
	(2.1905)	(7.0958)					
	−6.5898	0.9465	0.6090	0.0192	0.9889	1.7882	0.8116
	(2.1802)	(6.5445)		(2.0634)			
Electrical & electronic	−7.7306	1.0549	0.6445		0.9877	2.0284	0.8147
	(2.6547)	(7.4598)					
	3.1621	0.4923	0.3007	0.0326	0.9900	2.2138	0.6262
	(1.1435)	(3.4458)		(3.7912)			
Non-metallic mineral	−4.3149	0.6390	0.7488		0.9926	1.5145	0.7321
	(3.6876)	(15.1418)					
	2.5489	0.3744	0.4388	0.0233	0.9939	1.8073	0.5339
	(1.0361)	(3.9741)		(2.9443)			
Petroleum & coal	10.6563	0.1169	0.1282		0.9959	2.0562	0.9572
	(4.12639)	(1.2718)					
	8.5086	0.1301	0.1428	0.0409	0.9960	1.9612	0.8811
	(3.0538)	(1.2022)		(5.5843)			
Chemical	−5.4263	0.6860	0.7666		0.9944	1.3559	0.6325
	(6.8474)	(24.2226)					
	10.3237	0.0852	0.0953	0.0563	0.9970	1.4219	0.8773
	(3.4781)	(0.7569)		(4.7986)			

A—Efficiency parameter
α—Elasticity of response of output to labour
β—Elasticity of response of output to capital
λ—Contribution of technological change to output through time, while holding labour and capital constant
Q—Value added output
L—Total man-hours
K—Net capital stock in 1971 dollars
Source: Appendix B, Tables B-1 to B-20

TABLE D-2
CES PRODUCTION FUNCTION, MARGINAL CONDITION
(1971 Dollars)

$$ln\ Q = ln\ A + V\left[ln\ L - \frac{1}{\rho} ln\ \left\{\delta(K/L)^{-\rho} + (1 - \delta)\right\}\right] + \lambda t$$

	δ	σ	V	λ	$\bar{R}^2$	$D.W.$	ρ
Total Manu.	0.3088	1.4706	1.7306 (44.9781)		0.9976	1.8002	0.5838
	0.5385	0.6900	1.9996 (25.8736)	0.03199 (3.8382)	0.9972	1.7758	0.7403
Food & bev.	0.5860	0.9274	1.5429 (39.3162)		0.9974	1.5159	0.6226
	0.2390	0.9771	1.1957 (70.4063)	0.0492 (4.4294)	0.9986	1.5774	0.5046
Tobacco prod.	0.5886	1.2563	1.8992 (13.0792)		0.9000	0.5521	
	0.5491	1.4758	1.8647 (13.6235)	0.0490 (0.4750)	0.9701	0.5693	
Rubber & plastic prod.	0.4579	1.3957	1.1326 (16.9394)		0.9648	1.8193	0.4090
	0.3591	4.7338	1.0924 (18.7348)	0.0232 (2.0814)	0.9674	1.7891	0.3691
Leather	0.3538	1.0456	1.0375 (4.2107)		0.9186	1.5045	0.9786
	0.3534	1.0275	1.0336 (4.2058)	0.0005 (0.1349)	0.9186	1.5040	0.9786
Textile	0.6755	0.8148	0.4198 (0.7201)		0.9612	1.5905	0.8882
	0.4399	0.5888	0.9000 (3.3186)	0.1053 (2.5082)	0.9729	1.4054	0.9759
Knit. mills	0.1804	−5.2243	0.6666 (2.0639)		0.9754	1.5788	0.9072
	0.2287	1.2871	0.9847 (3.1001)	0.0502 (1.3237)	0.9668	1.1985	1.0501
Clothing	0.3787	1.2249	1.0497 (3.7213)		0.9876	1.8332	0.9460
	0.4220	1.4102	1.0932 (3.8113)	0.0116 (6.0850)	0.9877	1.8630	0.9427
Wood	0.5955	0.6486	1.3245 (8.9780)		0.9821	1.3764	0.7896
	0.5511	0.7813	1.2439 (8.5838)	0.0189 (1.1066)	0.9794	1.4699	0.7703
Furn. & fixt.	0.3875	1.0638	1.3903 (19.8835)		0.9747	1.5218	0.1325
	0.3930	0.8554	1.4352 (19.6327)	0.0122 (0.4411)	0.9732	1.4287	0.1198

136

TABLE D-2 (continued)

	δ	σ	V	λ	ρ	Q	K/L
Paper	0.6961	0.7146	1.2145 (23.0878)		0.9818	1.7498	0.4068
	0.7078	0.6995	1.2225 (22.8123)	0.0013 (0.0818)	0.9818	1.7465	0.4136
Print & pub.	0.4859	0.8811	1.6071 (15.3712)		0.9952	2.1208	0.7779
	0.4690	0.9539	0.8924 (3.2710)	0.0028 (0.2003)	0.9959	2.2259	0.9479
Primary met.	0.7735	0.6649	1.3800 (11.9672)		0.9633	1.6752	0.3407
	0.9749	0.3994	1.5178 (13.1176)	0.0342 (2.4486)	0.9682	1.6067	0.3290
Metal fab.	0.5007	0.8487	1.6155 (23.7968)		0.9886	1.8921	0.2813
	0.5568	0.6995	1.6773 (25.2017)	0.0129 (0.7904)	0.9893	1.8441	0.2658
Machinery	0.1519	15.7049	1.0078 (3.1891)		0.9840	2.1396	0.8874
	0.2164	1.5343	0.8961 (3.2045)	0.0328 (1.3990)	0.9841	2.2078	0.8986
Transport. equip.	0.7514	0.6886	1.6463 (7.8275)		0.9823	1.4943	0.8306
	0.3325	0.6158	1.2842 (7.4705)	0.0674 (2.5238)	0.9895	2.0597	0.9638
Electrical prod.	0.2539	2.0710	1.7156 (8.5999)		0.9888	2.1079	0.8014
	0.3531	0.4816	1.7183 (20.8505)	0.0691 (7.4089)	0.7555	1.8847	
Non-Metallic min. prod.	0.4999	1.0843	1.3849 (15.7447)		0.9926	1.5186	0.7229
	0.5053	1.0678	1.3880 (15.5632)	0.0006 (0.0743)	0.9926	1.5168	0.7261
Petroleum & coal prod.	0.1301	2.3053	1.6240 (12.7219)		0.8949	0.7908	
	0.6363	2.8758	1.8469 (13.3348)	0.0295 (2.9087)	0.9035	0.8120	
Chemicals & chem. prod.	0.2105	2.2670	1.4934 (57.8221)		0.9911	0.8693	
	0.2983	1.3733	1.5542 (25.3075)	0.0149 (1.1900)	0.9943	1.4049	

δ—Distribution of factor inputs for a given production technology
σ—Elasticity of substitution between factor inputs
V—Return to scale
ρ—Substitution parameter
λ—Technological change through time, holding labour and capital constant
Q—Value added output
L—Total man-hours
K/L—Capital labour ratio
Source: Appendix B, Tables B-1 to B-20

TABLE D-3
VES PRODUCTION FUNCTION, MARGINAL CONDITION
(1971 dollars)

$$ln\ Z = \alpha_0 + \alpha_1\ ln\ K + \alpha_2\ ln\ W + \lambda t$$

	α_0	α_1	α_2	λ	$\bar{R}^2$	D.W.	ρ
Total manu.	0.4716 (6.4627)	−0.1635 (1.3615)	1.4075 (9.5128)		0.9919	0.7319	
	0.8245 (10.3051)	−0.0294 (0.3402)	0.3146 (1.4451)	0.0286 (5.6916)	0.9962	0.9696	
Food & bev.	0.8064 (10.4380)	0.0923 (0.9584)	0.8214 (7.7108)		0.9908	0.6389	
	0.8429 (7.6542)	0.06103 (0.5548)	0.8031 (6.3377)	0.02050 (0.4108)	0.9917	0.6921	
Tobacco	0.6912 (6.83166)	0.4632 (2.8944)	0.6656 (4.1142)		0.9898	1.2785	
	1.2005 (5.1925)	0.37146 (2.5181)	0.1735 (0.5909)	0.0236 (2.3920)	0.9924	1.4816	
Rubber & plastic prod.	0.61071 (6.9059)	0.5291 (3.2276)	0.3763 (1.5236)		0.8714	1.1146	
	0.7295 (2.0144)	0.5843 (2.5084)	0.05186 (0.05236)	0.00653 (0.3386)	0.8719	1.1735	
Leather	0.4391 (20.3213)	0.0323 (0.5170)	0.9882 (19.3069)		0.9843	1.7170	0.1903
	0.5418 (10.5207)	0.1104 (1.5650)	0.4396 (1.7769)	0.01385 (2.2542)	0.9867	1.8010	0.2779
Textile (1957-1977)	−0.3137 (2.5077)	−0.1203 (0.9939)	2.0269 (14.7919)		0.9936	1.6731	0.5857
	−0.8720 (0.6348)	−0.1299 (1.2681)	0.9071 (2.6593)	0.03403 (3.4902)	0.9956	1.6309	0.5905
Knit. mills	2.2362 (4.6033)	0.8605 (3.2374)	−1.2138 (2.1896)		0.9819	1.5238	0.9180
	−0.1101 (1.4327)	0.4356 (2.3109)	−1.8150 (3.5366)	0.0985 (5.8788)	0.9912	1.5935	0.4522
Clothing (1957-1977)	0.6172 (24.1420)	0.1248 (2.9461)	0.8552 (41.0817)		0.9914	2.0666	
	0.8259 (8.2159)	0.1655 (3.8355)	0.4416 (2.2677)	0.01234 (2.1347)	0.9932	1.7489	
Wood (1957-1977)	0.8069 (14.0519)	−0.3637 (2.7966)	1.2293 (7.8845)		0.9725	0.7200	
	0.9857 (4.3662)	−0.3302 (2.4023)	0.8479 (1.7264)	0.01513 (0.8197)	0.9736	0.7016	
Furn. & fixt.	0.4175 (2.3365)	−0.00954 (0.0474)	1.0883 (3.5549)		0.9465	1.0244	
	0.9888 (3.2681)	0.1164 (0.6232)	−0.8769 (0.9449)	0.05155 (2.2141)	0.9612	1.5109	
Paper	0.7852 (4.6008)	0.063769 (0.43111)	0.6956 (3.6902)		0.9662	1.0042	
	1.0676 (5.1996)	0.03114 (0.2228)	0.3134 (1.2638)	0.01361 (2.2023)	0.9712	1.3182	

TABLE D-3 (continued)

	α_0	α_1	α_2	λ	$\bar{R}^2$	$D.W.$	ρ
Print. & pub.	0.6475 (11.1155)	0.03667 (0.00227)	0.9352 (6.2002)		0.9889	0.8527	
	1.0420 (9.3548)	−0.2176 (1.5194)	0.5334 (3.3246)	0.0197 (3.9181)	0.9928	1.1880	
Primary met.	1.6536 (4.0930)	−0.6088 (2.0168)	1.4624 (4.4323)		0.9382	1.8008	0.2203
	2.2258 (4.6228)	−0.5593 (1.9368)	0.4981 (0.9134)	0.0257 (2.0439)	0.9531	1.5266	0.3708
Metal fab.	0.5599 (9.1140)	−0.2674 (2.3844)	1.3188 (10.9311)		0.9745	0.9579	
	0.1934 (0.5884)	−0.4695 (2.2373)	2.2890 (2.6515)	−0.0222 (1.1347)	0.9768	1.1374	
Machinery	−0.3826 (2.8594)	0.1247 (0.6734)	1.5344 (6.4736)		0.9527	1.0645	
	0.2592 (0.6644)	0.1412 (0.8137)	0.5946 (1.0139)	0.0227 (1.7310)	0.9616	1.0609	
Transport. equip.	1.4520 (2.0295)	−0.1139 (0.9183)	0.8774 (2.2584)		0.9859	1.6351	0.9629
	0.4985 (1.6139)	−0.1478 (1.1762)	0.5679 (1.3508)	0.0405 (2.7153)	0.9874	1.8349	0.8549
Electrical prod.	−0.1123 (1.3214)	−0.4536 (3.4542)	2.0179 (10.1721)		0.9548	1.3284	
	1.4241 (7.5899)	0.06300 (0.6725)	−1.0023 (2.6848)	0.06212 (8.4452)	0.9873	1.9377	
Non-metallic min. prod.	0.6544 (4.7691)	0.0739 (0.6593)	0.9653 (7.8587)		0.9903	1.6895	0.4764
	0.7939 (3.9996)	0.0639 (0.5625)	0.6544 (1.9288)	0.0110 (0.9772)	0.9906	1.6653	0.5225
Petroleum & coal prod.	0.2433 (0.5069)	−0.00962 (0.0434)	1.4475 (5.0602)		0.9426	1.0669	
(1957-1977)	2.1677 (5.8141)	0.5923 (4.0991)	−2.0358 (3.9089)	0.0826 (6.9829)	0.9852	1.6623	
Chemicals & chem. prod.	−0.1046 (0.6117)	0.4194 (2.9488)	0.8068 (3.8379)		0.9894	1.5305	0.6365
	0.6065 (2.6135)	0.2363 (1.9178)	0.0405 (0.1485)	0.0353 (3.6927)	0.9929	1.5791	0.5528

α_0—A coefficient containing market imperfection and substitution parameters
α_1—A coefficient containing parameters of labour efficiency and substitution
α_2—A coefficient approximately neutral elasticity of substitution
λ—Technical change over time
Z—Output per man-hour
K—Net capital stock per man-hour
W—Real earning per man-hour
t—A time variable
Source: Appendix B, Tables B-1 to B-20

TABLE D-4
TRANSLOG PRODUCTION FUNCTION, MARGINAL CONDITION
(1971 dollars)

$$\ln Q/L = \alpha_0 + \alpha_1 \ln L + \alpha_2 \ln (K/L) + \alpha_3 [\ln (K/L)^2] + \lambda t$$

	α_0	α_1	α_2	α_3	λ	$\bar{R}^2$	D.W.	ρ
Total	−0.2405	0.1721	0.0320	0.0298	0.0298	0.9880	1.7816	0.5014
manufacturing	(0.1920)	(0.5635)	(0.1468)	(0.3602)	(2.3786)			
	−3.9594	0.8658	0.0756	0.1774		0.9913	1.7149	0.3595
	(9.3245)	(10.5040)	(0.4124)	(3.4171)				
Food &	7.0207	−0.4395	−0.2832	0.0615	0.0385	0.9331	0.6676	
beverages	(1.6214)	(1.3128)	(1.9613)	(0.5653)	(2.7103)			
	−4.0844	0.4139	−0.3788	0.3371		0.9912	0.7505	
	(2.6346)	(3.2888)	(2.4426)	(7.8661)				
Tobacco	0.7544	0.0686	1.3126	0.0077	0.0627	0.9982	1.1399	
(1957-77)	(0.1760)	(0.1700)	(2.5974)	(0.1955)	(4.1881)			
	3.1232	−0.2626	−0.2429	−0.1455		0.9961	0.9273	
	(0.5234)	(0.4724)	(0.5045)	(7.1987)				
Rubber &	8.4848	−0.6817	−2.0793	0.6272	0.0544	0.8986	2.0761	0.1478
plastic	(3.1190)	(2.5078)	(3.6151)	(4.1514)	(2.7567)			
	1.0898	0.0557	−1.1125	0.6172		0.8589	1.8923	0.1893
	(1.6944)	(0.8585)	(2.1239)	(3.5404)				
Leather	6.2178	−0.4098	0.0026	0.0047	0.0214	0.9881	2.0595	−0.1330
	(1.3010)	(1.0836)	(0.0099)	(0.0292)	(7.6869)			
	0.4627	−0.2056	−0.3729	0.8077		0.7688	2.0592	0.8754
	(0.8368)	(0.5466)	(1.0163)	(3.2881)				
Textile	16.5972	−1.7631	4.7317	−1.6640	0.1015	0.9935	1.9067	0.1050
(1957-1977)	(6.2917)	(6.4620)	(5.1415)	(5.9426)	(11.8864)			
	1.6509	−1.3562	0.5189	−0.3641		0.3456	1.4354	0.9196
	(2.5838)	(2.1996)	(0.2305)	(0.5511)				
Knitting	1.3228	−0.1847	0.1297	−0.0183	0.0506	0.9337	1.4228	0.5116
(1961-77)	(0.6355)	(0.4064)	(0.1071)	(0.0241)	(3.0972)			
	0.0338	0.1403	−1.5275	1.3248		0.6480	1.4565	0.8215
	(0.0445)	(0.3731)	(1.2180)	(1.8753)				
Clothing	−1.6136	0.2405	0.7841	0.9207	0.0242	0.9922	1.9730	0.0920
(1957-1977)	(0.6081)	(0.9832)	(2.5544)	(1.9723)	(16.9862)			
	−0.1819	0.3251	1.0801	0.8838		0.5480	2.0239	0.9247
	(0.5595)	(0.9947)	(2.4241)	(1.2408)				
Wood	2.8022	−0.4229	−0.1298	−0.0391	0.0583	0.9165	1.7502	0.5611
	(1.7093)	(1.5595)	(0.1598)	(0.2056)	(3.3467)			
	−0.7839	−0.3474	1.4269	−0.2863		0.5413	1.1810	0.8203
	(1.8822)	(2.1127)	(1.7013)	(1.2390)				
Furniture &	2.1530	−0.2693	0.0973	−0.2225	0.0428	0.8616	1.4817	0.4919
fixtures	(0.8518)	(0.6088)	(0.1774)	(0.4093)	(1.8961)			
	−3.1381	0.4497	0.1654	0.3019		0.9205	1.5771	0.2047
	(1.7956)	(2.2622)	(0.3497)	(0.8636)				
Paper	−0.8143	0.1754	0.1272	0.0010	0.0170	0.9489	1.7148	0.2294
	(0.3034)	(0.6197)	(0.2926)	(0.0088)	(1.5980)			
	−3.9588	0.4979	−0.1070	0.1098		0.9489	1.6933	0.1860
	(1.9932)	(2.5816)	(0.2658)	(1.3104)				

TABLE D-4 (continued)

	α_0	α_1	α_2	α_3	λ	R^2	D.W.	ρ
Printing & publishing	3.9585 (3.4670)	−1.0294 (3.2382)	0.3203 (0.9026)	−0.4013 (2.1743)	0.0642 (4.6381)	0.9543	2.1642	0.7036
	−1.0683 (1.6571)	0.3399 (2.1573)	0.2651 (0.6021)	0.2109 (1.3012)		0.9341	2.0909	0.6665
Primary metal (1961-77)	19.7028 (4.5604)	−1.8186 (6.0249)	3.3443 (2.2507)	−0.9957 (3.8164)	1.1107 (8.0265)	0.9858	1.7479	0.0998
	−8.5800 (2.1618)	0.5924 (2.8292)	4.9444 (1.1758)	−0.7936 (1.0584)		0.8317	1.5593	0.3412
Metal fabrication (1961-77)	−1.6305 (0.7664)	0.1312 (0.4227)	3.6128 (2.2553)	−1.3164 (1.9855)	0.03445 (2.1345)	0.9581	1.6665	0.3850
	−6.1400 (4.5108)	0.7279 (5.7624)	0.9894 (0.8367)	−0.1173 (0.2822)		0.9558	1.7944	0.2816
Machinery (1961-77)	3.0890 (0.6959)	−0.3684 (0.8030)	2.6857 (1.5143)	−1.0680 (1.6012)	0.0541 (1.9316)	0.9462	1.9547	0.2406
	−2.6314 (2.3889)	0.4632 (2.3486)	2.1353 (0.9869)	−0.4807 (0.5988)		0.8277		
Transportation equipment	0.5077 (0.5856)	−0.0860 (0.2994)	−0.4956 (1.0114)	0.1074 (0.6611)	0.0590 (3.8897)	0.8075	2.0954	0.7741
	−3.8386 (4.9458)	0.9224 (5.8326)	−0.1805 (0.3297)	0.3618 (1.9274)		0.8568	1.7019	0.6460
Electrical	5.9285 (2.4307)	−0.3792 (1.9750)	0.0029 (0.0158)	−0.1209 (0.8707)	0.0564 (6.6485)	0.9899	2.0117	−0.1184
	−2.0492 (3.6638)	0.6047 (4.3896)	−0.3477 (1.2517)	0.4895 (3.6617)		0.7997	2.1553	0.6718
Non-Metallic mineral	0.9206 (0.7189)	−0.1050 (0.3024)	−0.0751 (0.0841)	0.0299 (0.1234)	0.0352 (2.3437)	0.9339	1.7473	0.6099
	−1.7089 (3.4262)	0.6647 (5.3669)	−1.5564 (2.2834)	0.4918 (3.2488)		0.9052	1.6545	0.6498
Petroleum & coal (1957-1977)	−0.0559 (0.0120)	−0.5177 (2.3394)	3.5559 (2.4620)	−0.4261 (2.4371)	0.0415 (9.2053)	0.9891	1.4983	
	−32.6103 (4.4063)	0.9394 (2.4954)	11.7361 (4.2343)	−1.3522 (3.8846)		0.9316	0.7723	
Chemicals	9.9319 (2.8733)	−0.8377 (2.6461)	0.4273 (1.5919)	−0.0382 (0.6033)	0.0568 (4.2936)	0.9938	0.6521	
	−4.4509 (4.0980)	0.4514 (3.5318)	−0.0582 (0.1877)	0.1723 (3.4080)		0.9896	0.6411	

α_0—A coefficient containing the logarithmic value of the geometric means of capital/labour and capital/labour squared ratios.

α_1—Scale elasticity coefficient, whereas ($\alpha_1 + 1$) is returns to scale value.

α_2—A coefficient containing multiple values of the geometric means of capital/labour ratios.

α_3—A coefficient indicating the behaviour of economies of scale through time. I.e. a positive value means an increasing returns to scale at an increasing rate. The two estimated coefficients which are of interest to us are the returns to scale ($\alpha_1 + 1$) and its trend through time, α_3. Since this function is an approximation to the CES (as suggested by Griliches), the coefficients α_2 and α_3 contain distributive and substitutional parameters which are used to compute the value of the elasticity of substitution. See Appendix A for derivations.

Source: Appendix B, Tables B-1 to B-20

TABLE D-5
PRODUCTIVITY AND CAPITAL INTENSITY,
VES PRODUCTION FUNCTION
(1971 dollars)

	Total Manu.		Food & Beverages		Tobacco		Rubber		Leather		Textile		Knitting	
	Z	K	Z	K	Z	K	Z	K	Z	K	Z	K	Z	K
1946	2.68	3.25	3.55	2.71	3.03	2.12	2.98	1.95	2.31	1.04	1.46	3.14		
1947	2.80	3.21	3.36	2.86	3.17	2.28	4.08	2.19	2.20	1.16	1.39	3.11		
1948	2.88	3.41	3.43	3.18	3.27	2.48	4.06	2.68	2.01	1.24	1.41	2.89		
1949	2.92	3.55	3.41	3.40	3.34	2.42	5.21	3.03	2.11	1.25	1.40	3.47		
1950	3.07	3.65	3.59	3.70	3.73	2.67	4.06	2.86	2.12	1.30	1.52	3.48		
1951	3.19	3.67	3.66	3.82	3.66	2.82	4.29	2.98	2.26	1.44	1.69	3.93		
1952	3.25	3.90	3.84	3.95	4.57	3.04	4.21	3.34	2.24	1.28	1.61	4.26		
1953	3.39	4.12	3.98	4.14	4.89	3.05	4.73	3.53	2.46	1.32	1.80	4.56		
1954	3.53	4.64	4.18	4.41	5.16	3.12	4.44	4.16	2.53	1.43	1.75	5.00		
1955	3.75	4.73	4.26	4.57	5.71	3.23	4.85	4.13	2.54	1.32	1.94	4.66		
1956	3.93	4.87	4.47	4.75	6.26	3.56	5.31	4.19	2.71	1.29	1.98	4.66		
1957	4.02	5.42	4.62	4.93	6.76	3.97	5.45	4.81	2.81	1.37	2.18	5.24		
1958	4.17	6.06	4.78	5.10	6.88	4.19	5.95	5.37	2.79	1.34	2.26	5.68		
1959	4.41	6.12	5.00	5.33	7.16	4.51	6.44	5.11	2.89	1.30	2.47	5.41		
1960	4.53	6.43	5.14	5.62	8.15	5.01	5.93	5.84	2.88	1.35	2.66	5.59		
1961	4.42	6.20	4.88	5.42	8.05	4.91	5.39	5.77	2.82	1.19	2.75	5.21	2.08	1.96
1962	4.69	6.18	5.16	5.72	7.79	4.69	6.61	5.63	2.97	1.21	2.92	4.95	2.25	1.96
1963	4.86	6.19	5.40	5.97	8.32	4.90	6.62	5.53	3.03	1.24	3.08	4.84	2.54	1.99
1964	5.07	6.13	5.57	6.00	8.93	5.18	6.95	5.48	3.16	1.26	3.20	4.80	2.63	1.94
1965	5.24	6.16	5.61	6.07	9.93	5.75	7.09	5.55	3.22	1.27	3.26	5.10	2.63	1.86
1966	5.41	6.38	5.80	6.19	10.34	6.09	7.66	5.83	3.27	1.30	3.30	5.50	2.76	1.97
1967	5.62	6.89	6.17	6.53	10.57	6.24	8.78	6.65	3.32	1.40	3.41	5.79	2.86	2.09
1968	6.02	7.27	6.44	6.95	10.70	6.76	10.32	7.69	3.46	1.41	4.03	6.22	3.18	2.01
1969	6.38	7.46	6.79	7.36	11.38	7.12	11.16	8.30	3.60	1.51	4.47	6.17	3.38	2.08
1970	6.48	8.10	7.09	7.77	12.00	7.12	6.54	5.30	3.76	1.70	4.69	6.89	3.72	2.34
1971	6.90	8.55	7.59	8.29	12.71	7.55	6.89	5.91	3.92	1.71	5.14	7.02	3.98	2.41
1972	7.13	8.54	7.87	8.53	13.35	7.78	7.08	5.93	4.05	1.82	5.42	6.64	4.17	2.48
1973	7.51	8.57	8.14	8.89	13.93	7.89	7.32	5.84	4.21	1.93	5.61	6.66	4.37	2.60
1974	7.75	8.97	8.20	9.29	14.51	7.91	7.69	6.56	4.47	2.06	5.71	7.24	4.35	2.80
1975	7.57	9.74	8.27	9.52	14.44	8.19	7.39	7.17	4.40	2.09	5.90	8.11	4.49	2.93
1976	7.84	9.96	8.66	9.79	15.78	8.68	8.27	6.88	4.24	2.12	6.20	8.55	4.73	3.02
1977	8.26	10.42	10.82	12.26	16.79	8.71	9.39	6.85	5.00	2.39	6.65	8.82	5.58	3.28

	Clothing		Wood		Furniture & Fixtures		Paper		Printing & Publishing		Primary Metals		Metal Fabrication	
	Z	K	Z	K	Z	K	Z	K	Z	K	Z	K	Z	K
1946	1.80	0.52	1.55	1.53			3.72	6.30	3.18	2.56				
1947	1.68	0.54	1.60	1.46			3.74	6.30	3.32	2.53				
1948	1.65	0.54	1.60	1.50			3.86	6.74	3.53	2.60				
1949	1.71	0.55	1.62	1.59			4.04	7.27	3.35	2.46				
1950	1.71	0.55	1.70	1.58			4.29	7.54	3.66	2.59				
1951	1.85	0.61	1.79	1.65			4.42	7.75	3.70	2.71				
1952	1.89	0.55	1.79	1.70			4.38	8.72	3.78	2.83				
1953	1.95	0.58	1.86	1.70			4.68	9.46	4.02	2.80				
1954	2.00	0.63	1.93	1.85			4.78	9.68	4.17	2.84				
1955	2.04	0.60	2.07	1.83			4.81	9.78	4.33	2.98				
1956	2.14	0.59	2.07	1.91			5.02	10.50	4.59	2.97				
1957	2.83	0.77	3.03	3.16			5.02	12.08	4.85	3.27				
1958	2.83	0.76	3.17	3.26			5.03	12.96	4.83	3.52				
1959	2.88	0.74	3.23	3.24			5.28	12.84	5.07	3.61				
1960	2.90	0.73	3.50	3.55			5.48	13.01	5.13	3.74				
1961	2.92	0.70	3.77	3.84	3.27	1.41	5.43	13.12	5.18	3.79	5.78	13.82	4.73	4.05
1962	3.12	0.71	3.99	3.89	3.41	1.39	5.53	13.22	5.37	3.96	6.09	13.90	4.76	3.70
1963	3.23	0.68	4.12	3.84	3.49	1.39	5.71	13.35	5.45	4.11	6.34	14.04	4.96	3.63
1964	3.28	0.67	4.32	3.86	3.56	1.41	5.97	13.33	5.48	4.30	6.62	13.63	5.08	3.45
1965	3.33	0.66	4.34	3.96	3.80	1.43	6.06	13.93	5.60	4.32	6.75	13.31	5.24	3.30
1966	3.44	0.67	4.51	4.22	4.02	1.49	6.17	14.58	5.78	4.33	6.71	13.53	5.45	3.37
1967	3.42	0.67	4.69	4.46	4.11	1.64	6.10	15.99	5.91	4.42	6.54	14.52	5.70	3.78
1968	3.58	0.67	4.81	4.57	4.33	1.83	6.45	16.94	6.08	4.56	7.13	14.79	5.83	4.04
1969	3.64	0.67	5.03	4.93	4.46	1.87	6.93	16.85	6.36	4.69	7.44	15.45	6.16	4.16
1970	3.67	0.68	5.18	5.88	4.48	2.06	7.00	17.93	6.62	5.00	7.55	15.41	6.28	4.48
1971	3.84	0.67	5.45	6.07	4.49	2.03	7.17	19.47	6.92	5.20	7.70	16.71	6.56	4.73
1972	3.96	0.67	5.17	5.82	4.67	1.90	7.66	19.88	7.16	5.19	7.96	17.27	6.66	4.75
1973	4.14	0.71	5.34	6.05	4.95	1.99	8.06	20.05	7.35	5.15	8.44	17.36	7.06	4.71
1974	4.27	0.78	5.54	7.36	4.94	2.13	8.10	19.31	7.66	5.35	8.73	17.43	7.39	4.77
1975	4.38	0.82	5.65	8.64	4.74	2.40	6.70	20.47	7.89	5.62	8.22	19.14	6.94	5.10
1976	4.56	0.84	6.29	8.31	5.25	2.50	7.45	20.27	8.12	5.72	8.19	20.16	7.09	5.07
1977	4.87	0.93	6.79	8.43	5.77	2.72	8.36	21.89	8.52	6.05	8.64	20.07	7.28	5.29

TABLE D-5 (continued)

	Machinery		Transpor-tation Equipment		Electrical & Electronic		Non-Metallic Minerals		Petroleum & Coal		Chemicals	
	Z	K	Z	K	Z	K	Z	K	Z	K	Z	K
1946			2.38	2.96	2.54	1.25	2.95	5.68	2.72	8.55	2.98	5.32
1947			2.74	2.71	2.76	1.22	3.25	5.40	2.76	9.66	3.06	5.63
1948			2.89	2.74	2.80	1.34	3.36	5.72	3.02	11.60	3.13	6.14
1949			2.91	2.67	2.93	1.57	3.57	5.96	3.04	12.91	3.14	6.36
1950			3.10	2.68	3.07	1.67	3.74	5.76	3.33	13.94	3.50	6.78
1951			3.31	2.50	2.97	1.77	3.98	5.80	3.69	15.54	3.65	6.62
1952			3.16	2.26	2.96	2.04	4.18	6.21	3.71	16.99	3.85	7.59
1953			3.40	2.45	3.24	2.15	4.27	6.13	4.01	19.54	4.06	8.79
1954			3.28	3.24	3.41	2.52	4.31	6.33	4.21	21.81	4.37	9.42
1955			3.63	3.55	3.75	2.60	4.42	6.12	4.87	25.26	4.74	9.57
1956			3.61	3.44	3.06	2.62	4.95	7.09	5.76	28.55	5.10	10.20
1957			3.51	3.57	3.50	2.74	5.36	8.84	6.76	35.61	5.53	11.57
1958			3.52	4.22	3.70	3.12	5.35	8.96	6.61	37.59	5.82	12.51
1959			3.85	4.81	3.90	3.18	5.40	8.73	7.95	44.66	6.02	13.10
1960			3.89	5.16	4.26	3.43	5.48	9.58	8.31	47.02	6.38	13.64
1961	4.31	3.44	4.20	5.70	4.00	3.08	5.52	9.43	7.69	41.36	5.75	12.11
1962	4.41	3.24	4.65	5.34	4.38	2.91	5.62	9.04	8.36	42.04	6.07	12.43
1963	4.41	3.13	4.95	5.05	4.56	2.88	5.92	9.12	9.39	44.53	6.35	12.56
1964	4.73	3.10	4.92	4.85	4.86	2.84	6.19	8.89	9.71	45.52	7.03	12.61
1965	4.74	3.02	5.60	4.97	5.06	2.77	6.41	8.94	10.50	46.82	7.33	12.99
1966	5.11	3.07	5.71	5.32	5.22	2.75	6.39	9.47	10.03	42.97	7.74	13.93
1967	5.11	3.22	6.56	5.80	5.27	3.00	6.30	10.83	10.05	43.86	7.84	14.92
1968	5.31	3.53	7.58	6.13	5.61	3.25	6.75	11.19	11.05	45.61	8.27	15.79
1969	5.68	3.46	8.07	6.09	5.93	3.31	7.03	11.63	11.50	48.20	8.94	16.48
1970	5.82	3.76	7.66	7.03	6.13	3.74	7.11	12.87	11.97	52.88	9.01	17.10
1971	6.80	4.45	8.85	7.28	6.29	3.85	7.96	12.78	12.88	58.68	9.78	18.25
1972	6.85	4.14	9.00	6.84	6.82	4.01	8.24	12.46	13.82	62.58	10.63	19.04
1973	7.20	4.07	9.50	6.39	7.18	3.94	8.93	12.57	14.86	63.67	11.47	18.93
1974	7.65	4.08	9.68	6.83	7.42	4.03	9.13	13.07	14.67	66.64	11.88	20.01
1975	7.40	4.26	10.14	7.72	7.26	4.42	9.17	13.95	14.63	73.03	11.17	22.50
1976	7.32	4.61	10.56	7.51	7.91	4.67	9.56	14.61	15.72	81.13	11.88	26.34
1977	7.48	4.88	10.95	7.41	8.34	5.15	10.81	15.93	15.29	77.94	12.64	29.08

TABLE D-6
ELASTICITY OF SUBSTITUTION AND TECHNICAL CHANGE, VES PRODUCTION FUNCTION, MARGINAL CONDITION
(1971 dollars)

	Total Manu.		Food & Beverages		Tobacco		Rubber		Leather		Textile		Knitting	
	σ_b	g	σ_b	g	σ_b	g	σ_b	g	σ_b	g	σ_b	g	σ_b	g
1946	0.989	0.924	0.972	0.973			1.07	1.01	0.978	0.998				
1947	0.995	0.930	0.978	0.979			1.09	1.03	0.976	0.996				
1948	1.009	0.945	0.973	0.975			1.09	1.03	0.975	0.995				
1949	1.003	0.938	0.977	0.978			1.10	1.04	0.975	0.995				
1950	1.013	0.949	0.975	0.976			1.09	1.03	0.975	0.996				
1951	1.019	0.956	0.973	0.975			1.09	1.03	0.975	0.996				
1952	1.002	0.937	0.974	0.975			1.09	1.03	0.976	0.996				
1953	0.991	0.926	0.979	0.980			1.09	1.03	0.975	0.996				
1954	0.991	0.926	0.979	0.980			1.09	1.03	0.975	0.996				
1955	1.005	0.940	0.980	0.981			1.08	1.02	0.976	0.997				
1956	1.007	0.943	0.979	0.980			1.08	1.02	0.977	0.997				
1957	1.001	0.936	0.982	0.982	2.32	0.72	1.08	1.02	0.976	0.997	0.43	0.57		
1958	1.007	0.942	0.979	0.980	2.32	0.72	1.08	1.02	0.976	0.997	0.49	0.66		
1959	1.020	0.957	0.979	0.980	2.20	0.70	1.08	1.02	0.977	0.997	0.57	0.77		
1960	1.019	0.955	0.980	0.981	2.04	0.68	1.08	1.02	0.976	0.997	0.58	0.79		
1961	0.997	0.932	0.995	0.994	2.23	0.71	1.09	1.03	0.975	0.996	0.58	0.79	1.89	1.44
1962	1.011	0.947	0.991	0.991	2.34	0.72	1.09	1.03	0.975	0.996	0.61	0.83	1.90	1.37
1963	1.018	0.955	0.987	0.987	2.21	0.70	1.09	1.03	0.976	0.996	0.62	0.85	1.19	1.28
1964	1.027	0.964	0.985	0.985	2.16	0.70	1.08	1.02	0.976	0.997	0.63	0.86	1.20	1.28
1965	1.031	0.968	0.987	0.987	2.07	0.68	1.08	1.02	0.976	0.997	0.62	0.85	1.29	1.30
1966	1.032	0.969	0.986	0.986	2.03	0.68	1.09	1.03	0.976	0.996	0.60	0.82	1.27	1.30
1967	1.032	0.970	0.984	0.984	2.08	0.69	1.10	1.04	0.975	0.995	0.61	0.83	1.37	1.31
1968	1.043	0.981	0.982	0.983	2.18	0.70	1.09	1.03	0.975	0.996	0.67	0.92	0.84	1.22
1969	1.050	0.989	0.980	0.981	2.11	0.69	1.09	1.03	0.975	0.996	0.69	0.95	0.74	1.19
1970	1.042	0.980	0.981	0.981	2.13	0.69	1.09	1.03	0.976	0.996	0.69	0.95	0.54	1.14
1971	1.048	0.987	0.979	0.980	2.15	0.69	1.09	1.03	0.976	0.996	0.70	0.97	0.45	1.10
1972	1.053	0.991	0.979	0.979	2.12	0.69	1.08	1.02	0.976	0.997	0.71	0.98	0.40	1.09
1973	1.061	1.001	0.978	0.979	2.07	0.68	1.08	1.02	0.976	0.997	0.71	0.99	0.35	1.07
1974	1.060	0.999	0.982	0.983	1.94	0.67	1.08	1.02	0.977	0.997	0.71	0.98	0.51	1.13
1975	1.048	0.987	0.987	0.987	2.08	0.68	1.09	1.03	0.976	0.996	0.71	0.99	0.56	1.14
1976	1.058	0.998	0.991	0.991	2.03	0.68	1.11	1.05	0.973	0.993	0.71	0.98	0.53	1.13
1977	1.065	1.005	0.992	0.992	1.99	0.67	1.08	1.02	0.977	0.997	0.72	0.99	0.22	1.01

145

TABLE D-6 (continued)

	Clothing		Wood		Furniture & Fixtures		Paper		Printing & Publishing		Primary Metals		Metal Fabrication	
	σ_b	g	σ_b	g	σ_b	g	σ_b	g	σ_b	g	σ_b	g	σ_b	g
1946							0.79	1.00	0.94	1.00				
1947							0.80	1.00	0.94	1.00				
1948							0.79	1.00	0.94	1.00				
1949							0.79	0.99	0.94	1.00				
1950							0.79	0.99	0.94	1.00				
1951							0.79	0.99	0.94	1.00				
1952							0.80	1.00	0.94	1.00				
1953							0.80	1.00	0.94	1.00				
1954							0.80	1.01	0.94	1.00				
1955							0.81	1.01	0.94	1.00				
1956							0.81	1.01	0.94	1.00				
1957	1.25	1.08	0.62	0.84			0.81	1.02	0.94	1.00				
1958	1.24	1.07	0.64	0.87			0.81	1.02	0.94	1.00				
1959	1.25	1.08	0.65	0.89			0.81	1.01	0.94	1.00				
1960	1.24	1.07	0.65	0.90			0.81	1.01	0.94	1.00				
1961	1.32	1.13	0.65	0.89	0.86	0.93	0.82	1.02	0.94	1.00	0.60	0.87	0.79	0.91
1962	1.29	1.11	0.66	0.90	0.86	0.94	0.82	1.03	0.94	1.00	0.62	0.91	0.79	0.91
1963	1.27	1.09	0.66	0.90	0.87	0.94	0.81	1.02	0.94	1.00	0.63	0.93	0.81	0.93
1964	1.28	1.10	0.67	0.92	0.87	0.94	0.81	1.01	0.94	1.00	0.64	0.96	0.81	0.93
1965	1.29	1.11	0.65	0.90	0.88	0.96	0.81	1.01	0.94	1.00	0.64	0.97	0.82	0.95
1966	1.29	1.11	0.65	0.89	0.88	0.96	0.81	1.02	0.94	1.00	0.64	0.95	0.82	0.95
1967	1.32	1.13	0.65	0.89	0.88	0.96	0.82	1.03	0.94	1.00	0.61	0.90	0.82	0.95
1968	1.30	1.12	0.64	0.88	0.89	0.97	0.82	1.02	0.94	1.00	0.64	0.97	0.82	0.94
1969	1.33	1.14	0.64	0.88	0.89	0.97	0.81	1.01	0.94	1.00	0.65	0.98	0.83	0.95
1970	1.33	1.14	0.63	0.86	0.88	0.95	0.81	1.02	0.94	1.00	0.64	0.95	0.82	0.94
1971	1.32	1.13	0.62	0.85	0.87	0.95	0.82	1.03	0.94	1.00	0.62	0.92	0.82	0.94
1972	1.33	1.14	0.58	0.78	0.88	0.96	0.81	1.02	0.94	1.00	0.62	0.91	0.82	0.94
1973	1.29	1.11	0.57	0.76	0.88	0.96	0.81	1.01	0.94	1.00	0.64	0.95	0.83	0.96
1974	1.30	1.12	0.54	0.72	0.87	0.95	0.81	1.02	0.94	1.00	0.64	0.96	0.83	0.97
1975	1.33	1.14	0.55	0.72	0.85	0.93	0.84	1.05	0.94	1.00	0.60	0.88	0.80	0.92
1976	1.36	1.16	0.57	0.76	0.87	0.95	0.85	1.06	0.94	1.00	0.59	0.85	0.80	0.92
1977	1.30	1.11	0.59	0.79	0.89	0.97	0.83	1.04	0.94	1.00	0.61	0.90	0.80	0.93

TABLE D-6 (continued)

	Machinery		Transpor- tation Equipment		Electrical & Electronic		Non-Metallic Minerals		Petroleum & Coal		Chemicals	
	σ_b	g	σ_b	g	σ_b	g	σ_b	g	σ_b	g	σ_b	g
1946			0.51	0.69	0.83	0.74	1.14	1.00			3.92	1.20
1947			0.62	0.86	0.87	0.78	1.13	1.00			4.20	1.24
1948			0.64	0.89	0.86	0.77	1.12	0.99			3.49	1.15
1949			0.64	0.89	0.86	0.77	1.12	0.99			4.00	1.22
1950			0.66	0.91	0.89	0.79	1.12	0.99			3.23	1.11
1951			0.67	0.93	0.83	0.74	1.11	0.98			3.09	1.08
1952			0.64	0.89	0.77	0.67	1.11	0.98			3.18	1.10
1953			0.62	0.86	0.82	0.72	1.12	0.99			3.27	1.11
1954			0.60	0.82	0.80	0.70	1.13	0.99			3.13	1.09
1955			0.62	0.86	0.92	0.83	1.13	0.99			2.84	1.04
1956			0.61	0.83	0.57	0.47	1.12	0.99			2.69	1.00
1957			0.57	0.78	0.71	0.61	1.11	0.98	1.16	0.98	2.56	0.98
1958			0.54	0.73	0.75	0.65	1.11	0.98	1.46	1.06	2.45	0.95
1959			0.57	0.79	0.82	0.72	1.12	0.99	0.92	0.90	2.43	0.95
1960			0.58	0.79	0.86	0.77	1.12	0.99	0.88	0.88	2.40	0.95
1961	2.65	1.24	0.61	0.83	0.77	0.67	1.13	1.00	1.18	0.99	3.30	1.11
1962	2.59	1.22	0.64	0.89	0.86	0.76	1.12	0.99	1.00	0.93	2.98	1.06
1963	2.67	1.25	0.66	0.91	0.88	0.79	1.12	0.99	0.77	0.84	2.87	1.04
1964	2.45	1.17	0.65	0.90	0.93	0.84	1.12	0.99	0.76	0.83	2.44	0.95
1965	2.47	1.17	0.67	0.94	0.95	0.88	1.12	0.99	0.70	0.80	2.35	0.93
1966	2.37	1.13	0.68	0.94	0.97	0.89	1.12	0.99	0.77	0.84	2.26	0.91
1967	2.51	1.19	0.70	0.98	0.95	0.87	1.13	1.00	0.82	0.86	2.30	0.93
1968	2.45	1.17	0.71	1.00	0.98	0.91	1.12	0.99	0.72	0.81	2.25	0.91
1969	2.38	1.14	0.72	1.01	1.00	0.93	1.12	0.99	0.73	0.82	2.15	0.89
1970	2.45	1.17	0.71	0.99	0.98	0.90	1.13	1.00	0.73	0.82	2.35	0.94
1971	2.18	1.06	0.72	1.01	0.97	0.89	1.12	0.99	0.72	0.81	2.15	0.89
1972	2.18	1.06	0.72	1.01	1.02	0.95	1.12	0.99	0.68	0.79	2.03	0.86
1973	2.12	1.03	0.72	1.02	1.05	0.99	1.11	0.98	0.63	0.76	1.93	0.83
1974	2.10	1.02	0.72	1.02	1.05	0.99	1.11	0.98	0.66	0.78	1.92	0.83
1975	2.13	1.04	0.73	1.02	1.02	0.96	1.11	0.99	0.71	0.81	2.02	0.86
1976	2.17	1.05	0.73	1.02	1.04	0.98	1.12	0.99	0.70	0.80	2.02	0.85
1977	2.17	1.05	0.73	1.02	1.06	1.00	1.11	0.98	0.73	0.82	1.97	0.84

TABLE D-7
REAL WAGES RATE AND LABOUR SHARE IN VALUE ADDED, VES PRODUCTION FUNCTION, MARGINAL CONDITION
(1971 dollars)

	Total Manu.		Food & Beverages		Tobacco		Rubber		Leather		Textile		Knitting	
	W	S_w	W	S_w	W	S_w	W	S_w	W	S_w	W	S_w	W	S_w
1946	1.65	0.613	1.46	0.412	1.32	0.44	1.64	0.55	1.34	0.58	1.39	0.95		
1947	1.69	0.605	1.46	0.434	1.39	0.44	1.78	0.44	1.40	0.64	1.38	0.99		
1948	1.69	0.586	1.43	0.417	1.50	0.46	1.75	0.43	1.34	0.67	1.43	1.02		
1949	1.74	0.595	1.46	0.430	1.56	0.47	1.82	0.35	1.41	0.67	1.49	1.06		
1950	1.78	0.580	1.52	0.423	1.70	0.46	1.84	0.45	1.40	0.66	1.52	0.99		
1951	1.82	0.571	1.53	0.418	1.75	0.48	1.96	0.46	1.46	0.65	1.63	0.96		
1952	1.94	0.596	1.62	0.420	1.91	0.42	2.04	0.48	1.43	0.64	1.61	0.99		
1953	2.07	0.611	1.74	0.437	2.00	0.41	2.18	0.46	1.60	0.65	1.76	0.98		
1954	2.15	0.611	1.83	0.438	2.07	0.40	2.21	0.50	1.65	0.65	1.75	0.99		
1955	2.22	0.592	1.88	0.441	2.18	0.38	2.23	0.46	1.58	0.62	1.78	0.92		
1956	2.31	0.589	1.95	0.436	2.25	0.36	2.35	0.44	1.66	0.61	1.83	0.92		
1957	2.40	0.597	2.06	0.445	2.37	0.35	2.50	0.46	1.78	0.63	1.92	0.88		
1958	2.46	0.589	2.09	0.438	2.40	0.35	2.42	0.41	1.74	0.62	1.91	0.85		
1959	2.51	0.569	2.19	0.438	2.40	0.34	2.55	0.40	1.76	0.61	1.93	0.78		
1960	2.59	0.572	2.26	0.440	2.55	0.31	2.61	0.44	1.81	0.63	2.04	0.76		
1961	2.66	0.603	2.36	0.483	2.74	0.34	2.72	0.51	1.86	0.66	2.11	0.77	1.72	0.83
1962	2.73	0.583	2.44	0.473	2.74	0.35	2.78	0.42	1.93	0.65	2.15	0.74	1.73	0.77
1963	2.78	0.572	2.50	0.462	2.81	0.34	2.78	0.42	1.95	0.65	2.22	0.72	1.79	0.70
1964	2.83	0.559	2.54	0.456	2.95	0.33	2.87	0.41	2.00	0.63	2.27	0.71	1.86	0.71
1965	2.90	0.553	2.59	0.462	3.15	0.32	2.93	0.41	2.04	0.63	2.34	0.72	1.89	0.72
1966	2.98	0.551	2.65	0.457	3.21	0.31	2.97	0.39	2.12	0.65	2.45	0.74	1.97	0.71
1967	3.09	0.550	2.79	0.452	3.37	0.32	3.15	0.36	2.22	0.67	2.52	0.74	2.08	0.73
1968	3.21	0.533	2.88	0.447	3.57	0.33	3.26	0.32	2.26	0.65	2.58	0.64	2.08	0.65
1969	3.31	0.519	2.99	0.441	3.68	0.32	3.37	0.30	2.35	0.65	2.66	0.59	2.16	0.64
1970	3.46	0.534	3.13	0.442	3.91	0.33	3.19	0.49	2.41	0.64	2.76	0.59	2.22	0.60
1971	3.61	0.523	3.32	0.438	4.18	0.33	3.32	0.48	2.50	0.64	2.89	0.56	2.28	0.57
1972	3.67	0.515	3.43	0.436	4.34	0.33	3.40	0.48	2.55	0.63	2.92	0.54	2.34	0.56
1973	3.75	0.499	3.54	0.435	4.41	0.32	3.38	0.46	2.62	0.62	2.95	0.53	2.39	0.55
1974	3.89	0.501	3.66	0.447	4.29	0.30	3.49	0.45	2.77	0.62	3.05	0.53	2.56	0.59
1975	3.96	0.523	3.82	0.462	4.60	0.32	3.55	0.48	2.83	0.64	3.09	0.52	2.70	0.60
1976	3.95	0.504	4.09	0.473	4.90	0.31	3.66	0.44	3.02	0.71	3.31	0.53	2.81	0.59
1977	4.06	0.491	5.15	0.476	5.11	0.30	3.72	0.40	3.07	0.61	3.41	0.51	2.83	0.51

148

TABLE D-7 (continued)

	Clothing		Wood		Furniture & Fixtures		Paper		Printing & Publishing		Primary Metals		Metal Fabrication	
	W	S_w	W	S_w	W	S_w	W	S_w	W	S_w	W	S_w	W	S_w
1946	1.44	0.80	1.28	0.83			1.81	0.49	1.80	0.57				
1947	1.49	0.89	1.38	0.86			1.90	0.51	1.85	0.56				
1948	1.42	0.86	1.34	0.84			1.88	0.49	1.82	0.52				
1949	1.48	0.87	1.39	0.86			1.92	0.47	1.85	0.55				
1950	1.46	0.86	1.43	0.84			1.97	0.46	1.95	0.53				
1951	1.53	0.83	1.46	0.82			2.09	0.47	1.92	0.52				
1952	1.46	0.77	1.49	0.83			2.23	0.51	2.05	0.54				
1953	1.59	0.81	1.59	0.86			2.42	0.52	2.22	0.55				
1954	1.60	0.80	1.66	0.86			2.54	0.53	2.28	0.55				
1955	1.57	0.77	1.74	0.84			2.58	0.54	2.39	0.55				
1956	1.63	0.76	1.80	0.87			2.73	0.54	2.45	0.53				
1957	1.72	0.61	1.92	0.63			2.83	0.56	2.61	0.54				
1958	1.68	0.60	1.92	0.61			2.81	0.56	2.73	0.56				
1959	1.74	0.60	1.92	0.59			2.86	0.54	2.81	0.55				
1960	1.73	0.60	2.06	0.59			2.98	0.54	2.89	0.56				
1961	1.88	0.64	2.25	0.60	2.11	0.64	3.12	0.58	3.02	0.58	3.36	0.58	2.82	0.60
1962	1.96	0.63	2.33	0.58	2.17	0.64	3.20	0.58	3.13	0.58	3.39	0.56	2.83	0.60
1963	1.98	0.61	2.41	0.58	2.18	0.63	3.21	0.56	3.19	0.58	3.45	0.54	2.88	0.58
1964	2.05	0.62	2.47	0.57	2.25	0.63	3.25	0.54	3.22	0.59	3.47	0.52	2.90	0.57
1965	2.10	0.63	2.55	0.59	2.27	0.60	3.29	0.54	3.28	0.59	3.51	0.52	2.94	0.56
1966	2.16	0.63	2.68	0.59	2.38	0.59	3.43	0.56	3.35	0.58	3.56	0.53	3.06	0.56
1967	2.21	0.65	2.80	0.60	2.46	0.60	3.57	0.58	3.45	0.58	3.69	0.56	3.20	0.56
1968	2.27	0.63	2.90	0.60	2.52	0.58	3.69	0.57	3.57	0.59	3.72	0.52	3.27	0.56
1969	2.36	0.65	3.04	0.60	2.59	0.58	3.78	0.55	3.67	0.58	3.80	0.51	3.39	0.55
1970	2.38	0.65	3.21	0.62	2.72	0.61	3.91	0.56	3.84	0.58	4.00	0.53	3.54	0.56
1971	2.47	0.64	3.42	0.63	2.74	0.61	4.13	0.58	3.99	0.58	4.26	0.55	3.68	0.56
1972	2.57	0.65	3.48	0.67	2.81	0.60	4.23	0.55	4.03	0.56	4.42	0.55	3.74	0.56
1973	2.61	0.63	3.66	0.69	2.92	0.59	4.28	0.53	4.11	0.56	4.49	0.53	3.82	0.54
1974	2.71	0.64	3.95	0.71	3.02	0.61	4.47	0.55	4.41	0.58	4.57	0.52	3.98	0.54
1975	2.85	0.65	4.00	0.71	3.09	0.65	4.28	0.64	4.39	0.56	4.72	0.57	4.09	0.59
1976	3.02	0.66	4.32	0.69	3.26	0.62	4.84	0.65	4.53	0.56	4.84	0.59	4.14	0.58
1977	3.08	0.63	4.52	0.67	3.28	0.57	5.10	0.61	4.63	0.54	4.87	0.56	4.21	0.58

TABLE D-7 (continued)

	Machinery		Transportation Equipment		Electrical & Electronic		Non-Metallic Minerals		Petroleum & Coal		Chemicals	
	W	S_w	W	S_w	W	S_w	W	S_w	W	S_w	W	S_w
1946			2.00	0.84	1.73	0.68	1.50	0.51	2.04	0.75	1.72	0.58
1947			1.98	0.72	1.81	0.66	1.60	0.49	2.09	0.76	1.80	0.59
1948			1.98	0.69	1.85	0.66	1.59	0.47	2.06	0.68	1.75	0.56
1949			2.00	0.69	1.93	0.66	1.65	0.46	2.16	0.71	1.82	0.58
1950			2.05	0.66	1.96	0.64	1.70	0.45	2.28	0.69	1.91	0.55
1951			2.08	0.63	2.02	0.68	1.77	0.44	2.34	0.63	1.96	0.54
1952			2.17	0.69	2.12	0.72	1.86	0.45	2.58	0.69	2.09	0.54
1953			2.46	0.72	2.24	0.69	2.02	0.47	2.68	0.67	2.22	0.55
1954			2.48	0.76	2.40	0.70	2.08	0.48	2.72	0.65	2.36	0.54
1955			2.62	0.72	2.33	0.62	2.13	0.48	2.84	0.58	2.45	0.52
1956			2.70	0.75	2.51	0.82	2.26	0.46	3.19	0.55	2.57	0.50
1957			2.77	0.79	2.64	0.75	2.37	0.44	3.33	0.49	2.71	0.49
1958			2.89	0.82	2.71	0.73	2.38	0.45	3.43	0.52	2.77	0.48
1959			3.02	0.79	2.70	0.69	2.43	0.45	3.62	0.46	2.84	0.47
1960			3.04	0.78	2.82	0.66	2.52	0.46	3.71	0.45	2.98	0.47
1961	3.03	0.70	3.13	0.75	2.89	0.72	2.68	0.48	3.80	0.50	3.16	0.55
1962	3.06	0.69	3.21	0.69	2.91	0.67	2.73	0.46	3.94	0.47	3.22	0.53
1963	3.11	0.71	3.28	0.66	2.96	0.65	2.75	0.46	3.90	0.42	3.31	0.52
1964	3.15	0.67	3.33	0.68	2.99	0.62	2.80	0.45	3.99	0.41	3.33	0.47
1965	3.18	0.67	3.49	0.62	3.01	0.59	2.89	0.45	4.07	0.39	3.38	0.46
1966	3.30	0.65	3.51	0.61	3.04	0.58	2.95	0.46	4.17	0.42	3.44	0.45
1967	3.47	0.68	3.57	0.54	3.16	0.60	3.08	0.49	4.33	0.43	3.56	0.45
1968	3.54	0.67	3.85	0.51	3.21	0.57	3.16	0.47	4.40	0.40	3.67	0.44
1969	3.69	0.65	3.92	0.49	3.26	0.55	3.32	0.47	4.62	0.40	3.79	0.42
1970	3.88	0.67	4.04	0.53	3.52	0.58	3.46	0.49	4.81	0.40	4.15	0.46
1971	3.93	0.58	4.29	0.49	3.66	0.58	3.63	0.46	5.11	0.40	4.14	0.42
1972	3.96	0.58	4.32	0.48	3.69	0.54	3.75	0.46	5.21	0.38	4.20	0.39
1973	3.97	0.55	4.36	0.46	3.65	0.51	3.83	0.43	5.17	0.35	4.19	0.37
1974	4.10	0.54	4.44	0.46	3.77	0.51	3.97	0.43	5.40	0.37	4.31	0.36
1975	4.11	0.56	4.50	0.44	3.88	0.53	4.11	0.45	5.76	0.39	4.36	0.39
1976	4.21	0.58	4.67	0.44	4.07	0.51	4.34	0.45	6.08	0.39	4.66	0.39
1977	4.28	0.57	4.76	0.43	4.12	0.49	4.50	0.42	6.13	0.40	4.78	0.38

TABLE D-8
NET CAPITAL-OUTPUT RATIO

	Total Manu.	Food & Bev.	Tobacco	Rub. & Plast.	Leather Products	Text.	Knit.	Cloth.	Wood	Furn. & Fix.	Paper
1946	1.210	0.763		0.654	0.449						1.693
1947	1.148	0.850		0.537	0.528						1.683
1948	1.181	0.926		0.660	0.617						1.745
1949	1.215	0.998		0.581	0.592						1.797
1950	1.186	1.030		0.705	0.613						1.758
1951	1.151	1.042		0.695	0.639						1.753
1952	1.201	1.026		0.792	0.573						1.992
1953	1.214	1.041		0.747	0.535						2.019
1954	1.317	1.055		0.937	0.567						2.025
1955	1.263	1.072		0.852	0.519						2.035
1956	1.239	1.062		0.790	0.476						2.091
1957	1.349	1.068	0.587	0.882	0.489			0.272	1.042		2.408
1958	1.452	1.068	0.610	0.902	0.479			0.268	1.030		2.577
1959	1.386	1.065	0.630	0.793	0.449			0.258	1.003		2.434
1960	1.420	1.095	0.615	0.975	0.468			0.253	1.013		2.375
1961	1.404	1.111	0.609	0.070	0.423	1.898	0.941	0.240	1.021	0.432	2.415
1962	1.318	1.109	0.603	0.852	0.407	1.694	0.874	0.226	0.973	0.408	2.389
1963	1.273	1.107	0.589	0.835	0.409	1.570	0.784	0.213	0.932	0.398	2.336
1964	1.209	1.079	0.581	0.789	0.400	1.501	0.739	0.204	0.894	0.395	2.232
1965	1.176	1.084	0.578	0.783	0.394	1.567	0.708	0.198	0.912	0.377	2.298
1966	1.179	1.067	0.590	0.761	0.397	1.667	0.714	0.193	0.937	0.370	2.363
1967	1.226	1.050	0.590	0.757	0.420	1.696	0.730	0.196	0.952	0.400	2.619
1968	1.209	1.079	0.632	0.745	0.407	1.544	0.631	0.188	0.950	0.422	2.626
1969	1.170	1.084	0.625	0.744	0.420	1.380	0.615	0.185	0.980	0.418	2.431
1970	1.249	1.096	0.593	0.811	0.451	1.470	0.628	0.185	1.134	0.460	2.563
1971	1.239	1.092	0.594	0.859	0.432	1.365	0.605	0.173	1.114	0.453	2.715
1972	1.198	1.083	0.583	0.838	0.450	1.226	0.593	0.170	1.125	0.406	2.595
1973	1.140	1.092	0.566	0.797	0.459	1.187	0.595	0.172	1.134	0.403	2.488
1974	1.157	1.133	0.545	0.853	0.461	1.267	0.645	0.182	1.329	0.432	2.383
1975	1.287	1.150	0.567	0.970	0.476	1.375	0.652	0.187	1.531	0.506	3.052
1976	1.269	1.131	0.550	0.832	0.501	1.379	0.637	0.184	1.320	0.478	2.721
1977	1.262	1.133	0.519	0.730	0.477	1.326	0.587	0.190	1.241	0.473	2.618

TABLE D-8 (continued)

	Print. & Pub.	Prim. Met.	Met. Fab.	Mach- inery	Trans. Equip.	Elec- tric. & Elec- tronic	Non- Met. Min.	Petr. & Coal	Chem- ical
1946	0.807				1.244	0.492	1.923		1.790
1947	0.763				0.989	0.407	1.662		1.837
1948	0.735				0.948	0.479	1.699		1.962
1949	0.734				0.918	0.538	1.670		2.023
1950	0.709				0.864	0.550	1.542		1.938
1951	0.732				0.754	0.595	1.459		1.813
1952	0.750				0.717	0.688	1.487		1.973
1953	0.696				0.721	0.663	1.436		2.166
1954	0.681				0.897	0.738	1.467		2.158
1955	0.687				0.979	0.695	1.365		2.020
1956	0.647				0.952	0.856	1.432		2.003
1957	0.673				1.017	0.782	1.649	5.266	2.092
1958	0.728				1.199	0.843	1.677	5.687	2.150
1959	0.712				1.250	0.816	1.617	5.622	2.176
1960	0.730				1.327	0.806	1.748	5.658	2.139
1961	0.731	2.391	0.856	0.800	1.358	0.771	1.707	5.382	2.108
1962	0.737	2.282	0.778	0.735	1.149	0.665	1.517	5.031	2.046
1963	0.753	2.215	0.732	0.710	1.018	0.632	1.539	4.741	1.977
1964	0.784	2.059	0.679	0.655	0.986	0.585	1.436	4.674	1.794
1965	0.771	1.974	0.630	0.636	0.888	0.546	1.395	4.457	1.772
1966	0.749	2.016	0.617	0.600	0.932	0.526	1.482	4.283	1.800
1967	0.748	2.220	0.664	0.631	0.884	0.571	1.718	4.365	1.903
1968	0.751	2.074	0.694	0.664	0.809	0.579	1.658	4.128	1.909
1969	0.737	2.077	0.676	0.609	0.755	0.558	1.653	4.193	1.843
1970	0.755	2.042	0.713	0.647	0.918	0.611	1.811	4.419	1.899
1971	0.751	2.169	0.721	0.654	0.823	0.611	1.606	4.558	1.866
1972	0.724	2.170	0.712	0.604	0.760	0.588	1.513	4.529	1.791
1973	0.701	2.058	0.667	0.565	0.672	0.549	1.407	4.283	1.650
1974	0.699	1.998	0.646	0.533	0.705	0.543	1.432	4.543	1.684
1975	0.712	2.327	0.735	0.576	0.761	0.609	1.522	4.993	2.015
1976	0.704	2.463	0.716	0.630	0.711	0.591	1.539	4.160	2.216
1977	0.710	2.322	0.727	0.652	0.677	0.617	1.474	5.095	2.300

TABLE D-9
NET OUTPUT-CAPITAL RATIO

	Total Manu.	Food & Bev.	Tobacco	Rub. & Plast.	Leather Prod.	Text.	Knit.	Cloth.	Wood	Furn. & Fix.	Paper
1946	1.826	1.311		1.529	2.227						0.591
1947	0.871	1.176		1.862	1.894						0.594
1948	0.847	1.080		1.515	1.621						0.573
1949	0.823	1.002		1.721	1.689						0.556
1950	0.843	0.971		1.418	1.631						0.569
1951	0.869	0.960		1.439	1.565						0.570
1952	0.833	0.975		1.263	1.745						0.502
1953	0.824	0.961		1.339	1.869						0.495
1954	0.759	0.948		1.067	1.764						0.494
1955	0.792	0.933		1.174	1.927						0.491
1956	0.807	0.942		1.266	2.101						0.478
1957	0.741	0.936	1.704	1.134	2.045			3.676	0.960		0.415
1958	0.689	0.936	1.639	1.109	2.088			3.731	0.971		0.388
1959	0.722	0.939	1.587	1.261	2.227			3.876	0.997		0.411
1960	0.704	0.913	1.626	1.015	2.137			3.953	0.987		0.421
1961	0.712	0.900	1.642	1.935	2.364	0.527	1.063	4.167	0.979	2.315	0.414
1962	0.759	0.902	1.658	1.174	2.457	0.590	1.144	4.425	1.028	2.451	0.419
1963	0.786	0.903	1.698	1.198	2.445	0.637	1.276	4.695	1.073	2.513	0.428
1964	0.827	0.927	1.721	1.267	2.500	0.666	1.353	4.902	1.119	2.532	0.448
1965	0.850	0.923	1.730	1.277	2.538	0.638	1.412	5.051	1.096	2.653	0.435
1966	0.848	0.937	1.695	1.314	2.519	0.600	1.401	5.181	1.067.	2.703	0.423
1967	0.816	0.945	1.695	1.321	2.381	0.590	1.370	5.102	1.050	2.500	0.382
1968	0.827	0.927	1.582	1.342	2.451	0.648	1.585	5.319	1.053	2.370	0.381
1969	0.855	0.923	1.600	1.344	2.381	0.725	1.626	5.405	1.020	2.392	0.411
1970	0.801	0.912	1.686	1.233	2.217	0.680	1.592	5.405	0.882	2.174	0.390
1971	0.807	0.916	1.684	1.164	2.315	0.733	1.653	5.780	0.898	2.208	0.368
1972	0.835	0.923	1.715	1.193	2.222	0.816	1.686	5.882	0.889	2.463	0.385
1973	0.874	0.916	1.767	1.255	2.179	0.842	1.681	5.814	0.882	2.481	0.402
1974	0.864	0.883	1.835	1.172	2.169	0.789	1.550	5.495	0.752	2.315	0.420
1975	0.777	0.870	1.764	1.030	2.101	0.727	1.534	5.348	0.653	1.976	0.328
1976	0.788	0.884	1.818	1.262	1.996	0.725	1.570	5.435	0.758	2.092	0.368
1977	0.792	0.883	1.927	1.370	2.096	0.754	1.704	5.263	0.806	2.114	0.382

TABLE D-9 (continued)

	Print. & Pub.	Prim. Met.	Met. Fab.	Mach- inery	Trans. Equip.	Elec- tric. & Elec- tronic	Non- Met. Min.	Petr. & Coal	Chem- ical
1946	1.239				0.804	2.033	0.520		0.559
1947	1.311				1.011	2.457	0.602		0.544
1948	1.361				1.055	2.088	0.589		0.510
1949	1.362				1.089	1.859	0.599		0.494
1950	1.410				1.157	1.818	0.649		0.516
1951	1.366				1.326	1.681	0.685		0.552
1952	1.333				1.395	1.453	0.672		0.507
1953	1.437				1.387	1.508	0.696		0.462
1954	1.468				1.115	1.355	0.682		0.463
1955	1.456				1.021	1.439	0.722		0.495
1956	1.546				1.050	1.168	0.698		0.499
1957	1.486				0.983	1.279	0.606	0.190	0.478
1958	1.374				0.834	1.186	0.596	0.176	0.465
1959	1.404				0.800	1.225	0.618	0.178	0.460
1960	1.370				0.754	1.241	0.572	0.177	0.468
1961	1.368	0.418	1.168	1.250	0.736	1.297	0.586	0.186	0.474
1962	1.357	0.438	1.285	1.361	0.870	1.504	0.659	0.199	0.489
1963	1.328	0.451	1.366	1.408	0.650	1.582	0.650	0.211	0.506
1964	1.276	0.486	1.473	1.527	1.014	1.709	0.696	0.214	0.557
1965	1.297	0.507	1.587	1.572	1.126	1.832	0.717	0.224	0.564
1966	1.335	0.496	1.621	1.667	1.073	1.901	0.675	0.233	0.556
1967	1.337	0.450	1.506	1.585	1.131	1.751	0.582	0.229	0.525
1968	1.332	0.482	1.441	1.506	1.236	1.727	0.603	0.242	0.524
1969	1.357	0.481	1.479	1.642	1.325	1.792	0.605	0.238	0.543
1970	1.325	0.490	1.403	1.546	1.089	1.637	0.552	0.226	0.527
1971	1.332	0.461	1.387	1.529	1.215	1.637	0.623	0.219	0.536
1972	1.381	0.461	1.404	1.656	1.316	1.701	0.661	0.221	0.558
1973	1.427	0.486	1.499	1.770	1.488	1.821	0.711	0.233	0.606
1974	1.431	0.501	1.548	1.876	1.418	1.842	0.698	0.220	0.594
1975	1.404	0.430	1.361	1.736	1.314	1.642	0.657	0.200	0.496
1976	1.420	0.406	1.397	1.587	1.406	1.692	0.650	0.194	0.451
1977	1.408	0.431	1.376	1.534	1.477	1.621	0.678	0.196	0.435

154

NOTES

Chapter 1

[1] D.J. Daly and S. Globerman, *Tariff and Science Policies: Applications of a Model of Nationalism,* (Toronto: University of Toronto Press, 1976).

[2] Y. Kotowitz, "On the Estimation of a Non-Neutral CES Production Function," *Canadian Journal of Economics,* I, 2 (May 1968); "Capital-Labour Substitution in Canadian Manufacturing, 1926-39, and 1946-61," *Canadian Journal of Economics,* 1, 3 (August 1968); and "Technical Progress: Factor Substitution and Income Distribution in Canadian Manufacturing 1926-39 and 1946-61," *Canadian Journal of Economics,* II, 1 (February 1969).

[3] H.H. Postner, *An Analysis of Canadian Manufacturing Productivity: Some Preliminary Results,* Economic Council of Canada, Staff paper #31 (Ottawa, 1971).

[4] D.J. Daly, "Productivity and Costs of Canadian Manufacturing: Some International Comparisons," mimeo, York University, 1976.

[5] D.J. Daly, B.A. Keys, and E.J. Spence, *Scale and Specialization in Canadian Manufacturing,* Economic Council of Canada, Staff Study #21 (Ottawa, 1968); James G. Frank, *Assessing Trends in Canada's Competitive Position* (Ottawa: Conference Board, 1977).

[6] K.J. Arrow, H.B. Chenery, B.S. Mikes, and R.M. Solow, "Capital-Labour Substitution and Economic Efficiency," *Review of Economics and Statistics* (August 1961), pp. 225-50.

[7] J.G. Frank, "The Route to Higher Living Standards," *Canadian Business Review,* 6, 1 (Spring 1979).

[8] E.G. Denison, "The Puzzling Drop in Productivity," *Brookings Bulletin,* 15, 2 (Fall 1978), pp. 10-12; *Accounting for Slower Economic Growth: The United States in the 1970s* (Washington, D.C., Brookings Institution, 1979).

[9] Denison, *Accounting for Slower Economic Growth.*

[10] J.A. Tatom, "The Productivity Problem," *Federal Reserve Bank of St. Louis,* 61, 9 (September 1979), pp. 3-17.

[11] W.D. Nordhaus, "Policy Responses to the Productivity Slowdown," R.M. Solow, Discussion to Nordhaus's "Policy Responses to the Productivity Slowdown," and M.L. Wachter and J.M. Perloff, "Productivity Slowdown: A Labor Problem?" in *The Decline in Productivity Growth,* Federal Reserve Bank of Boston, Conference Series No. 22 (June 1980).

[12] L.C. Thurow, "Survey of Factors Contributing to the Decline in U.S. Productivity Growth," in *The Decline in Productivity Growth*, Federal Reserve Bank of Boston, Conference Series No. 22 (June 1980), pp. 22-25.

[13] J.W. Kendrick, "Survey of the Factors Contributing to the Decline in U.S. Productivity Growth," in *The Decline in Productivity Growth*, Federal Reserve Bank of Boston, Conference Series No. 22 (June 1980); see also S. Maital and N.M. Meltz, *Lagging Productivity Growth, Causes and Remedies* (Cambridge, Mass.: Ballinger, 1980).

[14] S. Ostry and P.S. Rao, "Productivity Trends in Canada," in S. Maital and N.M. Meltz, *Lagging Productivity Growth, Causes and Remedies* (Cambridge, Mass.: Ballinger 1980).

Chapter 2

[1] G.L. Perry, "Capacity in Manufacturing," *Brookings Papers on Economic Activity*, 3 (1973), p. 722.

[2] *Ibid.;* see also L.R. Klein and V. Long, "Capacity Utilization: Concept Measurements and Recent Estimates," *Brookings Papers on Economic Activity*, 3 (1973), pp. 743-64; and F. De Leeuw, "Why Capacity Utilization Estimates Differ," *Survey of Current Business* (May 1979), pp. 45-55.

[3] De Leeuw, "Why Capacity Utilization Estimates Differ."

[4] See Daniel Creamer, *Capacity Expansion and Capacity in Post-War Manufacturing*, Studies in Business Economics No. 72 (New York: National Industrial Board, 1961).

[5] D.J. Daly, B.A. Keys, and E.J. Spence, *Scale and Specialization in Canadian Manufacturing*, Economic Council of Canada, Staff Study #21 (Ottawa, 1968).

[6] Paul Gorecki, *Economies of Scale and Efficient Plant Size in Canadian Manufacturing Industries*, Bureau of Competition Policy, Consumer and Corporate Affairs (Ottawa, 1976).

[7] Donald Le Craw, *Economies of Scale in Canadian Manufacturing: A Survey*, RCCC Study No. 29, (Ottawa, 1978), p. 20.

[8] *Ibid.*, pp. 50, 51.

[9] F.M. Scherer, "Economies of Scale and Industrial Concentration," in H.J. Goldschmid *et al.*, eds., *Industrial Concentration: The New Learning* (Boston: Little, Brown, 1974), p. 37.

[10] *Report of the Royal Commission on Corporate Concentration* (Ottawa, 1978), Chapter 3.

[11] D.J. Daly, *Canada's Comparative Advantage*, Economic Council of Canada, Discussion Paper No. 135 (September 1979), p. 28.

[12] *Ibid.*, p. 33.

[13] The debate culminated in an extensive and animated exchange between Jorgenson and Griliches and Denison. It is beyond the scope of the study to pursue the issue. But see D.W. Jorgenson and Z. Griliches, "The Explanation of Productivity Change," *Survey of Current Business*, 52, 5, Part II (May 1972) (with corrections), Part II, pp. 3-36, 65-94, 111, and Edward F. Denison, "Some Major Issues in Productivity Analysis: An Examination of Estimates by Jorgenson and Griliches," (May 1972), *Survey of Current Business* 52, 5, Part II pp. 37-65, 96-110. See also John W. Kendrick, *Productivity Trends in the United States* (New York: National Bureau of Economic Research, 1961); National Bureau of Economic Research,

Postwar Productivity Trends in the United States, 1948-1969 (New York, 1973); and Kendrick, *The Formation and Stocks of Total Capital* (New York: 1976). Also useful are Allen D. Searle and Charles A. Waite, "Current Efforts to Measure Productivity in the Public Sector: How Adequate for the National Accounts?" in J.W. Kendrick, ed., *New Development in Productivity Measurement and Analysis*, National Bureau of Economic Research (Chicago: University of Chicago Press, 1980), pp. 333-57; A.L. Gaathon, *Economic Productivity in Israel*, Bank of Israel (New York: Praeger, 1971); and D.J. Daly, "Combining Inputes to Secure a Measure of Total Factor Input," *Review of Income and Wealth*, Series 18, No. 1 (March 1972), pp. 27-53.

[14] For detailed methodology and statistical problems of the Translog function, see Z. Griliches and V. Ringstad, *Economies of Scale and the Form of the Production Function* (Amsterdam: North-Holland, 1971) Chapter 2, Appendixes C, D.

[15] A.A. Walters, *An Introduction to Econometrics* (London: Macmillan, 1970), pp. 323-40; "Production and Cost Functions": An Econometric Survey," *Econometrica*, 31 (1-2) (April 1963), pp. 1-66; M. Brown and J. Popkin, "A Measure of Technological Change and Returns to Scale," *Review of Economics and Statistics*, 44 (November 1962), pp. 402-11; M.I. Nadiri, "Some Approaches to the Theory and Measurement of Total Factor Productivity: A Survey," *Journal of Economic Literature* (March 1970), pp. 1168-70; R. Bodkin and L. Klein, "Nonlinear Estimation of Aggregate Production Functions," *Review of Economics and Statistics*, 49 (February 1962), pp. 28-44; R.K. Diwan, "Bias in the Measurement of Technical Change," *Journal of Finance and Quantitative Analysis*, 3 (1968), pp. 471-77.

[16] M. Nerlove, "Recent Empirical Studies of the CES and Related Production Functions," in the *Theory and Empirical Analysis of Production*, Studies in Income and Wealth, 31 (Cambridge: NBER, 1967), pp. 55-122; J. Kmenta, "On the Estimation of CES Production Function," *International Economic Review*, 8 (June 1967), pp. 180-89; R.G. Bodkin, "A Test of Specification of the Aggregate Production Function," Cowles Foundation, Discussion Paper No. 157, Yale University, 1963.

[17] Romesh K. Diwan, "Bias in the Measurement of Technical Change," *Journal of Financial and Quantitative Analysis*, 3 (1968), pp. 442-53; and "Alternative Specifications of Economies of Scale," *Economica*, (November 1966), pp. 442-51.

[18] The inclusion of the time variable resulted in high levels of multicolinearity and serial correlations. Consequently, the Cochrane-Orcutt technique was used to "untangle" the results.

[19] See Griliches and Ringstad, *Economies of Scale and the Form of the Production Function*.

[20] D.J. Daly and S. Globerman, *Tariff and Science Policies: Applications of a Model of Nationalism* (Toronto: University of Toronto Press, 1976).

[21] Daly, Keys, and Spence, *Scale and Specialization in Canadian Manufacturing;* see also D.J. Daly, "Size and Economies of Scale," in P.K. Gorecki and W.T. Stanbury (eds.), *Perspectives on the Royal Commission on Corporate Concentration* (Toronto: Butterworth, 1979), Chapter 8; S. Ostry and P.S. Rao, "Productivity Trends in Canada," (Mimeo), presented to a Conference on Lagging Productivity Growth, Toronto, May 24, 1979; and G. Lermer, "Evidence from Trade Data Regarding the Nationalizing of Canadian Industry," *Canadian Journal of Economics*, 6, (1973), pp. 248-56.

Chapter 3

[1] While studying the various classification methods, it would have been impossible to assemble a reliable and consistent set of data for the nineteen industry groups without the active help and co-operation of Statistics Canada personnel. I am deeply indebted to Dr. Koumanakas, Director of Capital Stock Division; Mr. J. Falardeau, Director of Labour Division; Mr. H. Potter, Director of Publications, Manufacturing Industries in Canada; Mr. B. McCormick, Director of Productivity Division; Mr. G. Finn, Senior Regional Advisor; and Mr. M. Williams, Senior Advisor on Data Retrieval.

[2] Z. Griliches and V. Ringstad, *Economies of Scale and the Form of the Production Function* (Amsterdam: North Holland Publishing, 1971), p. 108.

[3] Edward A. Carmichael, *Reassessing Canada's Potential Economic Growth* (Ottawa: Conference Board in Canada, 1979).

[4] Economic Council of Canada, *A Climate of Uncertainty*, Seventeenth Annual Review (Ottawa, 1980).

[5] It should be noted that measurements of capacity utilization are likely to be biased upward for several industries in the sector, because they lease rather than purchase equipment. Although the firms use capital, the amount does not appear in Statistics Canada publications as an increase in capital stock, but is recorded as current expenditure. Only a study at the micro level could overcome such a bias. *Ibid.*, p. 116.

[6] *Ibid.*, p. 89.

[7] *Ibid.*, p. 86.

[8] The focus of our analysis is the measurement of technological progress and the impact of technology on labour efficiency and other variables that are calculated and estimated from the VES reproduction function. Diwan's method is indeed a side issue (as pointed out rightly by one of the referees of this book), which comes to show that it is consistent as well with our overall findings. R.K. Diwan, "Bias in the Measurement of Technical Change," *Journal of Finance and Quantitative Analysis*, 3 (1968), pp. 471-77; and "Alternative Specification of Economies of Scale," *Economics* (November 1966), pp. 442-54; and R.M. Solow, "Technical Change and the Aggregate Production Function," Review of Economics and Statistics, 39 (August 1937), pp. 312-20.

[9] Z. Griliches, "Issues in Assessing the Contribution of Research and Development of Productivity Growth," *Bell Journal of Economics*, 10, 1 (Spring 1979), pp. 92-115.

[10] Economic Council of Canada, *A Climate of Uncertainty*, p. 90.

[11] *Ibid.*

Chapter 4

[1] See Richard D. French, *How Ottawa Decides* (Ottawa: Canadian Institute for Economic Policy, 1980), p. 105.

[2] *Financial Times*, July 22, 1974.

[3] An exception to this can be found in Albert Breton's *A Conceptual Basis for an Industrial Strategy* (Ottawa: Economic Council of Canada, 1974) in which five pages are devoted to the development of a rigorous definition of industrial strategy.

158

Breton defines industrial strategy as an attempt to reduce the gap assumed to exist between the actual output of industrial goods and the desired output (p. 31).

[4] *Financial Times,* July 22, 1974; emphasis added.

[5] Canadian Manufacturers' Association, Discussion Paper, *"Trade-offs: Some Crucial Choices"* (February 1980).

[6] Some might argue that Canada has an "implicit" industrial policy that has evolved more by accident than by design through assorted eclectic tax, expenditure, and regulatory policies.

[7] D.J. Daly, "Remedies for Increasing Productivity Levels in Canada," in S. Maital and N.M. Meltz (ed.), *Lagging Productivity Growth* (Cambridge, Mass.: Ballinger, 1980), chapter 7; J.J. Shepherd, *The Transition to Reality: Directions for Canadian Industrial Strategy* (Ottawa: Canadian Institute for Economic Policy, 1980).

Appendix A

[1] The formulation of the VES production function is identical to that of R.K. Diwan, "About the Growth Path of Firms," *American Economic Review,* LX, 1 (March 1970), pp. 30-43.

[2] The method used here to derive the rate of return is consistent with Arrow *et al.,* P.J. Dhrymes, and Diwan. Arrow's "total returns to capital" were taken to be equal to gross profit from operations (excluding other income) minus depreciation. They use rate of returns (r) to estimate their capital stock series via $K = (V - wL)/r$ where K = capital; V = value added, and wL = total factor payments to labour. Dhrymes used directly the relation $r = (Q - wL)/K$, stating it as requirement for the Arrow model. He called this relation "output per capital-rental relation." Diwan used the identical relation calling it "the rate of return on capital." West in using the "Griffen Method" to estimate capital stock used the same relation $K = (V - wLr)$, while defining r as the "factor payment to capital" and $V - wL$ as the "absolute amount of the return to capital" (p. 75).

At first glance the above look like different names for the same relation. In relating it to the CES or VES production functions "things however do matter." First, there are grounds to debate whether Arrow's method or Stigler's method is superior as a measurement of the aggregate production function. It seems to me that West's definition of r as "factor payment to capital" rather than as a rate of return eliminates plausible confusion between this and the financial-accounting concept of rate-of-return. Second, one should be cautious in interpreting results from both concepts. Generally, $(Q - wL)/k$ gives us a greater r than the r obtained from industry's balance sheets. Thus in the case of the VES, the size of r affects σ_b significantly, through the labour share variable S_1 since,

$$\sigma_b = \frac{1}{1 + \rho - (m\rho/s_1)}$$

If r is lower, then σ is lower and g might become lower depending on the values of ρ and $m\rho$.

See K.J. Arrow, H.B. Chenery, B.S. Minhas, and R.H. Solow, "Capital Labour Substitution and Economic Efficiency," *Review of Economics and Statistics,* 43, 3, pp. 225-50; Phoebus J. Dhrymes, "Some Extensions and Tests for the CES Class of Production Functions," *Review of Economics and Statistics,* 47, 4, (November

159

1951), pp. 357-66; R. Diwan, "Alternative Specification of Economies of Scale," *Economica* (November 1966), pp. 442-54; E.C. West, *Canada-United States Price and Productivity Differences in Manufacturing Industries 1963*, Economic Council of Canada, Staff Paper #32 (Ottawa, 1971).

3 Z. Griliches and V. Ringstad, *Economies of Scale and the Form of the Production Function* (Amsterdam: North Holland Publishing, 1971), Chapter 2.

4 R.K. Diwan, "Bias in the Measurement of Technical Change," *Journal of Finance and Quantitative Analysis*, 3 (1968) pp. 471-77.

Among "all the factors" Diwan (and others) include non-neutral technical change, imperfect competition, increasing returns to scale. R.G. Bodkin pointed out the same problem in his article, "A Test of the Specification of the Aggregate Production Function" Cowles Foundation, Discussion Paper No. 157, Yale University, 1963. See also M. Brown and Joel Popkin, "Measure of Technological Change and Returns to Scale," *Review of Economics and Statistics* (1962) pp. 402-11.

5 Diwan, "About the Growth Path of Firms," p. 32.

6 See J. Kmenta, "On the Estimation of the CES Production Function," *International Economic Review*, 8, 2 (June 1967), pp. 180-89; M.S. Feldstein, "Alternative Methods of Estimating a CES Production Function for Britain," *Economica* (November 1967), pp. 384-94; Dhrymes "Some Extensions"; and Bodkin, "A Test of the Specification."

7 R.K. Diwan, "On the Cobb-Douglas Production Function," *Southern Economic Journal*, XXXIV, 3 (January 1968), pp. 410-14; see also A.A. Walters, "A Note on Economics of Scale," *Review of Economics and Statistics* (1963), pp. 425-27.

8 P.J. Dhrymes, "On Devising Unbiased Estimators for the Parameters of the Cobb-Douglas Production Function," *Review of Economics and Statistics* (1957), pp. 312-20.

9 Z. Griliches and V. Ringstad, *Economies of Scale and the Form of the Production Function*, Chapters 1, 2.